THE HIDDEN HOUSES
OF IRELAND

Where to find them

THE HIDDEN HOUSES OF IRELAND

Where to find them

Marianne Heron

Gill & Macmillan

Gill & Macmillan Ltd

Goldenbridge

Dublin 8

with associated companies throughout the world

www.gillmacmillan.ie

© Marianne Heron 1999

0 7171 2730 3

Illustrations by Michael Fewer

Index compiled by Helen Litton

Design by Identikit Design Consultants, Dublin

Print origination by Carole Lynch

Printed by ColourBooks Ltd, Dublin

This book is typeset in 10/13pt MBembo.

A CIP catalogue record for this book is available
from the British Library.

1 3 5 4 2

CONTENTS

PREFACE

There is nothing quite so satisfying as contemplating a trip into the Irish countryside, especially if you live in a city, or in exile as I do at present. There is the romance of pleasures to come: the sweet scent of the air, the sound of rooks, the freedom to walk in the calm of pastures and hills. It is a voyage that begins with putting wellies and waterproof in the boot of the car, and ends, if you are lucky, in a house filled with the evidence of country pursuits, in a land where horse is king and fishing unrivalled.

Researching this book has given me the opportunity for many such trips but, however appealing, the exercise would not have been viable without the sponsorship of REDGEWOOD Town and Country. Their association with *The Hidden Houses of Ireland* has been a happy and very appropriate one. The original inspiration for the REDGEWOOD range had its roots in the 'hunting, shooting, fishing' tradition of the Big House, epitomised by the wearing of muted tweeds, heavy cords, and the ubiquitous - and usually imported - waxed jackets. The brainchild of Eddie and Patricia Cullen, REDGEWOOD Town and Country has now evolved into a sophisticated range of coats and jackets, as likely to be worn in Dublin, Paris or London as on a day's racing at the Curragh or Leopardstown.

The Cullens' enterprise is based in Thomastown, County Kilkenny, one of the most beautifully situated towns in Ireland. And their garments, evocative of a distinctively Irish way of life, are named after some of the great Irish Houses: Straffan, County Kildare; Norelands on the Mount Juliet Estate, County Kilkenny; and Woodstock at nearby Inistioge, Co. Kilkenny. They are also just the kind of thing to wear when visiting historic houses and gardens - a favourite pastime both of the Cullens and of this author.

INTRODUCTION

To travel through Ireland is to be constantly reminded of history. You can never go far without seeing traces of a ringfort or a prehistoric tumulus, glimpsing a ruined tower or catching sight of the remains of abandoned cottages or the roof of a handsome mansion behind the high walls of a demesne. The dwelling places of the past are a tantalising aspect of the landscape, provoking curiosity that is not easily satisfied.

Even in the small corner of Wicklow where I lived until recently, I was constantly made aware of the past by the ruins of an O'Toole tower, sacked by Cromwell as he marched south in 1650; by St Valery's eleventh-century cross and its eerie double shadow; by the house I lived in for fifteen years where diaries and records on loan from the original family provided a picture of everyday life in the years after it was built in 1836. One of the things that enthrals me about Ireland is the way the veil between past and present is so diaphanous that what went before is apparent but yet remains mysterious.

Houses and the clues they provide about social history have always had a special fascination for me. On one level, they provide insights into previous lifestyles; on another, homes provide tantalising clues about the families and individuals who lived in them. And in Ireland especially there is a strong connection between the wider context of history and its impact on families, their fortunes and their homes. To open a door on a house with a past is, in effect, to gain an intimate perspective on history.

There are now more houses open to the public in Ireland than ever before, for a number of reasons. In the south, Dúchas - The Heritage Service (formerly known as the heritage section of the Office of Public Works) have recently added a number of notable houses - among them Castletown, Emo Court and Rathfarnham Castle - to the number of heritage sites in their care. (In the north of Ireland the exemplary National Trust are the main guardians of historic properties and sites.) Individual county councils and local conservation bodies have also been involved in imaginative restoration and opening schemes. More individuals are generously opening their houses to the public and the Great Houses, Castles and Gardens of Ireland marketing group list dozens of properties and gardens which are open throughout Ireland, in their excellent brochure.

Most interesting of all, for those who enjoy roads less travelled, are the houses which are now open under the Properties of Significant Architectural and Historic Interest scheme. Designed to aid conservation of such properties, owners qualify under a Finance Act for tax relief on their buildings or gardens and are required to open to the public for 90 days a year. Not all of those listed are included in this book, for a variety of reasons, but the list is available on request from Bord Fáilte.

There is no comprehensive guide at present to those houses which are open to the public on a full- or part-time basis and this book is designed to fill that gap. It is a very personal guide, reflecting personal taste, and includes the kinds of places that I know people like me who love pottering about and discovering intriguing aspects of Ireland will enjoy. As in my previous book, the suggestions for places to stay are not typical B&B type accommodation but interesting homes, with histories and owners to match, and the pubs and restaurants are chosen for their surroundings and original food. The term 'house' covers every kind of furnished or semi-furnished dwelling, from castles to cottages and from mansions to modest terraced dwellings. The majority of the houses listed are of the larger kind - this is a reflection of history and of the type of houses that are open. Perhaps in future we can look forward to the opening of further small homes, which, like the excellent Shaw birthplace in Dublin, are intimate, easier to relate to than the 'big house' and reflect different strata of Irish life. These houses are now valued in a way that they were not in the recent past and their architecture and furnishings are seen as offering examples of the finest crafts of the day and as repositories of both personal and domestic history. Some of the more spectacular ruined houses and historic sites are also featured.

The very nature of Irish history and politics makes the strong connection between individual lives and homes inevitable. The arrival of Christianity, the foundation of great monastic centres, invasion, colonisation, plantation, wars, plagues, Cromwell's pogrom, the seizure and confiscation of Irish-owned land, the Penal Laws, the Famine, Land Commissions, the Troubles, all affected how and where people lived. Similarly, architecture was subject to a whole variety of influences, particularly the trends in English architecture from the eighteenth century onwards, and these influences were in turn Irish-ified.

Ireland has a very rich legacy from the past, stretching back to the first Neolithic farmers and their great megalithic tombs. There are traces of Bronze Age houses – at Lough Gur for instance – and the countryside carries innumerable traces of raths, hillforts, crannógs and ringforts, dating back to the Bronze and Iron Ages. Mass conversion to Christianity followed the mission of St Patrick in the last half of the fifth century and the great monastic settlements were eventually to make Ireland into an island of saints and scholars. By the time the first Viking invasions occurred there had been a distinctive Celtic culture for over a millennium where a pastoral people were organised along tribal lines and the Brehon Law system was established. The longships of the Norsemen came nosing up Irish inlets and harbours in search of plunder, and the Vikings stayed to found coastal settlements at Dublin, Wicklow, Wexford, Arklow, Waterford, Cork and Limerick, from the 840s until their overthrow by Brian Boru.

The arrival of the great monastic orders – first the Cistercians and then the Augustinians at the start of the twelfth century – heralded the introduction of a new form of church architecture, just as the invasion by the Anglo-Normans in 1169 laid the foundations of modern architecture and of our towns and cities. The Normans rapidly overran large areas of the country, particularly Wexford, Carlow, parts of Waterford, Tipperary, Meath and Dublin, and later most of Tipperary, north Cork and east Limerick, turning up their long noses at anything but the best land. Motte and bailey forts, constructed to defend their territories, were replaced by strong stone castles like Trim Castle in County Meath. Land was worked on a manorial system, with moated farms surrounded by farm buildings and cottages. As towns grew they were usually walled; Fethard and Kilmallock are good surviving examples. However, Norman dominance was dealt a body blow in the fourteenth century by a combination of a worsening of the climate, the Black Death and the Bruce invasion.

After Mary Tudor went to her grave with the loss of Calais engraved on her heart, England began to see a French invasion via the backdoor of Ireland as a threat. The Tudors took drastic action to secure their exposed flank, and ruthless suppression of the Irish followed. Laois and Offaly were planted, the colonisation of Munster followed and then Ulster. In those perilous times, defensive tower houses for the gentry and cabins sheltering within the safety of walled towns predominated throughout the fifteenth and sixteenth centuries. The first undefended manors - like Ormond Castle at Carrick-on-Suir - began to be built during Elizabeth I's reign, but few of them survive.

With the final breaking of Celtic resistance and the Flight of the Earls in 1607, the plantation of Ulster followed, bringing in its wake plantation houses and villages. Resentment over plantation and the rise of Nonconformism sowed the seeds for the 1641 rising, in which the Old Irish were joined by the Old English for the complexities of the Eleven Years War, ultimately leading to Cromwell's terrible pogrom of 1649 to 1650. These years of war, famine and plague reduced the population of Ireland to a mere half a million and their impact is vividly revealed in the stories of families and their houses. Fourteen Talbots of Malahide breakfasted together before the Battle of the Boyne; none of them returned. The Rothes, a family of merchants in Kilkenny, lost their home and regained it twice over, like scores of other families.

Only after the Restoration of Charles II did anything like stability return. The Duke of Ormonde, on his return from French exile, gave Dublin the Royal Hospital to rival Les Invalides in Paris. Some confiscated estates were restored, only to be lost again when Ireland became the battlefield for the right to the British throne. The defeat of James II's forces at the Boyne, Aughrim and Limerick brought about the final reversal of fortune for the Old Irish aristocracy; many joined the flight of the Wild Geese into exile, others converted expediently to the Protestant faith.

Very few houses still survive from the end of the seventeenth century - Beaulieu, with its steeply pitched roof and panelled interiors, is one of the rare exceptions. Many were demolished to make way for later houses.

A golden age of architecture was about to begin, albeit in the shadow of mass dispossession and the Penal Laws. At the beginning of the seventeenth century Catholics owned ninety per cent of the land in Ireland, but after the Siege of Limerick Catholic ownership had shrunk to fourteen per cent and would be reduced still further by the restrictive Penal Laws. In the 100 years of peace that followed the Battle of the Boyne, the rich and secure built magnificent follies de grandeur. As Lady Louisa Conolly of Castletown House remarked, 'there are few occupations more entertaining than building'. And build the new Ascendancy did, on a scale that frequently beggared their heirs.

The first and grandest of the great Palladian houses was Castletown House, built in 1722 for an Irishman of humble Donegal ancestry, Speaker (William) Conolly. Others followed, like Strokestown and Florence Court. Dublin boomed, and fine public buildings and ordered squares appeared. Architectural practices flourished and Edward Lovett Pearce, Richard Castle and James Gandon reigned supreme, while stuccodores like the Lafrancini brothers and Robert West clothed ceilings and walls in a plaster artwork of miraculous beauty. Tastes shifted; neo-classical style defined great houses like Castle Coole by James Wyatt and became a glorious exercise in perfection with the Marino Casino, built for the Earl of Charlemont by his architect and friend William Chambers. Improving landlords built model estate villages; the 1st Earl of Sligo had James Wyatt design Westport, and Lord Hartland made the main street at Strokestown wider than the Ringstrasse in Vienna. In many of the provincial towns fine streets grew up around market houses.

As the rise in Gothic style took hold in the imaginations of the affluent at the turn of the century, vast baronial castles were built from scratch, and classical houses which sometimes cloaked earlier castles were turned back into castles again. Nothing pleased better than excess. William Bury, 1st Earl of Charleville commissioned Francis Johnston to design Charleville Forest in 1798, leaving his estate severely embarrassed; the Pakenhams enlarged Tullynally Castle yet again and by the time Richard Morrison - Johnston's rival - designed a further addition in 1839 it had become the largest castellated mansion in Ireland. The vogue for Gothic ran in tandem with Greek revival architecture, like Francis Goodwin's design for Lissadell commissioned by Sir Robert Gore-Booth, and, although development slowed in Dublin after the 1801 Act of Union, country house building continued unabated. At Castle Ward in County Down, Viscount Bangor and his wife Lady Bligh could not agree on a style and compromised with a mansion which had a classical front and a Gothic back. Handsome institutions were built with serious purposes in mind: to serve God, Mammon, the mad and the bad.

The Famine was a disaster waiting to happen. Subsistence farming, a population explosion, the subdivision of land, rack renting, dependence on a single crop, mismanagement, and landlordism all contributed. A million died, a million emigrated; one third of landlords took no rents, about ten per cent went bankrupt, and a quarter of the land in Ireland was sold off under the Encumbered Estates Act. Decades of land agitation, reform and land redistribution followed. The final fling of country house building, as the Italian palazzo style came into fashion, was based most often on wealth from trade, like linen tycoon Andrew Mulholland's Ballywalter Park in County Down. The leading architects of the day were Benjamin Woodward and Sir Thomas Deane, and Charles Lanyon of Lanyon and Lynn. Mass production and Victorian inventiveness made life comfortable for the rising middle classes as the suburbs spread and county councils began a programme of building cottages for labourers.

After the early twentieth-century upheavals of civil war, the foundation of the Irish state, two world wars and Troubles old and new, Ireland has, in the last decades, come of age as a nation. There was always a magnificent tradition of hospitality in Ireland; no house great or small was closed to strangers. Now houses themselves, from castles to cottages, are accepted for what they are - an open door on living history.

Oscar Wilde once said that he liked men who have a future and women who have a past. The open houses of Ireland hopefully have both.

The Swiss Cottage

VALLEY COUNTRY

Carlow, Kilkenny, Tipperary, Waterford

My heart always lifts at any excuse to explore different parts of Ireland, and especially at the prospect of heading south-east. It would be hard to put my finger on the reason for its fascination for me, and perhaps that is part of the charm of the place. It is a subtle landscape of intimate vistas, never fully revealed, whose secrets remain concealed by a fold of the hills or a bend in a river, so that their appearance comes as all the more enchanting.

For years I had joined the lemming-like rush for the wilder west, so that the discovery of this sunny corner of Ireland came as a delightful surprise. Now I have to keep going back to try to discover the essence of a place that has given me a wonderful store of visual memories, many of them centred on historical buildings in the most perfect of settings. Among these are the extraordinary sight of the medieval silhouette of the town of Fethard in County Tipperary, or the prospect of the Blackwater River seen from Dromana, a house built on a FitzGerald stronghold hundreds of feet above the river, or Huntington Castle revealed at the end of an avenue of limes in the village of Clonegal.

Both the Normans and the Vikings found the south-east coast of Ireland the most accessible part of the country. The Viking influence can still be seen in the names of their favoured landing places - Wicklow (from *Viking* and *ló*), Waterford, Arklow. The rich land, capable of growing wheat and even wine, also drew the monastic orders to found abbeys like Jerpoint, Kells and Ferns.

To the north, the Wicklow mountains formed a natural barrier against the influence of English rule in the Pale and a haven for the Irish, especially Irish rebels, in country as wild as anything the west could offer. To the south, the character of the landscape is dictated by the valleys of the Slaney, the Barrow, the Suir, the Nore and the

Blackwater. Wherever there is a river you will find not only the most beautiful countryside - rounded hills, wooded slopes and verdant water meadows - but the most interesting of houses, villages, castles and abbeys. Modest mountain ranges also produce some of the most beguiling scenery: the Blackstairs, dominated by Mount Leinster; the Comeraghs; the Knockmealdowns, with a spectacular drive over the pass known as the Vee; the Galtees; and the Ballyhouras.

Taking to roads least travelled often produces the most memorable discoveries in Ireland. It is also a good way to get lost - given Irish signposting - but you won't have to endure the horrors of being pursued by thundering lorries, à la Steven Spielberg's *Duel*.

EXPLORING

Starting from Dublin, if I wanted to give myself a wonderful treat I would take the back roads over the Wicklow mountains and head south for County Carlow. For glorious mountain scenery there is a detour over the Sally Gap before heading down to Laragh through the beautiful wooded valley, then on to Clonegal with its extraordinary watch-house village and intriguing castle. Duckett's Grove, an 1830 Gothic fantasy near Carlow, is one of the more spectacular ruins. The towns and villages of the river valleys - Tullow and Bunclody on the Slaney, Graiguenamanagh on the Barrow (don't miss the restored medieval abbey of Duiske), and especially Thomastown, Inistioge and Bennettsbridge on the Nore - are all rewarding to visit, and drives along the river valleys take in some beautiful countryside.

Medieval Kilkenny is a good central point for exploring the surrounding area and has St Canice's Cathedral, the Tholsel, Kilkenny Castle and wonderful shops (don't miss the Kilkenny Design Workshops in the castle stables). The ruins of the fortified priory of St Mary at Kells are very impressive. Tintern Abbey, founded in 1200 by William the Earl Marshall, has recently been restored, and opened in June 1998. The slightly later Jerpoint Abbey at Thomastown is outstanding and opens daily (except Tuesday) from March to October (10am-5pm). There is a delightful *cottage orné* in the glen and a waterfall garden at Kilfane, Thomastown (open May-September, Tuesday-Sunday, 2-6pm). This is also an outstanding area for crafts and there is a craft trail which includes names like Nicholas Mosse of Bennettsbridge and the Kiltrea Bridge Potteries.

Shankill Castle, Ballysallagh House and Dunleckney Manor are all near to Kilkenny city and make a good mini tour. East of Kilkenny city at Tullaroan is Curragh, a seventeenth-century two-storey thatched farmhouse, its interior furnished to give an insight into the lifestyle of a prosperous Irish farming family in the 1880s (open March-November, 10am-5.30pm, Sunday 2-6pm; teas are served in the old dairy). The name Smithwick is famous for beer made at the family brewery in Kilkenny and Kilcreene Lodge is the Smithwick family home on the outskirts of Kilkenny. The oldest part of the house dates from 1670 and the main part of the house dates from 1863 (open 14 April-4 July).

Among the impressive ruins which you won't find mentioned in guide books are the 1840s classical mansion Castleboro House, seat of the Carews, Coolbawn House, an 1840 Tudor revival fantasy, and Wilton Castle, near Enniscorthy, designed by Daniel Robertson in the early nineteenth century. Near Waterford are the ruins of a Le Poer castle at Granny, dating in part back to the thirteenth century. Also dating from the thirteenth century, Enniscorthy Castle, in the centre of

Huntington Castle

9

Enniscorthy, is the setting for the County Museum commemorating the county's history, particularly local participation in the momentous events of 1798. Berkeley Forest, built in 1780, houses the Berkeley Costume and Toy Museum, a magnificent collection of costumes and toys from the eighteenth and nineteenth centuries.

One of the best ways to see the river valleys is by boat, and the Galley Cruising Restaurants, based at New Ross and Waterford, not only cruise the rivers but can also wine and dine passengers in the heated saloons from April to October (tel. 051-421723). Also at New Ross is intriguing slate-faced Dunamin, with unusual hexagonal towers at either end of the building and a history dating back to the seventeenth century. It is said to be the haunt of not one but two ghosts (open June-September, Thursday and Sunday, 2-5.30pm, or by appointment). A visit to Ballyhack Castle at Ballyhack on the north shore of the Waterford harbour, a 1450 tower house built by the Knights Hospitaller of St John (open daily July-August, 12 noon-6pm), provides an excuse for another voyage on the ferry between Ballyhack and Passage East. Worth a detour are the pretty fishing village of Dunmore East and Ardmore, which climbs the hill above Ardmore strand and has fine ecclesiastic remains, including St Declan's oratory and a round tower that is 97 feet high.

The Blackwater has to be Ireland's answer to the Loire or the Rhine. This majestic river flows through glorious countryside where the roofs of great houses can be glimpsed through the surrounding trees. You could hardly see anything more dramatic than Lismore Castle rising above trees on a cliff top or Dromana House high on a crag above the Blackwater. Nor is there anything more extraordinary than the follies of Ballysaggartmore. High in a beautiful wooded glen, these Gothic gateways - one built over a cascade - are a symbol of sibling rivalry between a Mrs Keily and her brother; the grandiose castle which she planned, to match the follies, never materialised, due to shortage of funds.

Lismore Castle, dating back in part to the early seventeenth century, was mainly constructed to the design of Joseph Paxton, of Crystal Palace fame, and is owned by the Duke of Devonshire (the gardens are open daily, 11 April-27 September, 1.45-4.45pm). Portlaw is a model Quaker village which was laid out by the Malcolms for their millworkers and nearby is the magnificent demesne at Curraghmore, seat of the Le Poers and their descendants since 1170. The house, incorporating a medieval tower, dates mainly from the eighteenth century and has wonderful plasterwork. The house is open to group tours only, on application to Lord Waterford (tel. 051-387102). The grounds, with an arboretum and shell grotto created by the Countess of Tyrone in 1754, are open Thursdays and bank holidays only (2-5pm).

Tipperary, the largest county in the valley country, is one of the great undiscovered secrets of Ireland, and I have often wondered, considering the Golden Vale of the Suir, whether Giraldus Cambrensis had this countryside in mind when he described Ireland as a 'land of milk and honey'. This is Butler country. Carrick-on-Suir grew up beside their Ormond Castle, Clonmel has many reminders of Norman times and the Butler castle at Cahir is a major attraction. Don't miss the Aladdin's cave of Fleury Antiques in the main square at Cahir. Also look out for the distinctive brick frontage of the Cashel Palace, built for Bishop Bolton in 1730 (now a hotel), and his 1744 library (now the GPA Library) in the grounds of the cathedral (open June-August, 11am-4.30pm). The group of medieval buildings perched on the Rock of Cashel is a breathtaking sight and Cahir Castle in the centre of Cahir, built for the Butlers in the thirteenth and fifteenth centuries, is one of the largest and best preserved castles (open March-October daily). Fethard is a medieval town with a 1303 Augustinian friary, and Kilcooley Abbey, founded by the Cistercians, has a magnificent rose window. Thomastown Castle at Golden, built in 1812 to Richard Morrison's Tudor revival design, is a memorable ruin. Knitwear designer Cyril Cullen and his wife Margi have set up a porcelain and knitwear gallery and home in fascinating Farney Castle, incorporating a fifteenth-century round tower and 1800 Gothic house, near Holycross. Harp recitals by their four harpist daughters can be arranged, tel. 0504-43281.

Tipp is certainly worth the trip. And where else would you find a village with a name like Twopothouse?

PLACES TO STAY/EAT

S et in a most glorious garden, Altamont, near Tullow, is also a base for residential courses, including those in flower painting and historic houses. Accommodation is in a seventeenth-century building, tel. 0503-59444; the gardens are open on Sunday afternoons, 2-6pm.

Friends wax lyrical about the original food at Danette's Feast at Urglin Glebe just outside Carlow (tel. 0503-40817). Foxmount Farm, near the pretty fishing village of Dunmore East, has a charming Georgian façade and offers the best of home-grown produce cooked to perfection, tel. 051-874308.

Dating to 1700, Sherwood Park House near Balloon offers candlelit dinners and canopy beds, tel. 0503-59117. The views and interiors at eighteenth-century Clomahon on the Slaney are a treat in themselves, but then there is also Maria Levinge's wonderful food, using home-grown organic foods whenever possible, tel. 054-77253. Richmond House, a comfortable hotel in a Georgian house just outside Cappoquin, I remember both for its friendliness and for a superb dinner, tel. 058-54278; ditto Penny and Rafa Alvarez's eighteenth-century Cedarfield House, just outside Carrick-on-Suir, tel. 051-640164. For culinary treats Mary Bowe's Marlfeld House at Gorey is especially recommended; guests eat in the conservatory dining-room and the bedrooms in the 1830s house are splendid, tel. 055-21124.

I have memories of the most superb breakfast at Flemingstown House, a farm just outside Kilmallock, where, not surprisingly, Mrs Sheedy King has won national prizes for her breakfasts, tel. 063-98093. Friends loved their stay at Lismacue (included in this chapter) for its views of the Knockmealdowns and the relaxed atmosphere in this 1813 family home, tel. 062-54106. White's in the centre of Wexford acts as a gathering point during the Wexford Opera Festival. It is a characterful former coaching inn dating back to 1779; try the Country Kitchen for snacks and Captain White's for dining. The Neptune, appropriately for a restaurant on Ballyhack harbour, specialises in seafood, from hot buttered lobster to scallops in orange and ginger sauce, tel. 051-89284.

THE SWISS COTTAGE

Cahir, County Tipperary

The setting for Ireland's most outstanding *cottage orné* remains as sylvan as any world-weary nineteenth-century aristocrat in search of the simple life could wish. The approach is through Kilcommon forest and visitors emerge from a woodland path to cross a bridge with a wonderful prospect down the River Suir as it meanders through water meadows towards Cahir. And the fact that the cottage remains hidden, while the entrance is through a mysterious tunnel, only serves to enhance the surprise in store. Visitors then climb spiral stairs to the entrance hall and have to step outside before they can absorb the full impact of the building. The place has a gingerbread charm all its own. The cottage crouches down, its feet in old-fashioned flowers, its mullioned windows peering from under a heavy fringe of thatch. It seems to have a life of its own, sprouting a whimsical balcony here, a dormer there, its duck-egg blue walls decorated with dark green trellis where no two patterns are alike.

The building is a highly sophisticated expression of an architectural fantasy in the picturesque style, where everything was inspired by nature. The billowing thatched roof is as undulating as the slopes and hollows of the surrounding glade. Artful boughs support the projecting roof to form a veranda, leafy branches frame mirrors and edge overmantels, and even the circular floor in the entrance hall mimics the pattern of a spider's web.

Here was an elegant sylvan retreat where the privileged could ape the simple pleasures of country life in a manner totally divorced from the squalid realities of the lives of the poor. The cottage was an expression of the new fashion for the picturesque, a reaction against the fashion for the mannered manipulation of the landscape and a move towards an appreciation of nature for its own sake. The concept also derived from the French ornamental farm at Hameau de Trianon, popularised by Marie Antoinette, which offered a respite from the excesses of life at Court.

The creation of this idealised version of a peasant cottage - probably to the design of the celebrated architect John Nash - was all the more remarkable since Richard Butler Lord Caher (the title is spelt differently from the town), for whom the cottage was built, had once known abject poverty himself.

The story of Richard's inheritance of the title and the fortunes of the Butlers of Cahir outdoes the plot of the most melodramatic novel. And had it not been for the interference of a good-hearted busybody his story might have ended very differently. The Butlers concerned were descendants (on the wrong side of the blanket) of the Earls of Ormonde and their seat was Cahir Castle. When James Butler Baron Caher died in 1786, the estate passed from his nephew to an impoverished cousin, both of whom died in quick succession. When scheming relatives discovered that Richard was next in line they had the lad, together with his sibling, kidnapped from his destitute mother and sent to France.

Diarist Dorothea Herbert tells the story: 'Mrs Jeffries, sister of the Chancellor, passing through Cahir heard at the inn the history of the old beggar woman and her two children. She sent for the woman, took notes of her tale, which she laid before the Chancellor Lord Fitzgibbon. On further investigation the whole story was proved fact and the Chancellor procured warrants for bringing the children over. Miss Jeffries was in a convent in France. Mrs Jeffries sent over for her daughter and undertook guardianship of the lost children. They were found in a miserable garret, all overgrown with hair. Mrs Jeffries had them educated and then made up a match for her daughter and the young Lord Caher.'

The pair were just 16 and 17 when they married and the couple soon became leading social lights. The new Lord Caher was an improving landlord, sat in the British House of Lords after the Act of Union and was created Earl of Glengall, while vivacious dark-haired Lady Glengall was a great promoter of amateur theatricals.

The cottage was used for summer entertainment, for picnics, tableaux and outdoor concerts, and possibly also as a place of dalliance for the Earl and his mistress. But, like its creator, the cottage had its own reversal of fortune. Together with the estate it remained in family hands and was used variously as a fishing and a shooting lodge until it was sold to the Land Commission in 1961 following the death of Richard Butler Charteris. The cottage was bought from the Commission by its caretaker William Heavey for £50, but after he died in 1980 the cottage remained empty for a number of years and was badly vandalised. It was rescued thanks to the intervention of Bill Roth of the New Inn, who offered some finance if the OPW would take over the building, which it duly did, backed by the Irish Georgian Society, the Cahir Community Council, the Irish-American foundation and SERTO. Further funds for completing the restoration came from the American philanthropist Mrs Sally Aall through her family trust, the Port Royal Foundation.

Designer Sybil Connolly succeeded admirably in reinterpreting the interiors, allowing the mood of the cottage itself to dictate the style, rather than attempting to reproduce a historic interior. The rooms are decorated and furnished in keeping with a mood of Regency frivolity. One can readily imagine ladies withdrawing in the heat of the day to rest on the sleigh bed in the upstairs bedroom, cooled by the breeze from the balcony and soothed by the blue-and-white toile wallcovering copied from a 1770s fragment in the National Museum and made by Robinsons of Ballsbridge. Wallpapers were specially designed by Ms Connolly for the music room and second bedroom, the former featuring a small leaf design, the other a trellis print combined with lily of the valley chintz.

It would be easy too to conjure up the company exclaiming over the beechwood chairs which simulate knotted branches or the wonderful drawing-room wallpaper, some of which survived and was restored and copied. Intended as a conversation piece, the wallpaper, originally by Dufour of Paris, is titled Rives du Bosphore and depicts turbaned Turks going about their business amid idyllic surroundings of exotic mosques and lush gardens. Its mood perfectly reflects the elements of fantasy and escapism which make the Swiss Cottage so fascinating.

OPEN Mid March, Oct. & Nov., 10am-4.30pm; April, 10am-5pm; May-Sept., daily 10am-6pm. Access by guided tour only, tel. 052-41144.

ADMISSION £2, concession £1.50, children £1, family £5.

DIRECTIONS Follow the signs from the centre of Cahir.

DAMER HOUSE AND CASTLE

Roscrea, County Tipperary

The successful, the newly promoted and the *arriviste* very often mark their rising status by having a grand new house built and acquiring a new wife to complete the picture. John Damer was no exception. He obtained the town and lordship of Roscrea in 1722, married in 1726 and built a handsome new house within the curtilage of the old Ormond Castle he had bought in the centre of the town. Perhaps he liked the idea of being lord of all he surveyed when he built his three-storey town house there rather than in a rural setting; perhaps he preferred the security of high walls and the nearby defensive castle.

The brick house with its nine-bay front over a basement and bold doorcase topped by a scrolled pediment has a splendid pine staircase. The side of the risers are carved with roses, the newels are reeded and have Corinthian capitals, even the handrail is carved, and the broad shallow steps are a pleasure to climb. A similar staircase is to be found in the former Bishop's Palace at Cashel, designed by Sir Edward Lovett Pearce in 1730. Houses like John Damer's were a vote of confidence in peace and the growing prosperity of the privileged Ascendancy class.

The story of Roscrea Castle belongs to the previous turbulent centuries. Roscrea has a strategically important position, guarding the pass in the Slieve Bloom and Devil's Bit mountains, giving access from the east to the Shannon complex. The Normans secured with a motte and bailey fort the settlement that had grown up around the monastery founded by St Cronan, probably on the site of the present castle which was built from 1280. The Butlers were the dominant influence among the feudal Norman lords who had been granted lands in Tipperary by King John following the Norman invasion.

And the Butlers' royal connections gave the county semi-independent palatinate status. In 1315 Edmund Butler, Earl of Carrick, was granted the royal castle of Roscrea and the Butler family held it until the castle fell to Cromwell's men, who were garrisoned there. The Butlers regained their properties after the Restoration. During the Williamite wars, in the time of the pro-William 2nd Duke of Ormond, the castle became a centre for anti-Jacobite forces. The 2nd Duke subsequently sold the property to Robert Curtis of Inane.

From the mid eighteenth century both the castle and house were used as a barracks. The house also served a variety of purposes - school, sanatorium, civil offices and technical school - before being abandoned in the 1960s. By the 1970s it was threatened with demolition and was rescued and restored by the Irish Georgian Society and the Roscrea Heritage Society. Apart from local exhibitions and some lively cartoons hanging on the first floor, the Damer House is sadly empty and represents a missed opportunity to display early eighteenth-century furniture. The thirteenth-century tower house of the castle, with its impressive first-floor hall and second-storey chamber and all the intriguing devices of a medieval castle - from a trip stair to a windowless dungeon - is open to the public. A formal Queen Anne-style garden has also been created behind the Damer House. Conservation and restoration of the complex has been undertaken by the OPW since 1989.

OPEN June-Sept., daily 9.30 a.m.- 6.30 p.m. or by special arrangement, tel. 0505-21850.

ADMISSION £2.50, groups £1.75, children £1. Guided tours of castle. Toilets, parking.

DIRECTIONS Situated in the centre of Roscrea.

TOURIN

Cappoquin, County Waterford

Embraced by the Blackwater River, where it curves around a particularly lovely stretch of water meadows and woods, Tourin holds not one but three houses in a perfect illustration of the progression of building styles in Ireland through the seventeenth, eighteenth and nineteenth centuries.

The place name, Tourin - which means bleaching green - probably dates from Elizabeth I's reign, when Sir Walter Raleigh was given a 1,000-acre seigniory on land stretching up to the nearby village of Affane where he established cherry and apple orchards and grew flax.

At that time the lands at Tourin were owned by the Anglo-Norman Roche family who built the seventeenth-century tower house. The five-storey strong house is particularly well preserved and, unusually, the oak centring used to

support the vaulted ceiling survives, perhaps because the tower has always been in use.

In the early eighteenth century an E-shaped manor was built onto the old castle and a large section of this is incorporated into the present farm manager's house. The refinement of the building can be gauged by the pair of decorative urns - now relegated to the garden - which graced the parapet, and the handsome bolection moulded chimney piece, now in the nineteenth-century house.

The Roches, being Catholic Old English, supported the Royalist cause in the confused period of rebellion leading up to Cromwell's lightning strike on Ireland in 1649. Their estates were forfeited and the lands granted instead to a John Nettles, whose great-grandson either sold the property or lost it in a wager at poker to Richard Musgrave, a former steward, in 1780. The Musgrave family consolidated their position and 60 years later, in about 1844, built an Italianate mansion in the style popularised by Sir Charles Barry's Travellers Club in London. The architect may have been

Dubliner Abraham Denny, who designed Whitfield Court at Kilmeaden.

Tourin's architecture belongs to the interesting transitional period when taste began to move away from strict Georgian classicism towards the Italian and Renaissance style.

Here was a house designed for comfort and family life, as well as for status; a two-storey, five-bay fronted villa featuring a deep eaved roof supported by a bracket cornice, the horizontal interest being repeated in a pronounced string course. Inside, the main rooms lead off a splendid inner hallway and staircase hall which runs two thirds of the depth of the house and is dominated by an imperial staircase. The grained handrail at the foot of the staircase is supported by putti. The hall is lit from above by a lantern decorated with acanthus leaves and by three arch-headed windows and is overlooked on two sides by arched galleries linking the first-floor bedrooms.

The principal receiving room was the bow-windowed drawing-room, which has a frieze of oak and vine leaves denoting wisdom and hospitality. There is a floor with an inlaid border, and French doors sheltered by an elegant veranda. All the main rooms of the house have had fine eighteenth-century marble fireplaces fitted by Mrs T. Jameson, the mother of the present owners. The second drawing-room or morning-room features sun-filled landscapes by Kirstin Jameson, a descendant of the Musgrave family, whose studio now occupies the study.

Beside the house is a delightful informal shrub garden and arboretum filled with a fine collection of giant rhododendrons, camellias and magnolias and carpeted with bulbs in springtime. There is an ongoing restoration programme at Tourin.

OPEN 3 Feb.-30 June & 1 Sept.-28 Nov., 9.30am-4pm.

ADMISSION £3.50, children £2.

DIRECTIONS Take the wooden bridge over the Blackwater from the Lismore side of Cappoquin, follow the winding road, taking one left turn. Turn into Tourin after the second gate lodge on the left.

KILKENNY CASTLE

Kilkenny

The grey bulk of Kilkenny Castle occupies a commanding position overlooking the River Nore and dominates the city which grew up at its feet. In its 800-year history the castle has served many roles - as a major Norman stronghold, a medieval fortress, and a power base of the Butler dynasty. It fell to Cromwell's army, and was altered in the last century to become a Victorian version of a medieval castle. But the most magnificent period of its long and turbulent history undoubtedly came following the return from exile of James Butler, on the Restoration of Charles II.

James Butler, first Duke of Ormonde - known as the Great Duke - introduced a new chapter in the story of Irish architecture. He returned to Ireland in 1662, inspired by his sojourns in the courts of Europe, and transformed the grim fortress at Kilkenny into a comfortable château in the French style. The great corner towers of the castle, originally built around 1190, were given conical roofs topped with cupolas, ducal coronets and weather vanes. Steeply pitched roofs and a gabled garden front were also added and later, in the 1690s, a splendid entrance gateway. The castle was furnished in the most extravagant style - 'Rich on every side with marble and ornamented with many things so curious that those who have seen it say that it surpasses many palaces of Italy', according to contemporary observer Jorevin de Rocheford.

The Great Duke assumed the office of Lord Lieutenant of Ireland, based in Dublin Castle, and his greatest legacies to the city are the Royal Hospital at Kilmainham and the Phoenix Park.

The Butler dynasty in Ireland had been founded by Theobald Walter, who came to Ireland with the first Norman invasion. He laid the foundations for the family's wealth by acquiring the title of

Chief Butler to the King, with the lucrative right to a levy on wine imported by the King. The family name was changed to Butler and Walter's descendant, James Butler, 3rd Earl of Ormonde, bought Kilkenny Castle from the Marshall family at the end of the fourteenth century. Among the most colourful of the powerful Butlers was Black Tom, 10th Earl of Ormonde, an Elizabethan courtier and favourite of Queen Elizabeth. He updated the castle but made his principal Irish home at Carrick-on-Suir.

Two generations later, the Butler fortunes hung in the balance. James Butler, the 12th Earl, served as Lord Lieutenant and head of the King's army. However, following the civil war in England and the execution of Charles I he fled into exile and Cromwell brought his reign of terror to Ireland, attacking Kilkenny and its castle in 1650. The Butler estate was saved from confiscation by James Butler's wife and cousin, Elizabeth Preston, granddaughter of Black Tom, who succeeded in her claim that the lands and properties were her inheritance.

The Great Duke's heir, another James Butler, 2nd Duke of Ormonde, weathered the War of the Two Kings, having backed King William, only to lose everything through his support of the Stuart cause in 1716. The fortunes of both

the Butlers and the castle then went into decline for half a century. It wasn't until Walter Butler inherited the castle in 1766 and moved in with his son John and John's heiress wife Anne Wandesford that further work was carried out, including the creation of the park.

The castle owes its present appearance to the Kilkenny architect William Robertson, who, in 1826, apparently pointed out to the then Lady Ormonde that the castle wall was out of true and dangerous, landing a major commission as a result. Sadly, the Great Duke's restored interiors were swept away and the castle was given a rather uninteresting Gothic treatment. A vast picture gallery - inspired by medieval banqueting halls - and a new wing were added. The castle underwent further alterations, between 1859 and 1862. The gallery was remodelled by Benjamin Woodward, its timbers painted with extraordinary mythical beasts by John Hungerford Pollen. The Moorish staircase by Thomas Newenham Deane (Woodward's partner) and Gothic windows were also added at this time.

The Butlers had always had strong links with the British Crown, and this continued into the twentieth century and the twilight of the Ascendancy, when Edward VII and later George V were entertained at Kilkenny Castle. The Butlers left the castle in 1935. The contents were auctioned and, after standing empty for over 40 years, the castle was sold to the castle restoration committee for £50 and opened to the public in 1976.

One of the few pieces of original furniture, apart from the collection of family portraits and the magnificent Gobelin tapestries bought by the Great Duke, is the vast Georgian marble-topped table in the main hall, used on occasion for lying in state. Among the rooms which are open to the public is the dining-room in one of the twelfth-century towers and the first-floor library, restored to its original vibrant saffron yellow colour scheme. The bedrooms of the west wing are charmingly furnished in 1830s style, one with a delightful Chinese wallcovering with a pattern of pheasants and cherries. The most remarkable room of all is the Long Gallery, where it is still possible to imagine Victorian ladies taking their constitutionals up and down its 135-foot length, pausing no doubt to examine the white marble fireplace by John Hungerford Pollen depicting the extraordinary 800-year history of the Butlers.

OPEN April-May daily, 10.30am-5pm; June-Sept. 10am-7pm; Oct.-March, Tues.-Sun. 10.30am-12.45pm & 2-5pm. Access by guided tour only, tel. 056-21450.

ADMISSION £3, concession £2, children £1.25, family £7.70. Teas, guided tours, toilets, parking.

DIRECTIONS Situated in the middle of Kilkenny city.

SHANKILL CASTL

Paulstown, County Kilkenny

An Englishman's home may be his castle, but an Irish gentleman's home is often a castle, incorporated into a house, extended to become a mansion and finally Gothicised into a mock castle, with a conservatory or two added later for good measure.

Nowhere is this evolving approach to architecture more charmingly in evidence than at Shankill Castle. Here, the changing tastes of different generations have been added and subtracted to the extent that it is possible to see several different architectural styles in one room alone. The ante-room, for instance, features a Carolinian corner chimneybreast and tall, narrow doorcase with a wider Georgian door opposite and a Wyatt window which was installed during later Gothicisation of the castle.

The exterior of the castle belies its age. The original house had a shallow H-shaped front. A Gothic porch has been added and Wyatt windows installed in the three bays. One of the bays has been given a tower-like appearance and another has had small turrets added. The drawing-room wing to one side and a castellated kitchen wing are later additions.

The known history of Shankill, which takes its name from the old church, or 'Seanchill', in the grounds, begins with a minor branch of the Butlers of Ormonde who built a tower house on lands they held at Paulstown in the fifteenth and sixteenth centuries. The estate was inherited by Elizabeth Butler in 1708, and Peter Aylward married her, no mean feat for a member of the manor gentry whose family estates at Faithlegg in County Waterford had been confiscated by Cromwell. The Aylwards came from Bristol and were said to have provided the ships which brought the Anglo-Normans to Ireland in Strongbow's wake in 1170.

Peter Aylward had a house built in 1713 on the site of the tower. His

23

house may have incorporated some of the earlier building, and it was certainly quarried for his new home. When the Penal Laws - among them the 1704 Act for the Prevention of Further Growth of Popery - ruled out land ownership for Catholics, Peter Aylward 'turned'. Whether or not he was uneasy with his change of religion, he is said to haunt the house.

The central part of the castle - with its panelled hallway, its dining-room, boot room, study and ante-room - has not changed very much since Peter Aylward's day and many of the period details, including the handsome chimney pieces, remain intact. The typical symmetrical layout, with rooms ranged around a square central hall, can still be seen on the top floor, although the arrangement has been altered on the first floor.

The succeeding generations of Aylwards devoted their energies to public service and running the estate. The next building phase, by Nicholas Aylward IV, was in the 1820s, when the drawing-room wing was added and the Wyatt windows installed, together with crenellations and a Gothic tower and porch.

The next builder Aylward was James, who married Isabelle Newton Forbes, the Scottish widow of one of the Newtons of Dunleckney. The couple travelled to Italy and came

back with extravagant ideas and a magnificent Italian marble fireplace from Milan for the drawing-room. James and Isabelle were responsible for building the intriguing Gothic conservatory on the garden front of the house and for commissioning Daniel Robertson to design the hunt yard and the ostentatious castellated entrance gate and lodge at the end of the eighteenth-century *claire-voie*.

This entrance was known locally as the black gates, perhaps because local people objected to this new barrier on their path to the ancient burial plot at the pre-Reformation church. This old Catholic church may also be central to the tale of the priest who is said to haunt the avenue where legend has it he was the victim of a sectarian murder by his cousin, one of the Aylward ladies. But then Shankill lends itself to colourful stories and equally colourful arguments - experts don't agree, for instance, as to whether the 1861 conservatory (demolished a century later) outside the drawing-room was by Paxton or by Turner.

Was there an itinerant marbler at work in the big houses of Victorian Ireland? The *trompe-l'oeil* Siena marble paintwork in the late Georgian staircase hall is remarkably similar to the work in the halls of Dunkathel in County Cork and The Argory in County Armagh.

The march of domestic progress inside the house can be seen in the siting of the three different kitchens. Number one was in the basement under the hallway, number two was under the 1820s wing, while kitchen number three in the office wing added in the 1850s is still exactly as it was, complete with the original range (a miracle of modern convenience in its day) and bread oven. Shankill Castle and the house are now in the sympathetic hands of Geoffrey and painter Elizabeth Cope, who, as previous neighbours and visitors of twenty years standing, knew the place well, and all the stories connected with it.

Outside of the dining-room window is a breathtaking testament to the work undertaken by the Copes and the Conservation Volunteers of Ireland. The vanished long pond, a feature of the early eighteenth-century baroque design for the grounds, has been reinstated, acting as a mirror to the house. One of the three walled gardens has been restored and the Copes also have plans to restore the attics, with their intriguing box beds which were used by children and servants.

OPEN Easter weekend, Sundays and bank holidays; July-Aug., Sat. & Sun. 2-5.30pm, tel. 0503-26145.

ADMISSION £3 with guided tour of house, £2 grounds only. Groups at other times by appointment. Light refreshments in the 1850s kitchen; shop.

DIRECTIONS Shankill is on the N9 Carlow-Kilkenny road at Paulstown.

BALLYSALLAGH

Johnswell, County Kilkenny

One eminent historian maintains that it is still possible to this day to tell where the lines of Cromwellian settlement were drawn in some parts of the country simply by looking at the shape of the inhabitants' heads. The south-east corner of Ireland - where a heart-shaped tract of country in Kilkenny, Waterford and Wexford was allocated for settlement on Cromwell's under-paid soldiers - is as good a place as any to put this theory to the test. In 1653 the lands at Ballysallagh, owned by Nicholas Purcell of the prominent Kilkenny family, descendants of Sir Hugh Purcell, were forfeited. The 758 acres were granted to two Roundhead soldiers, William Gumble and Mark Moulde.

Nicholas Purcell died that year and his son Thomas - who had sided with the Catholic Confederates against Cromwell - was listed for deportation to Connacht in the winter of 1654/55. However, Thomas was not among the 44,000 Irish who were ethnically cleansed to beyond the Shannon, remaining instead in the Kilkenny area as a rapparee. As was often the case with settlers, Gumble and Moulde did not make a go of things. Times were hard, for Cromwell's nine months of terror in 1649/50 had left famine, plague and labour shortages in their wake and farms fared very badly. Local lore has it that Thomas Purcell succeeded in buying his land back from the pair for a sum of £20, with two horses thrown in.

A decade after the 1660 Restoration, a long period of expansion began for landowners. By the early eighteenth century the Purcells were prosperous enough to build a handsome house at Ballysallagh which bears the date of 1722. It seems probable that the house was built for Mary Purcell, granddaughter of Thomas, and her husband Gerald Byrne; the couple were married in 1707.

Ballysallagh is a charming example of an early Georgian house, with a characteristic steeply pitched roof and a Gothic door with fanlight and a lunette window in the break-front. The house has two unusual features: a limestone platband in place of a cornice and the character-istic gutters peculiar to the Kilkenny area. The house is largely unaltered except for some changes made in 1810 to the entrance and staircase hall, which include the addition of a handsome interior fanlight and a built-in Hepplewhite cabinet. A large family kitchen with double doors leading to the garden has recently been created in the basement.

The house is on a very pleasing scale, retaining delightful period details such as the built-in boot-check at the foot of the stairs and the original lime plaster in the basement. The timber of the roof trusses and rafters is all original and the attic provides a wonderfully timeless view of the joiner's skill.

The Purcell family and their descendants through marriage, the Doyles, remained at Ballysallagh for over 200 years and continued to hold the property despite the Penal Laws against Catholics. A measure of the family's prosperity can be gauged from the 1847 sale of the contents of the library on the death of Councillor William Doyle of Rutland Square West and Ballysallagh. The sale made £1,600, and one book alone fetched £60 (over £200,000 in today's terms).

When the present owners of the house, Kieran and Geralyn White, discovered the property, thanks to a small advertisement for a genuine Georgian house, it was badly neglected; the level of the soil had risen to the height of the first-floor windows. Now, twelve years later, Ballysallagh has been sensitively restored. All those details which help to give an old house an air of serenity and a sense of continuity with the past have been lovingly restored, including the sweeping driveway, the original farm buildings and the haha. There is even a new folly.

OPEN Feb. & 1 May–30 June, 9am–1pm.

ADMISSION £3 house, £2 garden.

DIRECTIONS Complicated, best to ask locally! 5 miles north-east of Kilkenny.

HUNTINGTON CASTLE

Clonegal, County Carlow

I t seemed inevitable that expectations were going to be surpassed when the weathered oak door of Huntington inched open to reveal Olivia Durdin-Robertson's pale Sitwellesque features. 'I can't let you in, I'm in the middle of a spell,' she intimated, vanishing into the panelled depths of the castle. But I was already enchanted - by the initial sight of the tower and by the appealing riverside village of Clonegal.

You come upon the castle unexpectedly, in the middle of the village, where a narrow gateway opens onto a magnificent avenue of ancient lime trees. Framed at the end is the square keep of the castle, its roof-line and porch modestly castellated. The drive sweeps past the front as the entrance is now at the rear of the house, through a

pretty courtyard, where the wonderful, eccentric accumulation of additions and alterations to the original 1625 tower house become apparent. The tower, which initially served as a garrison, was built for Laurence, the first and last Lord Esmonde, on what was formerly O'Kavanagh land, granted to the Neterville family by Elizabeth I before being sold to Lord Esmonde. Esmonde first married Eilis O'Flaherty, a granddaughter of Grace O'Malley the pirate queen, but then had his marriage annulled (thereby disinheriting his son, Thomas), on the grounds of her 'mere Irishry', and married one of the Butlers. Whether or not a curse was put on him by Eilis, who can say, but he never had an heir and he died on his way back to Huntington from the siege of Duncannon. Eilis can be seen waiting for him still (one of several ghosts that inhabit the castle) under a bush on the avenue, combing her long hair and accompanied by a white cat.

Cromwell took the castle, on his march south to Kilkenny, and stationed a garrison there. The village of Clonegal, with its watch-house village at one end and its prosperity based on six distilleries, was strategically important, guarding what was then a pass on the route from Dublin to Wexford. A member of the Colclough family who was left in charge of the castle had the temerity to present a bill for costs incurred by Cromwell's men and was shot for his pains. More wisely, Thomas Esmonde (son of Laurence) went into exile with Charles II in France and was created a baronet for his loyalty. Thomas's son - another Laurence - returned following the Restoration, imbued with French culture, and set about transforming Clonegal into his residence, enlarging the windows, partitioning the tower into manageable-sized rooms, adding the porch and planting the avenue of French limes. He also did his bit to rectify history by marrying Lucy Kavanagh, descendant of the O'Kavanaghs.

In the mid eighteenth century, the Huntington estate passed out of family hands and was sold to one of the ubiquitous Leslies for £2,000, but later it was rented by Esmonde descendants who had married into the Durdin family. Alexander Durdin II who inherited in 1849 made many additions to the back of the house, including the tapestry room and first-floor library which is rather like a miniature medieval banqueting hall, installed electricity (one of the first houses in Ireland to have that convenience) and plumbing. Alexander Durdin I took as his third wife the widow of William Penn, founder of Pennsylvania.

It is the proud boast of the Esmonde/Durdin/Robertson family that none of them has done anything in particular for the last 300 years. However, although they may not have had any involvement in war or politics, they were always creatively busy at Clonegal. Helen, Alexander's daughter, inherited and her husband, Herbert Robertson, continued making additions, including an Anglican chapel and a romantic balcony designed by his son Manning Robertson.

It is hard to say which is more diverting, the amazing collection of possessions packed into the house, with its bewildering changes of level, or the intriguing stories surrounding them and their owners.

There is the tapestry room, casually hung with a glorious 1750 Aubusson carpet. On another wall there is a picture of the Slaney Valley abandoned halfway through by the artist Cecil Lawson when he was rejected by Helen Durdin in favour of one of the other suitors who were in hot pursuit at the time, and a tiger skin rug, one of several big cats bagged by the intrepid Nora Parsons, wife of Manning, who was brought up as a boy and shot her first crocodile in India at the age of 17. There is a passageway so hung with clerical ancestors that it is known as the 'Vicar's Tea Party'. There is also a panelled tower bedroom, with a wonderful early fireplace and a four-poster bed (1835); a former occupant, Bishop Leslie, is said to haunt strangers. The castle was built 'on a batter' (diminishing) and at this point the window embrasure shows that the walls are five feet thick.

Nothing is quite as it seems. The dining-room chimney piece is original to the house, and carved with the date 1625, but the back of the fireplace rolls back to become a hatch to the kitchen. The strapwork ceiling looks appropriately Tudor, but was replaced after the original ceiling collapsed when Alexander Durdin tried to lighten the basement, and the walls are lined not with tapestry but with Bedouin tent hangings. Some of the wonderfully Gothic woodcarving around the castle turns out to be the recent work of David Durdin-Robertson, a talent which runs in the family; the oak mantelpiece in the drawing-room was carved by Alexander Durdin.

This is a home where the extraordinary becomes ordinary, perhaps inevitable when the tutor to the family - a friend of T. S. Eliot -

was chief of the English Druids and spent much of his time working on astrological charts. Every house has its own 'feel' and the atmosphere at Huntington Castle has an appeal all its own; perhaps there is literally an undercurrent there, attributable to the Temple of Isis in the basement. Far from being sinister, despite the presence of a dungeon (last used in 1921 by the IRA, who were involved in a battle there and then invited the family back to their home for afternoon tea), the place is positively cosy, with colourful shrines to the signs of the zodiac and a chapel of mothers and deities ranging from the mother-goddess Mut to the ram-headed god Amun-Ra. The Fellowship of Isis was founded by the Rev. Lawrence Durdin-Robertson, Baron of Strathloch (who ceased to minister when he became convinced that God is a woman), Pamela Durdin-Robertson and the Hon. Olivia Robertson in 1976, and attracts followers from all over the world.

OPEN June, July and Aug., 2-6pm; May and Sept., Sundays only.

ADMISSION £3, children £1.50.

DIRECTIONS Off the north side of Clonegal's main street.

DUNLECKNEY MANOR

Bagnelstown, County Carlow

For any enthusiast of Victorian Gothic architecture Dunleckney Manor is the place where Heaven and masonry meet. For here are all the turrets, tracery and towers - not to mention stained glass, fan vaulting and woodcarving - that any lover of wonderfully over-the-top Tudor Gothic style could wish for.

Built in 1850 for Walter Newton, heir to the Bagenal estates, the house shows Kilkenny-based architect Daniel Robertson at his imaginative best. If the building is reminiscent of the dreaming spires of Oxford it is no accident, for Robertson based the design of the oriel window over the front door on one of the college windows, no doubt evoking memories of both his own and Walter Newton's under-graduate days. Further Gothic details - gargoyles grimacing down from pediments and gutters, panels of lacy

tracery beautifully executed by local stonemasons - reinforce the idiom.

Every detail designed by Robertson, from the Italianate curvilinear stairs, a feature repeated throughout both house and garden, to the ornately carved screens in the window embrasures, remains wonderfully intact, despite the fact that in the 1970s the house lay empty - its only tenants bats and birds - for an eleven-year period.

Unusually, Dunleckney is not screened by demesne walls or announced by grandiose gates with a guardian lodge, so the vista of its silvery limestone façade at the end of a straight avenue is revealed unexpectedly from the road. The interior also provides a series of dramatic revelations. The front door, framed on the inside by a wonderful piece of Jacobean carving in bog oak taken from above the bishop's throne in St Canice's Cathedral, opens straight onto a great hall, where the Tudor mood is reinforced by a vast baronial-style carved chimney piece in dark oak. Expectations of what lies beyond the great Gothic door at the end of the hall are likely to be surpassed by the spectacular bifurcated staircase, surrounded by a lantern gallery and lit by enormous Gothic stained-glass windows, and with a fan-vaulted roof. The total bill for this splendour came to £10,000, an enormous sum by the standards of the day.

Each of the rooms that open off the inner hallway is highly individual. The drawing-room, with its ornate compartmentalised ceiling and ivy-leaf cornice, and the oak room on the first floor are particularly fine. Panelled in oak from St Canice's Cathedral, the latter features a window-seat in the oriel window (where the young Newtons could sit and watch the novel sight of the new steam trains chuffing by between Dublin and Kilkenny), a central ceiling boss from St Canice's carved with children's faces and an ornately carved chimney piece.

Dunleckney was designed very much as a family home and some of the rooms may have been designed specifically for certain members of the family. The romantic tower bedroom, with inset bookcases beside the seat in the oriel window, was designed with ladies in mind, while the red bedroom, with an immense carved screen and elaborate Tudor ceiling, is decidedly masculine. The servants' quarters were in a back wing formed by part of an older house dating back to 1612.

The founder of the Bagenal dynasty in Ireland was Nicholas Bagenal, who came from Staffordshire in England in 1538. The first house at Bagenalstown was built in 1612 by his son George, who amassed an estate of 25,000 acres. The Bagenal decendants were inevitably caught up in the turbulent events of the seventeenth century. Dudley Bagenal was involved in a dispute with the Kavanagh clan, who originally held the land, and was ambushed by them and killed, together with nine of his followers. George Bagenal was killed during the Cromwellian war and Dunleckney was forfeited and handed over to one of Cromwell's men, a man called Axtell. Following the Restoration of King Charles II, Axtell was executed for regicide. Like many Catholic landowners, in an effort to secure their lands the Bagenals backed James II, and Dudley Bagenal fought at the siege of Derry and the battle of the Boyne before fleeing into exile with the Pretender.

The Bagenal heirs managed to hold onto their lands through the settlement which followed the Treaty of Limerick. Later they formed strategic links through marriage with many leading Protestant families. Walter Bagenal, faced with the punitive consequences of the Penal Laws, put land before religion and conformed, on his marriage to Eleanor Beauchamp. Their son, Beauchamp Bagenal, inherited the estate at the tender age of ten. In the manner of the times, he later did the Grand Tour of Europe and was also very much given to duelling. He might have changed the course of the British monarchy had his romance with Princess Charlotte of Germany lasted, but the Princess went on to marry George III. Beauchamp didn't believe in doing things by half measure and enjoyed life to an eccentric hilt. As commander of the local yeomanry he would review his men from his carriage, driven through their ranks, a glass of claret in his hand. His officers had to be decanted home by the cartload following his copious hospitality. Flamboyant to the end, he fought a duel, seated, with a tenant farmer in a dispute involving some trespassing pigs.

Subsequent generations lived more quietly at Dunleckney. The estate passed, through the female line, to Beauchamp's daughter Sarah, who married a Captain Newton, and it was their son Walter who caused Dunleckney to be built but never lived to see the 25-year project completed. The house passed out of family hands in 1941, was subsequently run as a stud farm, then stood empty from the early 1970s before becoming a bed-and-breakfast venture.

The present owners, Derek and Helen Sheane, use the house as a showcase for their wallcovering and fabric business. The house is beautifully decorated and furnished with many interesting pieces, many of them of ecclesiastic origin. Richard Sheehan, who conducts the excellent guided tours, is a fund of knowledge on the Bagenal family history.

OPEN March, May & Aug., Mon.-Fri. 2-6pm, excluding bank holidays. Guided tours on the hour from 2pm.

ADMISSION £2.50 adults, £1.50 students and pensioners. The trade showrooms in the mews are open to the public for end-of-range bargain fabrics and wallcoverings on Fridays only, 9am-5pm.

DIRECTIONS Dunleckney is about 1 km west of Bagenalstown. From the Carlow-Kilkenny N9 take the R724 and at the outskirts of the town turn sharp left at the yellow-windowed warehouse and follow that road.

CAPPOQUIN HOUSE

Cappoquin, County Waterford

The lower reaches of the Blackwater River are Ireland's equivalent to the Loire or the Rhine valleys. The broad river flows serenely through a rolling landscape of woods, cornfields and rich pasture, its banks guarded by a succession of magnificent castles and mansions.

Cappoquin House, commanding the high ground above the town of Cappoquin, occupies one of the finest positions of all, overlooking the elbow of the Blackwater where the river turns at right angles and reaches a silver arm towards Youghal and the sea. Upstream there is a view of the fawn towers of Lismore Castle, built for the 'great' Earl of Cork. Downstream, Dromana - once the stronghold of the Earl of Desmond of the Anglo-Norman Fitzgeralds - can be seen perched dramatically on a beetling cliff edge.

All three locations were chosen for their strategic position - controlling the tidal river - and formed a chain of communication, sited within signalling distance of each other.

Like so many eighteenth-century homes, Cappoquin House was built on the site of an earlier castle, once owned by the Fitzgeralds, whose lands were confiscated by Elizabeth I after the long-running rebellion by the Earl of Desmond and granted to 'undertakers' as payment for monies advanced to the Crown. Two of Elizabeth's favourites - Sir Walter Raleigh of Youghal and her chancellor, Sir Christopher Hatton of Cappoquin - each took up a 10,000-acre seigniory.

Cappoquin House was built in 1779 by Cork architect Abraham Hargreave for the Keane family. The rectangular block, built in silvery ashlar, has a seven-bay front overlooking the river, with three round-headed windows in the break-front and a balustraded parapet. Were the Keane family to come back from the eighteenth century to haunt the house, they would find it changed in several surprising ways, not least that the main entrance has been switched from the front to the back, the roof is flat and the plasterwork is in mint condition. The explanation is that Cappoquin House rose phoenix-like from the ashes of 1922, when it was burnt by the old IRA in a move against senators like the then owner Sir John Keane, who supported the Cosgrave government. The house was one of the very few to be reinstated when the Irish State made reparation for the properties burnt in 1922/23.

The story of Cappoquin House is inextricably linked to the twists and turns of Irish history. The massive walls to the west are the remains of the Fitzgerald castle. The few original leaded windows in the building to the east side of the courtyard behind the main house indicate a Tudor date; this earlier house was built for Sir Christopher Hatton's land agent.

The Keane family, descendants of the Ulster O'Cahan clan, came to Cappoquin 200 years ago. Like many Catholic Irish families the O'Cahan's sided with King James II, fighting with him at the battle of the Boyne. Backing James and the House of Stuart had advantages: the outlook appeared to be improving for Catholics and James had signed an act promising full restoration of lands that had been confiscated by Cromwell and only partially restored

by Charles II. Following James's defeat and flight to France, the O'Cahan lands were duly confiscated, with 456 other estates.

In the next generation, George O'Cahan changed his name to Keane, expediently conformed to the Protestant faith and entered government service as a lawyer. He evidently recouped the family fortunes to some degree and, on retirement, was able to take three 999-year leases on lands at Cappoquin. George O'Cahan's heir had Cappoquin House built, consolidating the family's restored status.

Sir John Keane was part of a brave new chapter in the emerging Ireland. He was instrumental in starting up the Waterford Co-operative, part of the imaginative co-operative movement founded by Horace Plunkett, to bring Irish farmers together to process and market their produce. However, despite this, both Cappoquin House and Plunkett's home were burnt out by the Republicans. Sir John had the contents of his house sent to England and escaped being shot, having received a timely warning that there was a price on his head.

Sir John had the house rebuilt over a ten-year period, in consultation with Richard Orpen, brother of the painter, William. The plasterwork was recreated in all its original splendour, using old moulds which were available in London. However, Sir John never lived in Cappoquin House again.

The house was occupied for a time by Ireland's answer to the mounted cavalry, the Seventh Bicycle Brigade. There are still pencilled graffiti on some old shutters, with drawings of enemy aircraft and the legend 'Up Dev [de Valera], the Seventh Bicycle Brigade are behind you'.

Cappoquin House is now the home of Sir Richard and Olivia Keane. The principal reception rooms, the entrance and staircase hall, the dining-room, library and splendid drawing-room overlooking the Blackwater valley are open to the public.

OPEN April-July, 9am-1pm, except Sunday.

ADMISSION £4.

DIRECTIONS The entrance to the estate is in the centre of Cappoquin.

ORMOND CASTLE

Carrick-on-Suir, County Tipperary

T hose colourful characters who have built houses down through the centuries can still exert a spell on the imagination. None more so than Thomas Butler, 10th Earl of Ormonde and builder of one of the first unfortified houses in Ireland at Carrick-on-Suir.

Known as Black Tom, for his sallow complexion, the Duke was a remarkable man. A true son of the Tudor renaissance, he managed to bridge the wide gulf between the English and Irish cultures. He was raised a Protestant, brought up at the English Court and shared a tutor with the future King Edward VI. Ormonde adopted the manner and dress of an English courtier yet was able to inspire loyalty and respect among the Irish lords and acted as a mediator between English and Irish interests. He was one of Queen

Elizabeth's favourites, and the nature of her relationship with the man she referred to as 'my black husband' has always been a matter of speculation. The walls of the great gallery at the Carrick castle are adorned with flattering plaster friezes of his distant cousin, perhaps in anticipation of a visit by the 'Virgin Queen' which never materialised.

From the entrance front, Ormond Castle looks for all the world like a Tudor manor-house. The manor was Black Tom's expression of confidence in the future, built at a time when there were six uprisings by the 'Old English' alone against Queen Elizabeth, and Gaelic and Norman lords still sheltered in defensive castles and strong houses.

The house - an almost unique survivor among the few unfortified houses dating to this period - is built in a U-shape with a fifteenth-century Butler castle forming the fourth side of a courtyard. The house is three storeys high and a single room deep, with steeply pitched gables over the windows of the attic floor. The mullioned windows have curved eyebrow-like mouldings above them and there is a wide oriel window over the porch and another at the side of the house. Originally the rubble walls would have been rendered and whitewashed.

Black Tom succeeded to his title at the age of 15 but only came to his Irish estates eight years later, in 1554, to the welcome of a cheering multitude; his new home was completed some time later. The Butlers were one of the most powerful Old English families, the foundations of their wealth and privilege stretching back to Theobald Walter, who came to Ireland with Strongbow and was granted 'prisage' (a levy on wines imported by the monarch) and the title of Chief Butler. The lordship of Carrick was granted to the Butlers by Edward II and their power and influence continued to grow, particularly in counties Tipperary and Kilkenny where they held the great castle in Kilkenny city.

In 1559 Black Tom was appointed to the lucrative post of Lord Treasurer in Ireland, and when he was at Ormond Castle the household of over 100 was run like a miniature court, a lifestyle reflected in the layout and usage of the rooms.

The large hall, parlour and rooms on the ground floor would have been used by visitors and senior members of the household; the hall served both as a gathering place and dining-hall and the parlour as dining- or withdrawing-room for family members or gentlewomen. The parlour has a plaster frieze divided by plain mouldings into simple compartments within which are heraldic devices or badges of the Ormonde family.

The great glory of the house is the long gallery, 100 feet in length, which runs the whole length of the building. Richly decorated with plaster strapwork and Tudor devices and a repeating frieze of Queen Elizabeth, and designed to impress, it was also used for indoor exercise. The gallery has two great fireplaces, one featuring virile griffins and the Carrick Knot of the Butler arms, and the other a plasterwork frieze of Queen Elizabeth. Adjoining the room is the Earl's chamber, with an oriel window overlooking the River Suir. This would have served as a room for receiving important guests and would have been hung with rich tapestries and curtains. On the opposite side of the building is a dining-chamber for family and important guests. While the family and important members of the household lived in relative comfort, the lower servants had to sleep where they could, possibly amongst stored furniture and possessions under the great oak trusses of the attic roof with their wonderful timber joints. The fifteenth-century castle with its two five-storey towers was still very much in use and would have included halls and chambers, a withdrawing-room and chapel. However, the castle was attacked and seized by Cromwell in 1649 and the old part severely damaged, never to be repaired.

A great ladies' man, Black Tom is reputed to have fathered twelve illegitimate children, but, although he was married three times, he had no surviving legitimate male heir. On his death in 1614 his estate was left to his daughter Elizabeth while the title went to a male relative. In the next generation, land and title were brought together again by the marriage of Elizabeth's daughter - another Elizabeth - to her cousin James Butler. However, the couple had to flee Carrick after the outbreak of rebellion in 1641 and James went into exile in France with Charles II in 1650. After the Restoration, the Butlers used Kilkenny Castle, revamped in the manner of a French château, as their principal residence, while Carrick became a base for James Butler's stables. The house was subsequently let to tenants and never again regained its pre-eminence.

The castle was taken into the care of the OPW in 1947 and has undergone a series of restoration programmes - most recently by the OPW in conjunction with FÁS to restore the plasterwork. It remains essentially Black Tom's home and I like to think of him at the window of his great chamber watching the busy traffic on the river, brooding over his feud with the Earl of Desmond or parleying with the emissaries of his beloved Queen or of Hugh O'Neill, Earl of Tyrone, the last of the great Gaelic lords, who came nearest - with his Spanish allies - to overthrowing the Elizabethan state.

OPEN Mid June-Sept., 9.30am-6.30pm daily. Last access 45 minutes before closing.

ADMISSION £2, concession £1.50, children £1, family £5. Guided tours only. Parking, toilets.

DIRECTIONS On the edge of Carrick-on-Suir.

THE ROTHE HOUSE

Kilkenny

The Rothe House offers a unique insight into the comfortable lifestyle of a merchant in the sixteenth century. John Rothe was of Norman descent and built his house in Parliament Street in 1594 and the complex of buildings which grew up behind the arcaded façade and shop fronting on the street give practical meaning to the expression 'extended family'. As John's family from his marriage to Rose Archer grew - the couple had 12 children - so too did his premises and a second house was built around a courtyard behind the first, and then a further courtyard and house beyond that.

John and Alice's house was fairly typical of the prosperous middle-class houses that huddled behind the fortified walls of trading centres like Dublin and Drogheda, but the Rothe house is virtually the only intact example and it is interesting to speculate why, when England and northern France have so many examples of houses from this period, so very few survived in Ireland. Many of the town houses would have been built of half-timbered cagework (unlike the Rothe House, which is stone built), which didn't weather well. As many were not owner occupied, tenants would not have kept up repairs. Also some would have been destroyed by war. In time the houses were swept away to make way for more modern buildings.

The Rothes built their house nearly 50 years later than Black Tom, Earl of Ormonde, built his manor house at Carrick-on-Suir, but there are similarities between the two Tudor buildings. Both are very English in style; both have mullioned windows, buildings ranged round inner courtyards and a similar system of gables. Like Ormond Castle, the principal room in the Rothe House was at first-floor level, running the width of the building, with an oriel-window affording a fine view of the goings-on in the street. On the floor above, the magnificent timberwork roof, secured with wooden dowels rather than nails, is left open and the gable windows look out over the rooftops. The ground floor, fronting onto the street, was occupied by shops, and still is to this day. The well-to-do John, one of the first aldermen of the city, had a stone plaque with a carving of his arms and his name in Latin set above the central archway. By 1619 a third house had been built, with a brewhouse for making ale. One of the houses was occupied by Peter, the eldest of the Rothe's four sons, who married in 1610.

John Rothe died in 1620 and his will gives an idea of the sophisticated lifestyle his family enjoyed. His possessions included bedsteads with hangings and feather bedding, brass and pewter vessels, expanding tables, linens, cupboards, virginals (musical instrument) and a chest. Some of these were imported, as the Rothes would have had links with the Continent through trade.

The family were Catholics and Peter Rothe supported the Confederate cause (Kilkenny was the seat of the Confederate Parliament formed by the alliance of Catholic interests). After Cromwell had besieged and taken Kilkenny, the Rothes' property, together with land they held at Kilkree, was forfeited, and Peter and his family were transported to Connacht, where Peter died. The Cromwellian transplantation not only took land from Catholics but also the owner-ship of properties in towns that had been held by Confederate forces. Cromwell's radical plans (which even included the transportation of beggars to the West Indies) did not work out as intended - for instance, only a quarter of the 35,000 soldiers

granted land actually settled in Ireland - and by the 1680s the Rothes once again owned the Kilkenny house, only to lose everything again through the family's support of James II. The Rothes left Ireland, went into exile in France and founded the Rothe regiment there.

The Rothe House was purchased by Kilkenny Archaeological Society and sensitively restored by the OPW and now houses a number of exhibits: some seventeenth-century furniture, a costume exhibition and memorabilia which includes a Confederate banner which was discovered hidden behind the wainscot. Standing in the courtyard of the Rothe House with the summer martins swooping round the mellow stone walls, it is still possible to sense the peace and security which was to prove so short-lived for the Rothe family.

OPEN July-Aug., 9.30am-6pm daily; March-June & Sept.-Dec., Mon.-Sat. 10.30am-5pm, Sun 3-5pm; Jan. & Feb., Sun only 3-5pm., tel. 056-22893.

Admission £2, students £1.50, children £1. Guided tours, tea room, toilets, parking.

DIRECTIONS Situated in Kilkenny city in Parliament Street.

LISMACUE

Bansha, County Tipperary

O nce that turn is made through the entrance gates, anticipation is part of the pleasure of visiting a house hidden from view. At Lismacue that sense of anticipation is heightened by a dramatic avenue of limes apparently heading off into infinity.

Just at the point when the avenue begins to seem like an elaborate joke, it bends unexpectedly and there, at the end, lies an architectural treat. The central block at Lismacue is a Regency house, which remains exactly as it was designed by the architect William Robertson and depicted in the architect's drawings which hang in the library. The entrance front has three bays with a Gothic porch and the south elevation has five bays and two storeys with a battlemented pediment.

It is a wonderful light-filled house, the gracious pillared entrance and staircase halls lit by a tripartite Gothic window and a decorative feature of three interlinked arches used repeatedly in the detailing throughout the house. The plasterwork in the drawing-room and library, of an unusual pendulous Gothic design, is particularly pleasing and the wallpaper is original, probably French.

The house was originally designed to have two wings. The east wing, a church-like structure, houses the kitchen and servants' quarters. The west wing, planned as a ballroom, was never built. Descendants of William Baker VII, for whom the house was built, continue to live at Lismacue, but William Baker himself - portrayed in a small sketch in the library as an elegant Regency gentleman in cravat and knee-breeches - did not live long to enjoy his new home. Just two years after the house was completed in 1813 he was shot at the gates of Thomastown Castle in Golden as he returned from the Cashel assizes. His murder is not thought to have been connected with agrarian agitation but with a grudge.

The Bakers were originally a Norman family and came over from England in about 1600 and settled at Lattin, County Tipperary. A descendant - another William Baker (IV) - bought the 209-acre estate at Lismacue in 1704 from Colonel Charles Blount. The existing house was listed in the hearth tax records of 1665/66 as having five fireplaces, taxed at a rate of ten shillings a year. This house was subsequently destroyed by fire and Lismacue House was built to replace it, incorporating part of the stables of the original house in a back wing. The family still have in their possession a book of maps of the fields on the estate with lists of tenants, and many of those families are still there. The house has sweeping views towards the V of the Galtee Mountains and there are pleasant walks through an arboretum and along the Ara River. Lismacue is a member of the Hidden Ireland group, so it is possible to stay at the house; the rate is £40 per night and dinner is an option. The drawing-room, dining-room, library and hall are open to the public.

OPEN 1 May-30 June, 11am-3pm.

ADMISSION £3.

DIRECTIONS Lismacue is on the N24 from Cahir to Tipperary, on the eastern outskirts of Bansha, on the right coming from Cahir.

DROMANA

Cappoquin, County Waterford

The setting of Dromana is unbelievably dramatic. The fifteenth-century stronghold of the FitzGeralds, Lords of the Decies, is built at the edge of beetling cliffs which drop sheer into one of the most beautiful stretches of the River Blackwater. The view downward is vertiginous. Over a hundred feet below, a lone heron patrols the swirls and eddies of the lion-coloured water. Upstream are the tower and turrets of Lismore Castle, and the ranges of the Galtees and the Knockmealdowns rise blue in the distance.

This has been the home of the descendants of the Earls of Desmond for 700 years. There are no half measures here, and the extraordinary is only to be expected in a family history where wealth was matched by extravagance and bravura.

Ireland's most exotic gateway is a startling introduction to Dromana. The folly and gate lodge were designed by Martin Day in 1849, to give access to the railway system which was proposed to run through Cappoquin, and also to give work after the Famine. The bridge over the Finisk River and the gate lodge,

in the Hindu Gothic style, were inspired by the extravaganza of the Brighton Pavilion, with domes and minarets adding a wonderful air of frivolity.

Beyond the bridge the road winds over meadows and tunnels through woods to emerge high on a promontory beside the house - or what remains of it, for Dromana has a curious architectural history. What remains now is a late seventeenth-, early eighteenth-century two-storey building, with a handsome Gibbsian doorway, which was built on the foundations of the old FitzGerald castle. This was originally intended as a temporary measure to provide more comfortable accommodation when the castle was badly damaged, having been first held by the Irish rebels in 1642 and then taken by government forces in 1647.

From the far side of the river the base of the castle, complete with a medieval window, built by Gerald, son of the 7th Earl of Desmond, in the fifteenth century, can clearly be seen and the former dungeons of the castle form the basement of the present house. But of the tremendously grand house built by

George Mason-Villiers, 2nd Earl of Grandison, and further embellished by Henry Villiers Stuart in the 1840s there is almost no sign. It was demolished after most of the estate was sold to the Department of Lands in 1959 and the earlier house became once again a self-contained home.

The dining-room, cosy modern kitchen and drawing-room lead off from a long flagged passageway, and are pleasantly-sized rooms with Georgian friezes, Irish furniture and family portraits. The drawing-room is built over the old castle, and beyond it is a section of what was once an enormous ballroom, with a balcony offering stunning views of the river. At the other end of the house the old kitchen has a vaulted roof supported on Romanesque pillars.

Colourful ancestors run in the family. Katherine FitzGerald's maternal relatives, the Powers of Curraghmore, tried to unite the two estates by betrothing her at 12 to her cousin and heir to the Curraghmore estate - then the prospective groom aged just 7. However, Katherine ran off instead with Edward Villiers, Captain of Chelsea Barracks. Edward's cousin was Barbara Villiers, mistress of Charles II. Another Katherine, granddaughter of the builder of the castle, was reputed to be the oldest ever woman in Ireland. Claims over her advanced years vary between 120 and 160.

The Villiers family had extensive estates in England and spent a good deal of their time there. However, George Mason Villiers embarked on his large two-storey house in the 1780s but never finished it, due to his fondness for gambling (and losing), and the house was not finally finished until two generations later, in 1845.

Between the two world wars Dromana was the home of Elspeth and her husband Ion Villiers-Stuart, and they held many parties and had fleets of servants, but when Elspeth was killed in a fall from a bicycle in 1943 an era came to an end. By the 1950s, family members refused to live in the enormous house and when tea planter FitzGerald Villers-Stuart retired from Kenya and took on Dromana he also came to the conclusion that the place was impossible to live in without at least seven servants and so he took the decision to demolish Lord Grandison's mansion.

OPEN By appointment.

ADMISSION £2.

DIRECTIONS From Cappoquin take the Dungarvan road, then turn left for Villierstown.

Section Two

BARONIES AND
KINGDOMS

Clare, Cork, Kerry, Limerick

If there is one place in particular that explains a great deal about the south-west of Ireland for me, it is Derrynane, birthplace of Daniel O'Connell. Wild and remote, it has that typical combination of mountainous land meeting sea, with long fingers of rugged coastline reaching into the sea and sheltered inlets in between. At Derrynane there is a secluded cockle strand, a perfect base for the trade carried on by Daniel's uncle, 'Hunting Cap' - not all of which received attention from customs.

The west was always a law unto itself, and distance gave the counties of the south-west a detached attitude to Dublin-based authority. France was often seen as a place to find opportunities and allies; the southern ports traded mostly with France. Daniel O'Connell went to school in France, and another uncle, Count Daniel O'Connell, was a general in the French army. However, remoteness did not give immunity from history, far from it: one of the most tense episodes was played out when the French Armada brought the threat of invasion to Bantry in 1796. At Tarbert, Sir Edward Leslie invited Benjamin Franklin to Kerry in a bid to restore trade links between America and the Kerry port in the wake of the American War of Independence.

In the south-west the Normans followed their usual pattern, displacing the Irish from the best land. Cork, Limerick and Kerry became part of the palatinate of the Desmond FitzGeralds, together with Waterford, while the Butlers held sway in Tipperary and Kilkenny. The MacCarthys and O'Sullivans moved to the peninsulas. Later, lands in east Cork and Waterford were to become the prizes for Elizabethan adventurers and favourites like Sir Walter Raleigh, whose home was the manor house Myrtle Grove, in Youghal, County Cork. In the

Cromwellian land distribution of 1653, the Irish were transplanted to Connacht and to Clare, while Cromwellian soldiers were allocated land concentrated around the borders of Connacht and Clare. The effects of history can still be seen in the distribution of houses, castles, towns and ruins in the landscape.

The best scenery in the south-west is around the coastline and it is debatable which is the best direction to take: whether to start from the rolling dairylands of east Cork and build up gradually through the small hills of west Cork to the drama of the Beara, Iveragh and Dingle peninsulas and the Ring of Kerry, before a change of scenic gear to the richer pasturelands of Limerick, finishing with the bare, exhilarating landscape of Clare, with its magical flower carpet, lunar rocks and vanishing turlough lakes of the Burren; or whether to proceed in the opposite direction. Both William Makepeace Thackeray and Mr and Mrs Carter Hall went for the clockwise option on their respective tours of Ireland in 1842 and 1840.

There is a pleasant trip along the coast of east Cork taking in Youghal with its medieval walls and towers and the great church of St Mary. Walter Raleigh is meant to have sown the first potatoes, brought from the New World, near his house at Myrtle Grove. There is some pleasing scenery around the fishing village of Ballycotton. With its picturesque harbour, narrow streets and numerous restaurants, Kinsale is now a gourmet's paradise. The town had a turbulent past and was once an important base for the British navy. It was also seized by the Spanish, who were besieged there in 1601/2 by Mountjoy.

The Desmond castle there was built as a customs house in 1500 by the Earl of Desmond and became a workhouse during the Famine (open mid April-mid October daily, except Monday), and the nearby Charles Fort, dating back to the seventeenth century and garrisoned until 1921, is a classic example of a star-shaped fort (open mid April-October daily).

Inland there are rewarding drives through the Blackwater valley, through Tallow, Conna and Fermoy. Nearby are the spectacular ruins of Castle Lyons, a fortified mansion built in the sixteenth century for the powerful Anglo-Norman Barrymores and accidentally burnt in 1771. There is also the chance to see the garden of Annes Grove with its curious eighteenth-century 'mount' at Castletownroche on the Awbeg River (open daily 17 March-30 September, Sunday afternoons only). The park at Doneraile Court is a splendid example of an eighteenth-century landscaped park and is open daily to the public. The former seat of the St Legers, the house - dating back in part to 1730 - has been under restoration and will be open in the near future. There are colourful stories associated with the house. The 4th Lord Doneraile was subjected to the most terrible curse for exercising his *droit de seigneur* and he died - ironically for a hunting man - after being bitten by his rabid pet fox. Nearby are the ruins of Kilcolman Castle, where Edmund Spenser wrote *The Faerie Queene*.

Mallow Castle on the River Blackwater at Mallow comprises the ruins of a Desmond castle and a house, dating in part to the sixteenth and in part to the nineteenth century. County Cork has more than its share of ruined great houses, by no means all of which were burnt during the Troubles. Sir Walter Coppinger of Coppinger's Court in Rosscarbery (1618) told his servants to burn his house if he did not return after a certain time. Having wine taken, he forgot his instructions and Coppinger's Court has been a shell ever since 1641. Another Barry property at Rosscarbery, Castle Freke (1780), was partially dismantled in 1952.

The combination of river and hills gives Cork - once the butter exporting capital of the world - a lively air to match the atmosphere of the city. Aside from good shopping - Paul Street is an especially happy hunting-ground - there are some wonderful restaurants. Everyone knows about Blarney Castle and its famous kissing stone, but few of the adjoining baronial style Blarney House and Rock Close garden, which are worth a visit in their own right (open June-September, Monday-Saturday).

Everyone has their own favourite retreat among the balmy inlets of the west Cork coast and there are wonderful places to choose from. Schull is a favourite with yachtspeople and Barleycove has a fabulous strand. Castletownshend is where Edith Somerville, who collaborated with her cousin Violet Martin to write *Some Experiences of an Irish R.M.* and other acutely observed horsey tales of Irish life, lived at Drishane House. My own favourite haunt happens to be the fishing village of Baltimore, with a ruined castle of the O'Driscolls overlooking the harbour; nearby is the extraordinary Lough Hyne, a mix of salt and fresh water with unusual marine life. Unforgettable for 'scenaholics' are visits to the subtropical gardens of Ilnacullin Island, the beautiful wood-fringed inlets around Glengarriff, the sweep of island-dotted Bantry Bay and the mountain passes leading to the lake and woods of Gougane Barra.

Volume upon volume has been written about Ireland's most popular (and populous) scenic routes: the Ring of Kerry, Killarney's Lakes and the Dingle Peninsula. Less written about is the extraordinary archaeological wealth of the area, often in the most beautiful of sites: the ringfort on Tullig mountain which gives Caherdaniel its name, the Staigue Fort three miles away with its thirteen-foot ramparts, the extraordinary beehive huts of the early Christian anchorite settlement on the inhospitable Skelligs where blue-eyed gannets high-dive for fish, the anchorite ringforts and ogham stones around Caherciveen

The Gallarus Oratory on the windswept Dingle Peninsula has an almost eerie perfection in its boat-shaped form and drystone walls a thousand years after it was built. The area is rich in remains. Near Mount Eagle the Fahan group includes over 400 beehive huts, the earliest type of surviving house in Ireland, dating back to the pre-Viking era of saints and scholars The very interesting St Brendan's Cathedral, at Ardfert near Tralee, is the site of a monastery founded by St Brendan the Navigator.

Route 69 has beguiling views of the Shannon estuary, and Askeaton - a Norman town which has a ruined Desmond castle with a magnificent great hall and friary - Glin Castle, Tarbert House and the Tarbert Bridewell, which demonstrates the justice system of the 1800s, are points of interest. Inland there is the pretty, picture-postcard estate village of Adare and beside it is Adare manor, seat of the Earls of Dunraven. The Golden Vale drive runs north-south through voluptuous countryside and through historic towns like medieval Kilmallock. Nearby is Bruree, a picturesque village on the River Maigue and birthplace of Éamon de Valera, where the schoolhouse museum is open daily, except Monday. At Dromcolliher, the handsome Springfield Castle, an eighteenth-century house combined with a sixteenth-century tower house, has grounds and a deer centre that are open June to September, 1-6pm daily.

The words 'interpretative centre' normally make me run a mile, but anyone wishing to get an understanding of the complexities of Irish history should head for King John's Castle in Limerick. The castle, dramatically sited by a bridge over the Shannon in the centre of the town, is hugely impressive, while the exhibition covers history from the foundation of the city to the siege of Limerick and the Flight of the Wild Geese, open daily mid April to October. The Hunt museum in the

University of Limerick has a stunning exhibition of decorative art and antiquities (open Tuesday-Saturday, 10am-5pm; Sunday 2-5pm).

County Clare is O'Brien, MacNamara and McMahon territory, a landscape of limestone hills, bare of trees and peppered with ruined towers and castles, many of them abandoned after the seventeenth-century wars, others, like the famous Bunratty, magnificently restored as symbols of the might of Gaelic nobles.

Clare is definitely different and, in my experience, the unexpected can - and does - happen. The limestone geology plays tricks; an idyllic camping spot beside a dried-up river can be a raging torrent gnawing at your tent pegs by morning. It's a great county for music - traditional music, which breaks out at any time in the village of Doolin, and music and dancing which finishes in the early morning in Lisdoonvarna, the little spa town which is the centre for matchmaking in the post-harvest mating season.

The beetling cliffs of Moher wreathed in salt spray and reverberating to the thunder of Atlantic waves, the flowers and rockscapes of the Burren and the sylvan lakeside setting of Killaloe on the Shannon couldn't be more different, and each in their own way memorable. Killaloe was an important ecclesiastical centre in the Kingdom of Thomond and one of the most important buildings there is St Flannan's Cathedral. Near Mount Shannon is Holy Island, site of a seventh-century monastic settlement with the remains of five churches.

Around 3,000 castles or forts were built in Ireland between the arrival of the Normans and the seventeenth century. The biggest concentration of defensive buildings was in the south-west, and probably the best known of all is Bunratty. Built on the site of many previous castles, Bunratty Castle was an O'Brien stronghold. Now restored and furnished in seventeenth-century style, it is managed by the Shannon Development Company and is well and truly established on the tourist trail. The castle is also used for medieval banquets (open all year round, banquet 9pm). Also under the umbrella of Shannon Development is the Bunratty Folk Park, which has reproductions of farmhouses and town houses of the region at around the turn of the century, including a Golden Vale farmhouse and a stone farmhouse from the Moher area. An evening céilí is also an option (open May-September and 9pm for céilí). The Craggaunowen Project near Quin in County Clare features reproductions of Stone Age dwellings found around Lough Gur, one of the most important archaeological sites in the country (open May-September daily).

PLACES TO STAY/EAT

In Cork, Arbutus Lodge, St Luke's Hill, Montenotte (tel. 021-501237), and Cliffords, 18 Dyke Parade (tel. 021-275333), are renowned for gourmet dining, the Oyster Tavern in Market Lane for seafood and old-world charm, the Crawford Gallery in Emmet Place for original and reasonably priced food by the Allen clan, and Café Paradiso, 16 Lancaster Quay, for vegetarian food that even has the carnivores queuing up (tel. 021-277939).

Assolas House near Mallow is a particuarly charming seventeenth-century house with an award-winning garden, and I'm told it is a blissful place to stay (tel. 029-50015). Aherne's Seafood Bar in Youghal (tel. 024-92424) (the prawns are to die for) and Finns in Midleton are a must for fish fanciers. And Ballymaloe House at Ballycotton (tel. 021-652531) is fascinating, not only for its wonderful food but for Darina Allen's nearby cookery school and gardens complete with shell house (tel. 021-646785).

I have a friend whose eyes mist over at the memory of having freshly baked cake offered on her arrival to stay at Ballyvolane House (1728), set in parkland at Castlelyons and with salmon rights on the Blackwater River (tel. 025-36349). Blair's Inn, at Cloghroe in Blarney, is the place for superior pub food, featuring seafood, local cheeses and homemade ice-cream. Inland, Longueville House (1720), a lovely old-world place to stay, is also the pride and joy of the O'Callaghan clan. New Irish cooking from one of the country's most talented young chefs and wines from the O'Callaghans' own vineyards feature (tel. 022-47156). Glenlohane, a fine Georgian mansion, is still occupied by descendants of the same family that built it in 1741, near Kanturk (tel. 029-50014). On the coast, on the outskirts of Butlerstown, is the 1760 slate-faced Sea Court, built for the Longfield family and now a guest-house and part-time home of genial host American Professor David Elder, who has also been restoring the house (open 10 June-20 August, tel. 023-40151). The house is a listed historic building and, together with the grounds, is open to be viewed gratis during the summer months.

A romantic bow-fronted Georgian house, Beaufort, overlooks the River Luane, near Killarney (tel. 064-44764). The Blue Haven Hotel in Kinsale is justifiably bestowed with awards for its cuisine, especially seafood (tel. 021-772209). Small Hotel of the Year 1996, Caragh Lodge, is a Victorian fishing lodge at Caragh Lake, County Kerry (tel. 066-69115).

Among the intriguing range of culinary possibilities in Kerry are the Beginish Restaurant in Green Street, Dingle, where the fish from the adjacent pier is delish (tel. 066-51588). If something scrumptious in front of a cosy fire is called for, then Packies in Henry Street, Kenmare, is just the place (tel. 064-41508). You can watch the play of light on Tralee Bay and enjoy stylish Cal-Ital food at The Summit Restaurant, Ballyroe Hotel, Ballyhaigue (tel. 066-26796). Hidden away behind the duvet covers in the Munster Warehouse in Tralee is Dawson's Restaurant, source of fresh baking and tasty home cooking, daytime only (tel. 066-27745).

Freddy's Bistro in Theatre Lane, Limerick, has won accolades for its original Irish menu and has a selection of Wild Geese wines from the Irish Châteaux, so-called for the Irish who left for France after 1690 and married into the wine trade (tel. 061-418749). Quenelles Restaurant on Steamboat Quay, Limerick's smartest new restaurant, serves stylish food overlooking the Shannon (tel. 061-411111). Other recommended County Limerick eateries are The Wild Geese, Rose Cottage, Adare, for French/Irish cuisine in a *cottage orné* setting (tel. 061-396451), and Croom Mills at Croom, which is a charming old millhouse offering fresh baking and home-style cooking.

Ash Hill Stud at Killmallock, County Limerick, featured in this section of the book, makes an excellent base for touring the Golden Vale area. On the edge of the Burren in County Clare is Georgian Corofin House, overlooking Lake Inchiquin; the fare features produce from the family farm and the garden (tel. 065-37692). Lively Ennis is establishing a good food reputation; two recommendations from friends are Garvello's, Clareabbey, Limerick Road, for modern Irish food in a smart setting (tel. 065-40011), and An Gole Mór, 17 Salthouse Lane, for cheerful food with the emphasis on wholefood and vegetarian dishes (tel. 065-23080).

DERRYNANE HOUSE

Caherdaniel, County Kerry

Derrynane is known first and foremost as the family home and country seat of Daniel O'Connell, the 'Liberator', father of constitutional nationalism in Ireland. The house overlooks an idyllic inlet and natural harbour on one of the remotest peninsulas of Kerry, near Caherdaniel. The house takes its name from the Gaelic for 'the oak wood of St Fionnán' and from the abbey founded by the saint on Abbey Island in the bay.

This was Daniel O'Connell's childhood home, a place which had a profound influence on him and to which he returned throughout his life to spend at least part of every year. The story of the O'Connell family illustrates perfectly the strength of the links between the west and south of Ireland and continental Europe, particularly

France. And often it was to Europe, rather than distant Dublin or Britain, that the O'Connells turned for education, careers and a means of livelihood.

The O'Connells were an ancient Irish family, holding hereditary rights as constables of Ballycarbery Castle under the Gaelic Lord of Desmond. They were dispossessed by Cromwell in 1650. Predictably, the staunchly Catholic family later supported King James. Captain John O'Connell, great-grandfather of the Liberator, fought in the siege of Limerick and afterwards, in 1702, built a house on land leased from the Earl of Cork at Derrynane. His son Donal inherited, and he and his wife Mairie had a family of five sons and five daughters - one of the most colourful, Maurice, was known as Hunting Cap after the cap he habitually wore to avoid the tax on fashionable beaver hats.

At one point the O'Connells dropped the O in front of their name to avoid sounding too Catholic, but Hunting Cap (and his father Donal before him) had other reasons for keeping a low profile. He was, not to put too fine a point on it, a smuggler, running the 'free trade' of south Kerry like a fore-runner of Shannon Airport's Duty Free. Brandy, wine, tea, tobacco and fine fabrics and furniture came in to Derrynane's secluded harbour, and butter, hides, beef and 'Wild Geese' - the cream of young Irishmen bound for the Irish brigades of France and Spain - sailed out from there, all without the attentions of the revenue officers.

Another brother, Connell, studied navigation in France and was second mate on a British ship. The youngest, Daniel Charles, joined a Swedish regiment with the French army, eventually rising to become a general and a chevalier for his services. Morgan, the Liberator's father, helped Hunting Cap with his business and ran a general store near his home at Carhan house. Daniel and his brother Maurice were adopted by Hunting Cap, who had no heirs, and lived at Derrynane until General Count Daniel O'Connell arranged for them to attend schools in France. The Count also organised their hasty retreat when French revolutionaries closed the English College at Douai.

Daniel then studied law at Lincoln's Inn in London and had a successful career as a barrister at the Irish Bar, earning sums of up to £6,000 a year. His opposition to the 1801 Act of Union propelled O'Connell into politics and later he launched an imaginative and successful campaign for Catholic emancipation which anticipated the modern party political machine. In 1823 he formed the Catholic Association, which became a mass movement. Subscriptions of 1 penny a month supplied the funds to fight elections and to bring about change, including an end to discrimination against Catholics, by democratic means.

O'Connell won a seat for Clare in 1828, which of course he was barred from taking, but his victory prompted the Emancipation Act the following year and, after winning again in Clare, he took his seat as an MP. His epithet of 'Liberator' celebrated that he had given Irish people a voice after years of oppression. His campaign for the repeal of the Union generated even greater support, culminating in monster meetings, but was over-taken by tragic events. One of the greatest figures of Irish politics died in the midst of the Famine years in 1847.

When Daniel inherited Derrynane from 'Hunting Cap' at the age of 50 in 1825, he altered the original 1702 house considerably, adding two wings, one of which is slate faced and crenellated and houses the library. He also made the back of the house, with its three-sided courtyard, the front. He added a chapel in 1844 in thanksgiving for his release from prison, where he had been held on charges of seditious conspiracy. The drawing-room and dining-room look out over the sea and the latter still contains its original furniture. The charming, unpretentious house is filled with portraits and interesting mementoes of the Liberator, including his desk and rosary beads. Some of the features in the grounds also have strong links with Daniel O'Connell, especially the Gothic summer house which he used as a quiet retreat. The property remained in the O'Connell family until 1958, the house was opened to the public in 1967 and the 300-acre estate was opened as a national park in 1975 on the 200th anniversary of the Liberator's birth.

OPEN Nov.-March, Sat.-Sun. 1-5pm; April & Oct., Tues.-Sat. 1-5pm, Sun. 11am-7pm; May-Sept., Mon.-Sat. 9am-6pm, Sun. 11am-7pm. Park open during daylight hours, tel. 066-75113.

ADMISSION £2. Guided tours, audio-visual presentation, coffee shop.

DIRECTIONS Signposted from Caherdaniel on the Waterville-Kenmare road.

CRATLOE WOODS HOUSE

Shannon, County Clare

The thought of fearless Maire Rua O'Brien still lying in wait for enemies after three centuries sent me scuttling up the avenue, through billowing rain, to blood-red Cratloe Woods House. It is the only example of an Irish long house in use and is still lived in by the descendants of the family who built it and can trace their bloodline back to Brian Boru, the eleventh-century High King of Ireland.

The long house is peculiar to Ireland. Like a grand version of the vernacular long cabin, it was thatched and had rooms leading from one to the other. It was a form of building that became popular as Gaelic and Old English lords moved away from their defensive towers and castles, and it went out of favour with the advent of Georgian and Palladian styles.

Cratloe still retains its original late seventeenth-century form. On the garden front the long low house with its steeply pitched gables and tall chimneys stretches out thirteen bays long, the only major additions being a passageway and porch on the entrance front and a bay window.

Cratloe is a welcoming place, but it wasn't always so. Repeated in carvings around the building is a device from the family crest known as the Stafford Knot. This was a time-saver designed to hang three people at one time, something which would have been very much after the heart of flame-haired Maire O'Brien. This formidable woman, grandmother of the first recorded O'Brien of Cratloe House, married into the O'Brien family, and if it were not for her quick thinking the family lands at Dromoland and Lemaneagh might have been lost. When her husband Conor O'Brien was slain at the Inchicronan ambush in battle with the Cromwellian troops, Maire denied he was her husband. Instead of accepting the confiscation of her Royalist husband's land, Maire rode into Limerick and demanded an audience with Cromwell's commander, the fearsome General Ireton. To prove her denial of her late husband she offered to marry one of Ireton's men. Cornet John Cooper volunteered and, although the marriage was said to be a happy one, he may well have got more than he bargained for. Maire had thrown her first husband, Colonel Neylon, out of a window when he annoyed her and was later acquitted of his murder.

Maire's grandson Lucius preferred the life of a playboy. He came to live at Cratloe with his new bride, Catherine Keightly, in 1702. Lucius's half brother Henry tied the knot with heiress Susanna Stafford of Blatherwyke in Northamptonshire, establishing a link between the two families. There have been Stafford O'Briens at Cratloe ever since.

The interior of the house has changed very little since Victorian times. Rooms filled with family furniture and memorabilia lead off a long stone-flagged passageway, halfway down which is a Tudor revival staircase made by a ship's carpenter and carved with the Stafford Knot. The apple green drawing-room, with its 1844 bow window and gilt detailing, is hung with portraits of Stafford O'Brien ancestors.

Gordon and Sylvia Brickenden, the current descendants in residence, showed me some of the fascinating papers and objects associated with the long history of the house. There are beautiful estate maps of the O'Briens' original 11,000 acres drawn up by Stokes of Dublin, showing Garranon oak wood, the source of the timbers used for Westminster Hall in the Houses of Parliament and the Royal Palace in Amsterdam. There are also exquisite paper cut-work pictures made by Elizabeth Brickenden, who worked as an unpaid assistant to Mrs Delany. The Brickendens gave up a comfortable existence in County Wicklow, opening the house to the public and undertaking an ongoing restoration programme. It is a particularly good place to bring children, as there is an open farm, scrumptious teas and lots of interesting stories about the past. And you will discover the origin of the saying 'Are you coming for a jar?'

OPEN June-mid Sept., Mon.-Sat. 2-6pm; other times by arrangement, tel. 061-327028.

ADMISSION Adults £2.50, groups £2, children £1.50. Teas, tours, toilets, parking, wheelchair access.

DIRECTIONS Look for a scarlet gate lodge, 8 km from Limerick on the Limerick-Shannon road.

RIVERSTOWN HOUSE

Riverstown, County Cork

'A Bishop who eats, drinks and sleeps in taste, who travelled beyond the Alps and brought home to Cork to the amazement of our mercantile fraternity the Arts and Sciences that are the Ornament of Italy and the admiration of the European World', wrote Lord Orrery of Cork.

The bishop in question was Dr Jemmet Browne, who remodelled and enlarged Riverstown House around the time of his succession to the See of Cork in 1745. He commissioned the Lafrancini brothers to decorate the dining-room of his home with the rococo plasterwork which is the chief glory of the house.

Bishop Browne carried out his improvements at Riverstown in the dawn of a golden age of architecture. Castletown House, the first and finest example of Palladian

architecture, was begun in 1722, and other great houses, like Russborough (1741), followed. There was a movement to promote finer buildings, furniture and estates, encouraged by the writings of advocates of style like Samuel Madden in his 'Reflections and Resolutions to the Gentlemen of Ireland' and Bishop Berkeley's *Querist*, where he wonders of the Irish 'whether any people in Europe were so meanly provided with houses and furniture'. Bishop Browne was greatly influenced by his friend Berkeley, who became Bishop of Cloyne in 1737 and collected portraits, had a musical household and kept open house at Castlemartyr. Rich bishops were in the vanguard when it came to building and improving, witness Cashel Palace (1730) and Castletown Cox in County Kilkenny.

The double bow-ended house is two storeys high on the four-bay entrance front and three storeys at the back, where the ground falls steeply to the river. The house remained in the hands of the Browne family until this century and then lay empty for a while. Forty

58

years ago the property was bought by the Dooley family, mainly for the attached farm. John Dooley, however, was a passionate collector of antiques and architectural bits and pieces and undertook the sympathetic restoration of the house, in consultation with the Irish Georgian Society. The house has been a home for the last 30 years and is now owned by the next generation, Denis and Rita Dooley.

Today, Riverstown House is surrounded by a housing estate and a tarmac apron rolls up to the front door. Inside, though, there are architectural treats in store. The entrance hallway is the first surprise: a small semi-circular room with three pairs of pillared doorways, displaying the Georgian passion for symmetry, with a cornice featuring the classical device of ox skulls and shields. The two bow-windowed reception rooms are arranged back to back; the first has recently been fitted with pine panelling with rococo scrollwork, salvaged from another property of the same period. Bishop Browne's silver and documents relating to his family are displayed in glass cases. In the green drawing-room, the missing chimney piece has been replaced by a timber Adam-style mantelpiece and overmantel; there is a also a portrait of Miss Waterhouse, who became the bishop's wife.

The dining-room overlooks the river valley and is the showpiece of the house. The magnificent ceiling is literally a painting translated into plaster, based on the painting 'Time Rescuing Truth from the Assaults of Discord and Envy', which Poussin painted for Cardinal Richelieu in 1641. The best way to admire the work is to lie on the floor, the better to see the winged Father Time whisking a voluptuous Truth cloudwards, away from Discord's dagger and snake-entwined Envy. The walls are inset with ten panels of classical figures symbolising various virtues, as befits a bishop's house, including soldier Marcus Curtius personifying heroic virtue, Aeneas with his father Anchises on his shoulder representing filial piety, and Ceres the goddess of harvest representing abundance. The lobby, the bishop's bedchamber and the basement kitchen are also on view.

OPEN May-mid Sept., Wed.-Sat. 2-6pm; other times by appointment, tel. 021-821205.

ADMISSION £2. Guided tours, toilets, parking.

DIRECTIONS 6 km from Cork, off the old Cork-Dublin road.

DUNKATHEL HOUSE

Glanmire, County Cork

Big houses in Ireland were more than a little like islands, isolated behind high walls, self-sufficient and sometimes surrounded by hostile neighbours: the very conditions which allowed the owners to inhabit a world of their own. Dunkathel House is a case in point, for here a family of deaf sisters lived out an independent and fulfilling Victorian lifestyle which continued into the 1950s. The house is still very much as it was in their day and the benign influence of this all-female house-hold lingers, adding to the special personality of one of my favourite houses.

The building of Dunkathel began around 1790, for wealthy Cork merchant Abraham Morris, in a prime position overlooking the busy Lee estuary on the site of an earlier eighteenth-century house.

The main house is a solid nine-bay classical block, flanked, Palladian-style, by wings and pavilions. The front door with fanlight opens directly onto the entrance and staircase hall, which is the most splendid room in the house. The walls are painted to represent Siena marble blocks (in similar style to those at The Argory and Paulstown Castle), while on the painted ceiling in the outer hall gauzy clouds float in an azure sky. The decoration dates from the early nineteenth century.

At the back of the hall, beyond a segmented archway with Corinthian pilasters, rises a graceful bifurcated staircase of Bath stone with wrought-iron balustrades; the hall is lit by a round-headed window on the half landing. The architect is thought to have been a pupil of Davis Ducart. Among the pieces of interest in the hall are a handsome gilt mirror and a rare barrel organ designed by Imhoff and Muckle. To the right, the dining-room is hung with portraits of the Russell family who now own the house and the Gubbins family from whom they inherited it. The drawing-room is currently used for an interior decoration business and behind it is the small drawing-room, which was much used by the Gubbins sisters for bridge parties.

Upstairs landings were often used as family rooms in the past and the one at Dunkathel is particularly bright and pleasant. Off the landing is a room dedicated to a delightful collection of paintings by Beatrice Gubbins, a talented watercolourist. These include paintings of places seen on her extensive travels and some of her family.

Each of the sisters had a particular talent. Maude ran the house, Gertrude was in charge of the garden and its produce, Beatrice (who was only partially deaf) concentrated on her art and was responsible for the redecoration of the house in the 1930s, Kathleen was a talented photographer. The sisters also farmed and even had a Friesian dairy herd, one of the first in Ireland.

Marianne, the eldest sister, moved away, as did the two brothers in the family, leaving the four sisters and their mother at home. Life continued much as it always had since the last century. There were two maids, a butler, a chauffeur, a cook and gardeners who also cleaned the shoes. Fires were lit in the bedrooms and water was fetched from the spring each day.

OPEN May-mid Oct., Wed.-Sun. 2-6pm, or for groups by appointment, tel. 021-821014.

ADMISSION £2, children £1. Group lunches and teas by arrangement. Guided tour, toilets, parking.

DIRECTIONS Signposted just after a roundabout 5 km from Cork on the Cork-Waterford road.

TARBERT HOUSE

Tarbert, County Kerry

There is a charming picture of the vivacious Miss Leslies in the drawing-room of Tarbert House, painted by James Latham, the Irish portraitist, in 1740. The figures have such a lively contemporary air that you feel they might come to life and join the company. If they did, they would find very little had changed in this serene Carolinian house overlooking the broad reach of the Shannon estuary near the ferry crossing to Killimer in County Clare.

There are still Leslies in residence, as there have been ever since the house was built in 1690. The black-and-white flagged entrance hall looks much as it has always done; even the walls are still painted blue, as they have been for the last 300 years. The library is still panelled, picked out in shades of pale gold. Indeed, there is even another generation of lovely Miss Leslies at home. Where other families have won and lost and regained their properties through the vagaries of war, or have rebuilt their homes on an ever grander scale, the Kerry branch of Leslies have been content with their tall seven bay-fronted house, the only changes being the addition of a third storey and a front porch to provide shelter from the Atlantic gales. But then, perhaps the ability to stay put is only to be expected from a family whose motto is 'Grip Fast'. The Leslie family came to Ireland from Scotland in the fifteenth century. Their coat of arms bears a thistle and three buckles, whereby literally hangs a tale. One of the Leslie forebears was Lord Chamberlain to Margaret, Queen of Malcolm III of Scotland, and his duty was to carry the Queen pillion clinging fast to a strap buckled around his waist. After a narrow escape, two more buckles were added to the belt: hence the motto.

The Leslies are descended from the first Leslie to come to Ireland, John Leslie, known as the 'fighting bishop' for his defence of the archbishop's Palace of Raphoe against Cromwell.

Tarbert House is a delightful example of a late seventeenth-century house and its rooms suggest how different the lifestyle of that period was. The large entrance hall, for instance, served a multiplicity of purposes: it was frequently the scene of cock fights and gaming, and was very much used by the male members of the household. The women tended to use the corresponding first-floor room as the main dayroom for activities like painting, embroidery, music and receiving friends, while children were allotted the third-floor landing. The hall was also used as an armoury, and the walls are still hung with a fearsome array of guns and bayonets from the time of Sir Edward Leslie, who formed the Tarbert Fencibles (one of the local militias raised against the threat of a Napoleonic invasion). There are still trusses on the walls which were down to facilitate the loading of guns.

The main rooms would have been panelled and a first-floor bedroom and the library still have their original panelling. The library also features finely carved Corinthian pilasters. Much of the furniture - motley Irish pieces including a magnificent Irish Chippendale mirror complete with its original gilt - is original to the house and the charming chintz used for the drawing-room curtains, known as the Tarbert roses, has been copied by the US firm of Scalamanre and now hangs as curtains in the White House in Washington.

The Leslies' prosperity depended very much on agriculture and on salmon rights to the river. Tarbert was a busy port, exporting grain, butter and pigs, and the old pier near the house was built in 1854 to facilitate this trade. The Leslies ran their estates well and enjoyed a good relationship with their tenants. There is a chain which was presented by grateful tenants in 1848 during the Famine, and the family, having passed over ownership of all but 250 acres, were never under threat during the Troubles.

There have been many colourful visitors to Tarbert down through the centuries. Charlotte Brontë spent part of her honeymoon at Tarbert House and Sir Edward Leslie invited Benjamin Franklin there as part of his drive to restore Irish-American trade to Tarbert after the American War of Independence.

OPEN 15 June-30 Aug., 10am-12 noon & 2-4pm, tel. 068-36198.

ADMISSION £2.50, family £5. There is also an hour-long woodland walk through the grounds.

DIRECTIONS Tarbert House is just outside Tarbert on the road to the Killimer ferry.

ASH HILL TOWERS

Kilmallock, County Limerick

'The drawing-rooms upstairs are regular curio shops, the ceilings are beautiful and the fireplace is of Italian marble, beautifully carved. The ceiling was done by an Italian artist, also the fresco around the walls.' So wrote Eileen Weldon Foster in a letter to her American fiancé during a visit to her ancestral home at Ash Hill in 1908.

Ash Hill Towers is a castellated Georgian mansion and horses are - and always were - paramount here. The front door even looks out onto the stableyard, so that the owner never needed to be out of sight of his equine pride and joy. This is serious hunting country - home of the Limerick Hunt and the Scarteens. The rolling limestone pastures of the Golden Vale make this one of the premier bloodstock breeding areas. The house and its surrounding park is on the fringe of Kilmallock, which in medieval times was one of the most important towns in Munster.

The property was originally called Castle Coote and was built for Chidley Coote in the eighteenth century. The front of the house has an eleven-bay façade of limestone ashlar with a break-front pediment and a tripartite Venetian window over the handsome doorcase. The Coote family - known for their eccentricity - gave the expression 'mad as a Coote' to posterity. One of the more adventurous Cootes - Sir Eyre Coote - who had a romantic liaison with a black slave girl during a spell in Jamaica, provided a blood link between Ireland and the man once in the running to be America's first black President, Colin Powell.

Chidley Coote died in 1799 leaving a five-year-old heir, Charles Henry Coote, who later, thanks to an inheritance, built himself an even grander house at Ballyfin, County Laois. The house then passed out of the Coote family and became the seat of the Eyre Evans family. The house was given the Gothic treatment by architect Charles F. Anderson in 1833. Two battlemented and machicolated towers were added to the garden front, but these were subsequently demolished in the 1950s.

The great glory of the house is the first-floor drawing-room, where there is a breathtaking ceiling apparently executed by the stuccodore who worked on the ceilings at Glin Castle.

The charming bow-windowed drawing-room with Wyatt windows is part of the two-storey addition of 1800. There are plans to restore the original staircase hall. There are delightful architectural details, particularly in the Gothic entrance hall and in the room above it, which is lit by the Venetian window and would originally have been a ladies' drawing-room.

In the mid nineteenth century Ash Hill was leased to John Henry Weldon and it is now the home of a second generation of the Johnson family. The house is run as a guest-house and horses bred at the stud are sold at Newmarket each year. Life at Ash Hill revolves around horses, and the mood of the place is reminiscent of Molly Keane novels.

OPEN 20 April–20 June, 9am–1pm, by appointment, tel. 063-98035.

ADMISSION £2.

DIRECTIONS On the outskirts of Kilmallock.

GLIN CASTLE

Glin, County Limerick

G lin is a sham castle. It is, in fact, a gorgeous late eighteenth-century house with a Gothicised cloak, still awaiting the completion of its ghostly third storey. It was built between 1780 and 1789 for Colonel John FitzGerald, 24th Knight of Glin. The benign, double bow-fronted house with its entrance and fanlight faces the Shannon and the low meadows of County Clare on the far bank. The cost of the house and the colonel's habit of parading his cavalry and infantry, uniformed and raised at his own expense in the ferment leading up to the 1798 Rebellion, precipitated Colonel John's bankruptcy, and the builders left halfway through plastering the third floor. The colonel's portrait, in the uniform of the Glin Artillery, hangs in the hall.

The 25th Knight of Glin - the Knight of the Women - enjoyed better financial as well as sexual success. He added turrets and battlements to his father's house and built castellated gate lodges, their miniature turrets like so many chess pieces.

The Shannon acts as a mirror, sending light bouncing off the sugar-white exterior of the castle and accenting the details of magnificent interior stucco-work and the grotesque carving of fine Irish furniture. The entrance hall is divided by two great Corinthian columns and the neo-classical plasterwork ceiling still has its original terracotta and green colours. The feeling of light and space is enhanced by a pair of doorways with fanlights next to the airy staircase hall and its Palladian window. Two sets of stairs face the doorways from the hall and then unite at the half landing as a single free-flying flight.

The fine interiors - the drawing-room with its delicate naïve plasterwork and the library with its magnificent pedimented bookcase and secret doorway - are matched by the splendour of the contents of the rooms at Glin. But what looks like the accumulation of treasured family possessions is, in fact, mainly a wonderful representative collection of fine Irish furniture and paintings, put together by Desmond FitzGerald, art historian, Christie's representative in Ireland and farmer of Glin's 400 acres.

These days Glin radiates tranquillity and hospitality dispensed by the Knight and his wife Olda, Madam Glin, to their privileged guests. But earlier chapters of FitzGerald history were far more turbulent. The FitzGeralds are an Old English/Norman family and arrived in Ireland with Strongbow, establishing themselves in Limerick and Kerry. The Knights of Glin had their earliest stronghold at Shanid near Limerick and later at Glin, where the stump of the original castle can still be seen in the village.

Stories about the FitzGeralds abound and one of the best known concerns the final fall of the castle, which was under siege by Sir George Carew. Carew captured the then Knight's six-year-old heir, tied him over the mouth of a cannon and threatened to blow him to bits; to which the Knight replied that he was virile, his wife fertile and they could easily produce another son. The boy was spared, but the Knight was defeated. In the next generation, Richard FitzGerald was known as the duellist and his portrait

in the act of receiving a duelling challenge from a Spaniard hangs in the hall at Glin. This particular duel was nearly his undoing, since the Spaniard was wearing a concealed suit of chainmail. However, on the advice of his servant, FitzGerald 'stuck him where they stick pigs'.

The family were Catholic until the eighteenth century and naturally supported James II. After Desmond FitzGerald was slain at Derry's walls, they avoided forfeiture of their estate because it was entailed to his son, Thomas 'the snub nosed'. Of Thomas's sons, three conformed to the Protestant faith. The second eldest son died the day after celebrating his wedding. Richard, the duellist, despite being a great ladies' man, never had a legitimate heir and it fell to Thomas, the youngest son, to secure Glin by conforming and marrying a Cromwellian heiress.

OPEN 1 May-30 June, 10am-12 noon & 2-4pm. Open to groups at other times by arrangement, tel. 068-34112.

ADMISSION Adults £3, children £1. Guided tours, garden open, shop, wheelchair access. Meals for garden and cultural groups can be pre-booked.

DIRECTIONS On the Foynes-Tarbert road 9 km beyond Foynes.

BANTRY HOUSE

Bantry, County Cork

Remote as Bantry may seem, it nevertheless became the theatre for one of those points where the course of Anglo-Irish history hung in the balance. Inspired by the French Revolution and the American War of Independence, Wolfe Tone and Lord Edward FitzGerald, leaders of the United Irishmen, enlisted the aid of the French government in an attempt to overthrow the British.

In 1796 a French fleet set sail for Ireland, but a violent storm dispersed all but 16 of the original 43 ships, and by Christmas Eve these lay off Whiddy Island in Bantry Bay. In the event, the threatened invasion never happened, the ships were blown out to sea again, and 13 more French ships turned tail after being given false reports that the British fleet were nearby. But Richard White of Seafield handled the emergency so well that he was created a baron in 1797 and later Earl of Bantry for his services to the Crown.

His elevation gave White - whose grandfather had originally acquired the property having made his money from a variety of activities ranging from fishing to farming - a new social standing. In 1820 he enlarged his house - originally built for a Samuel Hutchinson in 1720 - adding two bow ends to accommodate two drawing-rooms. Richard's son, Viscount Berehaven, undertook the Grand Tour, becoming so addicted to travel that he made no fewer than 20 visits to Europe and travelled as far afield as Russia and Poland, amassing artefacts that he sent home by the shipload. When he inherited from his father in 1851 he enlarged the house to create a suitably magnificent setting for his collection, adding a fourteen-bay block to the back of the house and remodelling the garden in the Italian style. The contrast between the wildness of the surrounding countryside and the baroque splendour of the Earl's home gives the mansion and its treasure-trove contents the aura of an extravagant - though now slightly faded - dream.

The inner and outer entrance halls are floored in black-and-white flags, with inset panels of mosaic brought from Pompeii by Viscount Berehaven. The walls are hung with family portraits, including one of the current owner, Egerton Shelswell-White, with the trombone he plays in the local band. The Rose drawing-room overlooks Bantry Bay and takes its name from the Aubusson tapestries - made for Marie Antoinette's marriage to the Dauphin. The Rose room has its counterpart in the adjoining drawing-room, which is hung with Gobelin tapestries, acquired, like the Aubusson pieces, by Richard Viscount Berehaven.

The library runs the full width of the central block at the back of the house, with views of the 'Stairway to the Sky', 100 steps climbing to a magnificent vantage point overlooking Bantry Bay. The serious mood of the library is accentuated by the grey marble columns marching down the room, the heavily compartmented ceiling and the minimal furnishing. The most photographed room in the house is the spectacular blue dining-room, dominated by full-length portraits of George III and Queen Charlotte.

Richard, 2nd Earl of Bantry, died without heir in 1868, and the title and Bantry House passed to his brother William, who had five daughters and a son. The house became the focus of a gay social life, as the British fleet frequently anchored in the bay and the naval officers attended parties given by the Whites. William's son, another William, died just five years after inheriting and the title became extinct. However, the estate remained in the family and they have been there ever since.

The house was opened to the public in 1945 by Clodagh Shelswell-White, one of the first stately homes in Ireland to do so. Egerton Shelswell-White has shared his home with tens of thousands of visitors each year since he inherited Bantry House from his mother in 1978, and he and his wife Brigitte have undertaken an ongoing restoration programme. One of the wings of the house has been converted to provide bed-and-breakfast accommodation and the handsome cupola-topped stables now house a 1796 French Armada exhibition.

OPEN 1 March-31 Oct., 9am-6pm. Spring and summer evenings until 8pm.

ADMISSION House and gardens £6, groups £4, children free. Tea room, shop, toilets, guided tours.

DIRECTIONS On the outskirts of Bantry.

COLLIS-SANDES HOUSE

Tralee, County Kerry

W hile the majority of Irish country houses are Georgian, their architecture informed by the cool symmetry of classicism, the brick palazzo that is Collis-Sandes House provides a whiff of exotic high-Victorian taste. Arches and ogee windows reminiscent of medieval Venice, and trefoil windows suggestive of the East, are combined with an elaborate interior with all the colour and richness of a pre-Raphaelite painting.

Originally known as Oak Park, it is a romantic house, built between 1857 and 1860 for Maurice Fitzgerald Sandes, in late middle age, and in honour of his new bride, Ellen Louisa Dennis. It was financed with the fortune he had amassed in the tea plantations of India. It was designed by Cork architect William Atkins and owes its chief inspiration to John Ruskin's brand of Gothic

revival, which drew on the architecture of Renaissance Venice. The house is of red brick, decorated with horizontal bands of limestone, with finely carved windows of local limestone. It seems for all the world as though the house has been plucked from among the Victorian villas of Belfast and dropped into the unfamiliar surroundings of a wooded Kerry hillside.

For both owner and architect, the house must have represented the realisation of their particular dreams. Maurice Fitzgerald Sandes was a true Victorian, entrepreneurial and adventurous, and like many of his generation he looked not to the land, the army or the church for a career but to the expanding British colonies. A barrister by profession, Maurice joined the civil service in India, rising to become Registrar General of the State of Bengal. Other opportunities presented themselves in the development of new techniques for making indigo dye, a business which grew rapidly and allowed Maurice to invest in tea plantations, becoming a director of the Balijan Tea Company in Assam. He obviously harboured the expatriot dream of retiring to the old country, to Kerry, where his family were big landowners. In preparation he purchased the Oak Park estate from the Encumbered Estates Court (presumably the previous family, the Batemans, had been ruined by the Famine and the remains of their home still stand). When he retired from India at the age of 52 he married Ellen and organised the building of his new home on land near his brother's home at Oakvilla.

William Atkins' major work up to that date had been institutional and included the Cork Lunatic Asylum and Mount Jerome cemetery, Dublin. At Oak Park he had licence to engage in all the whimsy of the new Victorian Gothic ideals. The significance of the house for the now forgotten architect is signalled in his initials above the front door.

The entrance to the house begins with two very grand statements: a massive arched *porte-cochère*, resting on square stone columns and the sumptuous staircase hall. Ogee arches supported on purple marble columns open onto a staircase of polished wood with a balustrade glittering with wheat sheaves, offset by rich green marbled walls and wood-panelled ceilings patterned in gold, green and red.

The main reception rooms leading off the hall are similarly decorated, with painted wood ceilings by Frederick Taylor and detailing like the fleur-de-lys patterned Minton tiles, poppy head doorcases and the brass work hinges reminiscent of the other arch priest of Victorian Gothic, Augustus Pugin. Bow windows lined with finely detailed wood panelling afford vistas of the enclosing woods and of what in the heyday of the house would have been flower beds dotting the lawn, filled with a succession of precision-planted annuals. This is now owned by the Tralee Pitch and Putt Group.

The estate, also known as Killeen, has strong Cromwellian connections and was granted in the seventeenth century to Rowland Bateman, an officer in Cromwell's Irish army. William Sandes, founder of the Sandes dynasty in Ireland, was also a Cromwellian officer who was granted lands in Kerry. The Sandes family settled at Tarbert and obviously prospered, for Maurice Sandes inherited and acquired an estate of around 11,000 acres by 1876.

On his return from India he continued his involvement in public service, serving as a JP and High Sheriff for Tralee. The Sandes had no children and the estate was left to Maurice's youngest nephew Falkiner Collis. He followed in his uncle's footsteps as a lawyer, practising in

Calcutta, and was also a director of the Balijan Tea Company and an administrator in Bengal. While in India he met his future wife, Louisa Jane Young. The couple had four children and lived in Florence for a while before eventually returning to Oak Park in 1895. Maurice their only son did not escape the tragedy of the First World War in which 49,400 Irish men lost their lives. Two daughters of the house left to marry (Doris Rosa married into the Leslie family of Tarbert House, also featured in this book), leaving Joan alone at Oak Park. During the height of the Troubles the house was bought for a £4,000 song by the Bishop of Kerry, Charles O'Sullivan, to serve as a novitiate for the Presentation Order.

The nuns converted the conservatory at the back of the house into a chapel and, after the Order left in 1973, the house and estate were subsequently purchased for local government use and became the County Committee of Agriculture office. When the agricultural services were reorganised, two local businessmen, Enda O'Brien and Patrick Crean, purchased the house, renamed it Collis-Sandes House in honour of the family and instituted an imaginative scheme where the house and its stables have been restored and now serve as a hostel and an educational and cultural centre. No doubt Maurice Fitzgerald Sandes would approve.

OPEN 1 July-31 Aug., 9am-5pm, groups by arrangement outside these hours, tel. 066-28658.

ADMISSION £3, concessions £1.50. Toilets, wheelchairs.

DIRECTIONS 1 mile north from Tralee centre on the N69. Turn left at gate lodge and follow signs.

Section Three

CONNACHT ISLAND

Galway, Mayo, Roscommon, Sligo

A medieval tower which became the inspirational home of William Butler Yeats, the Victorian palazzo that is the present home of the direct descendant of a High King of Ireland, the splendid Renaissance manor of the Earl of Clanricard, the thatched cottage which was the retreat of Pádraic Pearse, the executed leader of the 1916 uprising, the open houses of the west – all could not present more of a contrast. The scenery varies widely, from the gentle lakescapes of lovely Leitrim to the living rock sculptures that are the Aran Islands, from the harmonious peaks, inlets and lakes of Connemara, dominated by the Twelve Bens, to the desolate grandeur of the Mayo bogs where the cone of Nephin Beg forms a dramatic backdrop.

Connacht is like an island within an island, cut off from the other three provinces by the Shannon complex. The Connacht counties share a lot of history: the native Irish population was pushed westward to the least productive bog and mountain landscape by the Normans and again by Cromwell's ruthless policy of sending the landed Irish 'to Hell or Connacht'. The western counties were by the early nineteenth century the most densely populated and the most dependent on subsistence farming and on the potato, so that when famine struck the west was sorely hit, particularly Galway and Mayo. Thousands died and thousands more emigrated. Urbanisation and generations of emigration dramatically depopulated the region, a trend which is only now starting to reverse, and then only in some areas.

The great dynasties were the O'Malleys, the Norman Burkes or de Burgos, the O'Flahertys, the O'Conors and the O'Rourkes of Leitrim. There was trade between Galway and Spain and southern France, and the west coast came to represent a back door for allies who wanted to rock the mutual British enemy. General Humbert and his French forces landed at Killala in support of the 1798 Rebellion.

On the Limerick side of Galway, near Gort, there is a trio of locations that give an insight into three leading literary figures: William Butler Yeats's Norman tower, Thoor Ballylee; Coole Park, home of Lady Gregory, founder of the Abbey Theatre (the house no longer exists but the garden and estate are open); and the sixteenth-century Dúnguaire Castle, once the home of author Oliver St John Gogarty, and now also the scene of banquets (all open April-September daily). On the Shannonside of east Galway, Portumna Castle and Clonfert - a monastic settlement founded by St Brendan the Navigator in the sixth century - are notable, and the walls of Athenry and the castle built there by Meiler de Bermingham in 1250 are an impressive medieval legacy. At Ardrahan there is the 150-year-old Rathbaun Farm, where you can sample traditional fare and see traditional farming practices, and there is a re-created traditional Irish cottage in North Gate Street, Athenry (both open daily).

Connemara has the kind of scenery that gives you 'round-the-corneritis'. With twisting roads where each turn brings an even more enchanting prospect of mountains, sea and lakes, it is hard to resist finding out what happens round the next bend. There is said to be an island for every day of the year on Lough Corrib, and on a promontory overlooking the lake between Oughterard and Moycullen is Aughnanure Castle, an O'Flaherty stronghold dating to 1500 (open daily mid June-September). One of the most atmospheric ruins in Galway is the 1779 mansion built for the St George family, overlooking the sea at Clarinbridge. It was burnt during the Troubles and the St George Gothic mausoleum is on a hill nearby.

Galway city is extremely lively, thanks in no small measure to the vibrant arts community and to companies like the Druid Theatre Company and Macnas. Interesting houses open to the public in Galway are Lynch Castle, supposedly the oldest medieval town house (on the corner of Shop Street), and the Nora Barnacle House Museum, dedicated to James Joyce's wife and muse and located in her home in Bowling Green (open daily 10am-5pm, closed Sunday.)

Some of the loveliest lake and mountain scenery lies between Maam Cross and Recess. Turn off at Maam Cross for Gortmore and then Rosmuck, where Pádraic Pearse used to stay in a small thatched cottage which now contains Pearse memorabilia (open mid June-mid September). There are wonderful beaches at Roundstone (where there is a lively social scene in the summer) and at Ballyconneely. The Connemara National Park is on the slopes of the Twelve Bens at Letterfrack and just beyond is romantic Kylemore Abbey, originally built to make a honeymoon wish come true.

Exotically named Delphi was named after the 2nd Marquess of Sligo visited Delphi in Greece with Lord Byron. Westport House overlooks Clew Bay, surely one of the most idyllic settings of any of the great houses of Ireland, and the principal buildings and main street of Westport town were designed by James Wyatt. Close to Castlebar, Ballintubber Abbey - founded in 1216 by Cathal O'Conor, King of Connacht - has been in use for 800 years. Also overlooking Lough Carra are the ruins of Moore Hall (1795), home of John Moore, who was appointed President of Connacht by General Humbert, and later the home of the writer George Moore.

The lakelands in the centre of County Mayo are great fishing country, especially around Pontoon. Pink-washed Enniscoe House looks out across Lough Conn, which is ideally situated for a fishing holiday or for tracing your roots, since there is a family history research centre there. The north coast has some of the most spectacular cliff scenery, especially around Portacloy. At Ballycastle the Ceide Fields centre reveals the extraordinary field systems, tombs and dwelling areas of this extensive Stone Age monument. The settlement was buried in the boglands near dramatic cliffs and rock formations. Killala Bay was the site of General Humbert's ill-fated landing in 1798 - in support of the rebellion raised by the United Irishmen, the French force took Killala and Ballina but were defeated at Ballinamuck in County Longford. On the coast road are the remains of fifteenth-century Moyne Abbey and, a little further on, Rosserk Abbey, also fifteenth century. Foxford's woollen mills - the source of wonderfully durable woollen rugs - was founded by a local nun, Mother Agnes Morrogh Bernard, in 1892 to provide employment in the area. The town is pleasantly situated on the River Moy.

County Sligo is Yeats country and visits to Lissadell House - home of the Gore-Booth family - where Yeats was an occasional visitor, and the simple, dignified graveyard at Drumcliff church are most rewarding.

There are also plenty of worthwhile diversions in County Roscommon, including Clonalis House. Boyle is beautifully situated on the banks of the River Boyle where the fine Cistercian abbey, founded by Abbot Maurice O'Duffy, has a commanding site beside the river. Boyle is situated in the centre of a lovely stretch of countryside at the foot of the Curlew Mountains. It is also beside Lough Key Forest Park, the former demesne of Rockingham, the 1810 John Nash mansion of the King-Harmon family which was burnt in 1957 and subsequently demolished. Nearby are the ruins of a McDermott castle and two medieval priories. The story of the King-Harmon family, who came to Boyle in 1603, is recorded in the interpretative centre which is in their earlier home, King House (1730), together with the history of Connacht and its kings and of the house, open April, Saturday-Sunday, 10am-6pm; May-October, daily, 10am-6pm; group tours May-October, Saturday-Sunday, 10am-6pm, tel 079-63242. Frybrook House (1750), an imposing three-storey house in the centre of Boyle, is open from April to September (Tuesday-Sunday, 2-6pm). Woodbrook, so vividly described in David Thompson's evocation of Anglo-Irish life, is also near Boyle (but not open to the public).

The Palladian Strokestown Park, at Strokestown, with its added attractions of a walled pleasure garden and Famine Museum, makes a good focus for an outing. This could be combined with a visit to Lough Rynn at Mohill, County Leitrim, former property of the Wicked Earl of Leitrim. At the centre of an ornamental estate and walled gardens, this 1832 Tudor revival mansion was designed by Woodward and Deane (the estate and gardens are open.) There is some beguiling countryside around Lough Gill, with woods sloping down to the water and Creevelea Friary, the Lake Isle of Inisfree and Parkes Castle as focuses. A sixteenth-century plantation castle, the restored Parkes complex comprises a tower house, a manor house and a gate house within a bawn fortified with turrets. The castle - built for the Parke family on the site of an earlier O'Rourke stronghold - has a fairytale setting beside the lake and there is an example of a sweathouse - a kind of early sauna - on the lakeshore.

Nearby Fivemilebourne is an attractive village and, at the curiously named Dromahair (from the Irish for 'ridge of the two air demons'), are the ruined castle of the O'Rourke kings of Breffny and the remains of Old Hall, built in 1626 for Sir William Villiers, who was granted the O'Rourkes' escheated lands. Dervorgilla eloped from Castle Breffny with the King of Leinster, Dermot MacMurrough, an act which eventually led to the Norman invasion (*cherchez la femme*). To the north-east of Manorhamilton, which is located at the meeting point of four valleys, is the ruined 1638 mansion of Sir Frederick Hamilton. This seventeenth-century fortified house is set in the valley of Glencar Lough, where the Glencar Waterfall can be seen, inspiration for Yeats's poem 'The Stolen Child'.

PLACES TO STAY / EAT

There can't be many places in the world where you order a picnic lunch and get your own tin box complete with label, but that is typical of the good old-fashioned comfort at Currarevagh House, a Victorian mansion overlooking Lough Corrib, owned and run by June and Harry Hodgson as a country house hotel with special emphasis on fishing (tel. 091-552313). Sweeney's Oughterard House is a must, either to stay or to drop in to the bar and socialise. At certain times of the year impromptu parties are liable to develop. The ivy-clad Georgian hotel overlooks the Owenriff River running through the grounds and has all the charm of a private country house (tel. 091-82207).

The Galway Oyster Festival is a wonderful excuse for concentrating on shellfish and good places to be are Clarinbridge or Kilcolgan. Morans Oyster Cottage (thatched) beside the weir is especially recommended for oysters, prawns, or smoked salmon, accompanied with brown bread and a lunchtime pint. De Burgos, 15/17 Augustine Street, in the vaults of a sixteenth-century wine merchant's house in Galway, has great atmosphere and their three fillets - beef, pork and veal - are an original experience for carnivores. Drimcong House at Moycullen is definitely on the foody trail: superb Irish and international cuisine in a 300-year-old house (tel. 091-85115). Renvyle House Hotel, near the little village of Renvyle, is good for turn-of-the-century charm and spotting Irish VIPs. Delphi, near Leenane - where Prince Charles stayed, at his own

request – is the former fishing lodge of the Marquis of Sligo. With an incomparable lake and mountain setting, guests sit at one big table and house parties are welcome. Self-catering accommodation is also available (tel. 095-42211).

Kieran and Thelma Thompson preside over Georgian Newport House, once the home of the Earls of Tyrconnell. There is fine 1820s plasterwork and views over the Newport River. Seafood is a speciality (tel. 098-41222). Friends keep going back for the convivial atmosphere at the Victorian Mount Falcon, family home of the Aldridges, where guests gather at the great dining-table and fruit and vegetables from the kitchen garden feature on the menu (tel. 096-70811). Coopershill House near Drumfin, County Sligo, a handsome 1774 house with a particularly fine entrance hall (complete with rent table), is home of the O'Hara family. This is one of the houses I remember with pleasure from my four-poster bed tour (tel. 071-65108).

On the outskirts of Ballina is Belleck Castle, a high Victorian Gothic mansion overlooking wooded grounds and the Brosna River now converted to an hotel. Apart from having a great atmosphere, the house has a panelled dining-room complete with minstrels' gallery (tel. 096-21033). Enniscoe House near Crossmolina features as an open house and also makes a wonderful base for touring north Connacht (tel. 096-31112). Another happy memory is of 1846 Temple House, on the estate where the Percevals have lived since 1665. There is a thirteenth-century castle in the grounds and the house has its original furnishings. Deb Perceval's cooking is superb (tel. 071-83329).

LISSADELL

Carney, County Sligo

Constance Markievicz, revolutionary and first woman member of the Dáil, once described her childhood home as a 'grey barrack of a place'. The description hardly does her ancestral home justice. Backed by the sphinx-like mountain of Ben Bulben and with grounds sloping down to the great sweep of Sligo Bay, Lissadell could not have a more spectacular setting. The exterior of the house is rather austere, and certainly grey, especially on a day when sheets of rain sweep in from Sligo Bay, but architecturally it is a fine example of the restrained Greek revival style reflecting the serious mood of the period.

A great deal of public building in this style was carried out in the provinces in the early nineteenth century - courthouses, prisons and churches - where buildings had a moral as well as a practical purpose. The Greek revival style depends for its impact not on decoration but on the play of contrasts, with massive geometric shapes. The house was built in the early 1830s for Constance's grandfather, Sir Robert Gore-Booth MP, and designed by the London architect Francis Goodwin. Sir Robert's choice of an English architect may have been based on his familiarity with Goodwin's work in Lancashire, where the Gore-Booths had estates.

The prelude of the grand porch is followed by the pillared entrance hall. To the left is a massive imperial staircase of black Kilkenny marble, and to the right the billiard room. Beyond the hall is an architectural tour de force, an internal apse-ended room on a cathedral-like scale which dominates the heart of the house. Two storeys tall, with a high gallery supported by four great Ionic columns on one side and engaged Doric piers on the other, the room is lit only from above by a series of skylights. The room was used by Sir Robert as a gallery and a music room, where his Gothic organ - made by Hull of Dublin in 1812 - occupied pride of place.

Beyond the gallery the bow-ended library forms a dramatic enfilade of rooms which runs from the front to the back of the house. In the dining-room the pilasters supporting the cornice have been enlivened by life-sized paintings of members of the family and members of staff. Constance's initials can be seen on a window pane, where she scratched them with a diamond, in the anteroom which she was allowed to use as a 'den', known as the Glory Hole. She sometimes wore her pet snake around her neck and also kept a pet monkey.

The comings and goings of servants were hidden from view and access to the domestic offices in the basement was via a sunken yard and underground passage.

At the turn of the century, like many large country houses, Lissadell was home to large house parties and to an extended family. The poet William Butler Yeats stayed at the house twice in the winter of 1894, while researching Irish fairy tales. Later he recalled the sisters as he remembered them in the bow-windowed library.

The light of evening, Lissadell,
Great windows open to the south,
Two girls in silk kimonos,
Both beautiful, one a gazelle.

The Gore-Booths were a remarkable family, where the pursuit of individual interests were encouraged. Sir Robert's son Henry (father of Constance and Eva) was a keen Arctic explorer - remembered for sailing to the rescue of another Arctic explorer, Leigh Smith - and many of the exhibits in the family museum in the billiard room recall his exploits. They include Sir Henry's shooting trophies and a stuffed bear killed by the gallant butler Kilgallon, who not only accompanied his employer on expeditions but on this occasion saved his life. Lady Gore-Booth ran a lace-making school in the area, Eva became a poet and her brother Josslyn was a keen gardener. Constance was a linguist, she rode, gardened, sailed and sketched endlessly - eventually, at the age of 25, winning her parents' consent to study at the Slade School of Art in London. Later she moved to Paris, where she met her future husband, the self-styled Count Casimir Markievicz. She was condemned to death, reprieved and imprisoned for her part in the 1916 Rising, before being elected as Sinn Féin candidate to Westminster - although she did not take her seat.

The first member of the family to come to Ireland was Paul Gore, and the Lissadell branch of the family is descended from one of his sons, Francis Gore, who owned Ardtermon Castle. By 1760, when his great-grandson Booth Gore was created a baronet, the family was living at Lissadell, in an earlier house down by the shore. Booth Gore's father Nathaniel's marriage to Letitia Booth brought estates in Manchester and Salford into the family.

Sir Robert Gore-Booth inherited early, at the age of nine. He was widowed at the age of 23 before marrying again two years later. After he attained his majority he mortgaged his English estates to purchase additional land at Ballymore, making him the richest landowner in the county. He set about modernising and improving his estate. During the Famine rents were waived, and Sir Robert spent over £5,000 helping tenants to emigrate and £34,000 on imported grain (something like £1.5 million in today's terms).

Sir Josslyn Gore-Booth survived his more famous sisters, Constance and Eva, and two of his sons died fighting against Hitler. His widow and daughters first opened the house to the public in 1967. The present owner is his grandson, and namesake, who continues the tradition of engaging in a programme of restoration of the house, generously assisted by the National Heritage Council and the Office of Public Works, and made possible by the skills of Sligo craftspeople.

OPEN 1 June-mid Sept., daily except Sun., 10.30am-12.30pm & 2-4.30pm.

ADMISSION Adults £3, children £1. Guided tours, parking, toilets.

DIRECTIONS Follow signposts on Sligo-Bundoran road, turning off at Drumcliff.

KEVINSFORT

Strandhill Road, Sligo

Kevinsfort stands as an elegant testimony to the rise of the middle classes in the early nineteenth century. A house of modest size, its surrounding demesne has now been swallowed up by a housing estate. Nevertheless it retains its dignity, confronting the world with a handsome portico, topped with a pediment with acanthus leaf finials supported on stout Ionic columns. The plasterwork in the drawing- and dining-rooms is also sophisticated, with an unusual design of strapwork squares and diamonds with central bosses; the theme is repeated in the original chimney pieces. The principal rooms lead off an internal staircase hall, with a graceful staircase lit by a glass rotunda.

The house was built around 1820 by George Dodwell, a former High Sheriff of Sligo. There are records of Dodwells in the area dating back to the 1590s and a William Dodwell was High Sheriff of Sligo in 1636. Records suggest that Henry Dodwell, who was Mayor of Oxford in 1592, settled in Ireland in Kildare towards the end of Elizabeth I's reign. Henry's son George settled at Tanragoa in Sligo. The Dodwell who built the house was the land agent for the Gore-Booths and presumably also acted for other landed families in the area. Being an agent could be both a lucrative and a risky business, since the agent collected rents from tenants and was entitled to a percentage of the takings.

The house was built on a 580-acre estate and was faced in cut and dressed local limestone of a sombre grey. The Dodwell family evidently believed in doing things in some style. There was a generous stable yard in cut stone faced in brick, and three carriage houses in addition to the usual farm offices. A pleasure ground was created in the estate featuring over 50 different varieties of trees, including Chilean and Monterey pines, which were exotic introductions in the nineteenth century.

The declining fortunes of the house over the next century may have helped to ensure that many of its domestic features were preserved intact. In the small return the dressed stone servants' staircase circles down three flights from the attic floor to the basement. Off the half landings of these stairs are two magnificent examples of Victorian plumbing: the lavatories, which still have their original lever-operated cisterns, and the system, which was fed with water pumped by hand from the yard to the attic. The splendid Victorian bath is of painted cast iron with a mahogany rim. Before the arrival of plumbed-in baths, a tin bath - filled by hand - was the only genteel solution to bathing. A special tap at the turn of the stairs was used by servants to fill water cans with hot water for the china wash-basins in the bedrooms.

Below stairs, the unaltered basement with its acres of Liscannor flags tells the story of the servants' conditions far more eloquently than any words could do. Among the warren of rooms are the servants' hall, cellars, pantries, linen cupboards and a coal cellar. Cast-iron ranges were first introduced in the late eighteenth century, a technological mercy for cooks used to toiling over open fires. The coal-devouring monster at Kevinsfort is an early model.

The deeds of Kevinsfort were burnt with millions of other documents when the Custom House was gutted by fire during the 1922 Civil War. Neither the architect nor the plasterer who worked on the house are known.

The Condon family now own the house. John Condon was the dairy manager there and later ran an ice-cream making business, which is still remembered in the district. In their early days there the Condons had to live in the lower floors and rent the upstairs part of the house. Now they are gradually restoring Kevinsfort and researching the history of the place; in the longer term, there are plans to restore the stable yard.

OPEN 1 Aug.-31 Oct., Mon.-Fri. except bank and public holidays.

ADMISSION £2.50 adults, £1.50 OAPs and children.

DIRECTIONS Kevinsfort is on the outskirts of Sligo on the Strandhill road. 2 km from the centre turn left opposite Kilcawly's flat-roofed premises.

ENNISCOE HOUSE

Crossmolina, County Mayo

It would be hard to imagine a more peaceful, remote retreat than Enniscoe House. Across the meadow Lough Conn gleams with the promise of good fishing, with the mountains and woods of north Mayo as a backdrop. The 200-year-old pink-washed house, with its symmetrical twelve-pane windows and five-bay front, conforms exactly to the ideal of what a Georgian home should be.

Yet to this day a laneway at the back of the house is known as the French Avenue, recalling the French army that marched there in the final abortive chapter of the 1798 Rebellion. General Humbert's men had landed near Killala and later bivouacked at Enniscoe House, using the scaffolding which was still around George Jackson's new house

and raiding his cellar. There was no countrywide support for the French, the leadership of the United Irishmen had already been betrayed, and the French surrendered after defeat by General Lake at Ballinamuck. The Ninth Mayo Militia, under the command of Colonel George Jackson II, showed rebels in the county no quarter, and their severed heads were impaled on pikes on the road to Crossmolina.

George Jackson was a descendant of Francis Jackson, an officer in Cromwell's army. North Mayo was one of the areas designated for redistribution as payment for soldiers, and some time after 1650 Francis was granted 50,000 acres of land which was previously held by the Anglo-Norman Bourkes and forfeited for their support of the Confederates.

It wasn't until the next century - probably around 1720 - that the Jackson family felt secure enough to build an unfortified, three-storey farmhouse on their land, moving out of the shelter of an old castle and recycling the stones for the new building. This house is still perfectly preserved and incorporated into the later 1790s section. George Jackson MP was rising in the world, helped by his brother-in-law James Cuffe's position as Barrack Master General, and when Cuffe built a grand house across the lake Jackson took the opportunity to commission the builder to add a fashionable two-storey front with two elegant reception rooms on to his home. This improved house was inherited by his son, another George Jackson.

Enniscoe House remains much as it was in George Jackson's day. The entrance hall has Adamesque plasterwork, which was probably added post 1798, and leads into the oval staircase hall with its graceful staircase, lit from above by a dome decorated with classical medallions. To the left of the entrance hall is the drawing-room, still with its original wallpaper, faded from blue to dusty pink, and with a delicate frieze of sphinxes and foliage picked out in blue and white. The second drawing-room (formerly the dining-room) has a similar frieze and both rooms are furnished with a pleasant mix of Georgian and Victorian family pieces. A stunning interior fanlight marks the transition from the 1790s section of the house to the older part, where the rooms are smaller, the ceilings lower and the staircase has the characteristic shallow treads, panelling and heavy banister rail of the earlier period.

In the next century Enniscoe came into the Pratt family, through the marriage of George's grand-daughter Madeline Jackson to her cousin Mervyn Pratt of Cabra Castle in 1834. Their son Joseph was one of the first landlords to sell off his tenanted lands for redistribution to his tenants under the various Land Acts. Joseph's sons Audley and Mervyn were among the thousands of Anglo-Irish who fought in World War One - Audley was killed and Mervyn badly injured. Mervyn devoted his energies to gardening and fishing, leaving Enniscoe in 1950 to his cousin Professor John Nicholson, who held the chair in veterinary medicine in Dublin.

Enniscoe is one of the very few country mansions left in north Mayo: shorn of their lands, many had their roofs taken off by farmers in order to avoid tax and fell into ruins. In the 1980s Susan Kellett, Professor Nicholson's daughter, found herself facing the challenge - how to create jobs and make a living from a non-viable small farm without capital. The way in which that challenge has been met is a success story which has created work in the area and put Enniscoe on the map as a heritage house offering hospitality and guest accommodation. Susan was the instigator behind the Family History Research Centre in the former farm building, which became a prototype for genealogical enquiries on a world-wide basis. There is also a blacksmith school, 'Forging Links', in the prize-winning heritage centre which also houses a collection of machinery and implements from the area. There are plans to open self-catering accommodation and last year the pleasure grounds and restored walled garden, complete with the extraordinary rockery created by Major Pratt, was opened to the public. All of which goes to show that historic houses don't have to be dinosaurs, but can be a very dynamic part of the twenty-first century.

OPEN By appointment only, tel. 096-31112.

ADMISSION £3.

DIRECTIONS On the R135 Crossmolina-Castlebar road. Enniscoe House is a member of the Irish Country Houses and Restaurants Association.

WESTPORT HOUSE

Westport, County Mayo

'Nature hath done much for the pretty town of Westport and after Nature, the traveller ought to be thankful to Lord Sligo who has done a great deal too', wrote William Thackeray in his 1842 Irish sketch book. Howe Peter, 2nd Earl of Sligo, with a foresight stretching beyond most improving landlords, grasped the tourism potential of Mayo's superlative scenery and established a 25-bedroomed inn, equipping it down to the well-stocked cellar before handing it over, gratis, to a local man as landlord.

Among the great houses, Westport's situation is unparalleled. To the west, island-dotted Clew Bay stretches out to the blue hump of Clare Island, and, beyond the landscaped grounds, with lake, woods and river, Croagh Patrick and the precipitous mountains of

Mayo rear against the sky. Westport House presents two faces to the world: the seven-bay entrance front designed by Richard Cassels - or Castle - in 1730 for John Browne, later 1st Earl of Altamont, and the later front overlooking the lake designed in 1778 by Thomas Ivory for the 2nd Earl. The entrance front, with its narrow windows, has two storeys over a basement with a curious little three-bay voluted attic floor over the front door and pediment. Ivory's building formed three sides of a hollow square with the earlier house.

Westport House represents a fascinating amalgam of work by different architects commissioned by members of the Browne family. The first of the Brownes in Ireland was John Browne, son of Elizabethan courtier Sir Anthony Browne. He succeeded in establishing himself only too well in Mayo, to the point that he was murdered by envious Bourkes (the leading Gaelicised Anglo-Norman de Burgos). John left an infant son, Josias, whose barrister grandson - another John Browne - chose to build the first Westport House in 1650 on the foundations of the Castle of Cahenamart, once the stronghold of Grace O'Malley, the legendary pirate queen. His bride Maude Bourke, great-great-granddaughter of Grace, may have been influential in the choice. John amassed a great deal of land, including much of the Bourke land, but his support of James II, for whom he raised two regiments, proved his ruin. Thousand of acres were confiscated to pay his debts and his heir Peter lived under a cloud in reduced circumstances at a smaller property, Mount Browne. His son John was cast in a different mould. He was determined to succeed and engaged Cassels to build his fine cut-stone house, laid out the park and established a highly successful linen industry in the town of Westport - which he had moved from its former position around the house to a site about a mile away.

In his later years John Browne, now 1st Earl of Altamont, decided to double the size of the house and commissioned Thomas Ivory. However, the plans drawn up by Ivory were not executed until after the 2nd Earl, Peter, inherited. The first phase was initiated in 1778, aided no doubt by the fortune of his wife Elizabeth Kelly, heiress to Jamaican sugar plantations. The 3rd Earl, John Denis, later 1st Marquess of Sligo, completed Ivory's plan, created the lake and engaged James Wyatt to decorate the interior of the house and to lay out the town of Westport, with its wide streets.

Howe Peter, the 2nd Marquess, was a typical dashing Regency buck, a friend of George IV and Lord Byron, with an over-enthusiastic passion for the new science of archaeology. One of his better-known exploits involved the tracking down and removal of the doorway from the Treasury of Artreus. Homeward-bound on a chartered brig with his loot, he went one too far and 'borrowed' two British sailors off a warship - a treasonable offence in 1812 and one for which he was fined and sentenced to jail. In a development worthy of a soap opera, his widowed mother was so impressed by the judge's firm handling of her son that she ended up marrying him, only to discover that stern judges are not necessarily good husband material. However, the 2nd Marquess did rather better at gambling, winning 22,000 guineas in stakes during his racing career, but he backed the wrong architect when he engaged Benjamin Wyatt (son of James), who built a library with a new-fangled heating system which caused a fire and the loss of valuable books and pictures. Wyatt also removed some of his father's interior plasterwork.

Howe Peter also had a serious side and, while Governor of Jamaica, voted for the abolition of slavery, which caused him to lose a large amount of revenue from his Jamaican estates. He also refused a dukedom. He died at the end of an era, just before the Great Famine.

The 3rd Marquess did what he could in the face of the disaster, opening the workhouse at his own expense and sharing in the cost of a huge cargo of meal to relieve local suffering. He closed up Westport House, moved into a small house in the town with his sisters and travelled the country attempting to find a solution. When the local economy - and with it his rents - recovered, he had an impressive marble staircase with a bronze balustrade designed by George Wilkinson built, in place of his father's library.

The interior of the house has not been hugely altered since then. Among the most notable rooms are Cassels' magnificent entrance hall with its splendid barrel-vaulted ceiling, which leads through arches to the Wilkinson staircase, the Wyatt dining-room, with its splendid plasterwork featuring classical figures and garlands, the oak staircase with its Wyatt ceiling and the Chinese room with its original hand-painted Chinese wallpaper.

The 4th Marquess made the farm profitable; the 5th, known as the Nabob, had a working career in the Indian civil service; the 6th introduced forestry to the estate. In the changed social climate of the 1950s, following drastic death duties and four deaths in the family, and derisory offers for Westport House, the 10th Marquess took the decision to open the house to the public. Since then, over 1.5 million visitors have been to see Westport House and its associated attractions.

Architectural purists may groan at the impact of tourism on Westport's demesne but the Brownes are the only original family still to live in a house designed by Cassels. And they share the house - with the accretion of furniture and family memorabilia that makes the place a living home - with the public, rather than have Westport turned into a hotel, another golfing venue or a state-run museum.

OPEN Weekends in May, 2-5pm; 30 May-26 June, 2-6pm; 27 June-22 Aug., 10.30am-6pm, Sun. 2-6pm; 24-31 Aug., 2-6pm; Sept., 2-5pm, tel. 098-25430.

ADMISSION Adults £6, children £3 (house only). Tours £3.50. Family ticket for zoo and house £25. Conducted tours, parking, toilets, zoo, restaurant, rowing boats, pitch and putt, etc.

DIRECTIONS Westport House is just outside Westport.

CLONALIS HOUSE

Castlerea, County Roscommon

Clonalis is a splendid example of a late Victorian palazzo in the Italianate style, designed by Pepys Cockerell for Charles Owen O'Conor Don MP and built between 1875 and 1880. The entrance front remains tantalisingly out of sight from the long curved drive, and the impact of the façade and imposing three-storey central tower topped by a pyramidal roof is revealed with a flourish as visitors arrive in the garden forecourt. The house has two storeys and a basement, is faced in cement and has a balustraded porch.

It would be an interesting house in its own right, but the remarkable history of the O'Conors, Kings of Connacht, makes Clonalis even more fascinating. The family claim to have the oldest traceable ancestry

in Europe, stretching back, through the last of the High Kings of Ireland and 96 generations, to 300 BC. The first O'Conor to build at Clonalis was Turlough Mór O'Conor, High King of Ireland from 1119 to 1156, who built a stone castle, the first in a series of castles and houses constructed for 25 generations of O'Conors at Clonalis. In the forecourt is the coronation stone of the Kings of Connacht bearing the footprint of the first High King of Ireland, its use supposedly dating back to 90 BC.

In the dining-room hang portraits of seven successive generations of O'Conors. The earliest of these is of Major Owen O'Conor, in whose time the family lands were lost twice. They were forfeited once under Cromwell when he was aged nine. He was reinstated following the Restoration, only to lose his property again when he raised three regiments of militia to fight on the losing side for James II in the Williamite wars. He was jailed in Chester Castle in 1692. His son Denis O'Conor (b. 1674), known as 'Denis the heir to nothing', worked as a labourer in County Roscommon and walked all the way to Dublin to undertake a famous law case in which he won back 800 acres of the family lands. Among the other notable O'Conors was Denis's great-grandson Charles Owen O'Conor Don, who was the first Catholic MP for Roscommon, and his grandson, another Charles Owen, who was responsible for having the Irish language introduced in the school curriculum. Another Charles (Don Carlos) became part of the diaspora known as the Wild Geese and fled Ireland in the wake of the 1798 uprising. He eventually went to the United States and founded Tucson, Arizona.

The ornate entrance and staircase hall is dominated by two Ionic pillars in unusual pink Mallow marble, with arches giving onto the pine staircase and an arched corridor - which doubles as a picture gallery - leading to the principal rooms. The drawing-room is furnished in late Victorian style, while most of the pieces in the dining-room are Georgian.

The O'Conors are one of the few families to retain both their lands and their Catholic faith, and one room in the house is a consecrated chapel. The inscription 'Altare Priviligiatum' over the altar - a reference to the family's right to hold the sacraments in the house and to appoint the local parish priest - comes from the previous O'Conor house.

The former billiard room now houses a display of papers from the O'Conor archive of over 100,000 documents. Among these are an agreement between Sir Charles Coote and Cromwell's forces over the surrender of Limerick in 1652 and letters from Daniel O'Connell and Charles Stewart Parnell. The harp of blind Turlough O'Carolan is also on display here.

The O'Conor family still live in a wing of the house. Pyers O'Conor Nash, the current O'Conor Don, is a great champion of heritage houses who once likened ownership of a historic home to trying to breastfeed a dinosaur. The house is also open to guests and is a member of the Hidden Ireland organisation.

OPEN 1 June-15 Sept., daily 11am-5pm; groups by arrangement, tel. 0907-20014.

ADMISSION £3, students £2, children £1. Tea room, guided tours, toilets.

DIRECTIONS On the outskirts of Castlerea on the Westport-Castlebar road.

THOOR BALLYLEE

Gort, County Galway

There are hundreds of forgotten medieval towers in the west of Ireland, in varying degrees of dereliction. Thoor Ballylee, formerly known as Islandmore Castle, is just one of 32 built by the Gaelicised Norman Burke clan around the borders of counties Clare and Galway. But it will always be remembered as the home and touchstone of inspiration for William Butler Yeats.

The four-storey tower stands in an intimate landscape of small hills, beside a bridge over the river Cloon on a narrow winding road. Yeats spent some of the happiest and most productive times of his life here, between 1918 and 1928, having found a new serenity in his marriage, at the age of 52, to Georgie Hyde-Lees, after his tortured love affair with Maud Gonne. To the west and north-east lies the web of influence which brought the poet to this particular corner of Ireland: the home of Lady Gregory at Coole Park and the home of Edward Martyn, Tullira Castle at Ardrahan. Both were friends, mentors and co-founders, with Yeats and George Moore, of

the Irish Literary Theatre in Dublin, precursor of the Abbey.

Years before he bought the tower in 1916, Yeats was already fascinated by its colourful associations, not only with medieval warriors but with the lore of Biddy Early, who held there was a cure for evil between the mill wheels, and with tales of the legendary beauty 'Mary Hynes, the shining flower of Ballylee'. He discovered the tower in 1896 while staying for the first time with Lady Gregory.

The poet became a frequent visitor to Coole Park and eventually decided he should have a place of his own nearby. He bought the tower, which had passed from the farmer to the Coole estate and on to the Congested Districts Board for redistribution to smallholders, for the grand sum of £35.

Plans for its conversion and designs for furniture were drawn up by William Scott, Professor of Architecture at the National University of Ireland, and the work was carried out by local builder Thomas Rafferty and joiner Patrick Connolly. Yeats was overseeing the work in 1917, and that summer he went to France to visit Maud's sister, Iseult Gonne. He proposed to her in August, was refused and went to London, where he proposed to George Hyde-Lees in September. The couple were married the following month. Work on the tower was slow, as the war had caused a shortage of materials. Yeats found a solution, purchasing wood and stone from an old mill for the restoration work. The couple were eventually able to move into their new home with their baby daughter in the summer of 1919.

True to its medieval plan, the tower was left with a single room on each floor, and a spiral stone staircase in the thickness of the walls. The dining-room, where Yeats often wrote, was on the ground floor, the living-room with its corner fireplace was on the first, and the bedroom, where George painted the ceiling with gold stars on black and gold - reminiscent of Yeats's 'blue and dim and dark cloths' in 'Aedh Wishes for the Cloths of Heaven' - was on the second. The kitchen and other bedrooms were housed in the thatched cottage and the furniture - beds, tables and chairs in wood - was part medieval, part Arts and Crafts, in inspiration. Symbolically, the third floor, which

was to be Yeats's secret, inspirational room, was never completed.

The bridge beside the tower was blown up and the tower used briefly by irregulars during the Civil War. In 1922 Yeats became a senator in the Irish Parliament and received the Nobel Prize for literature in 1923. Despite his commitments, he managed to spend some of his time at Islandmore, which he renamed 'Thoor Ballylee'. In 1932 the death of Lady Gregory severed one of his main links with the place and Ballylee was left to the weeds and the weather until, through the combined offices of Bord Fáilte and the Kiltartan Society (dedicated to the literary history of the district), the tower and cottage were restored and reopened by poet Pádraic Colum in 1965, the centenary of the birth of the great poet of the Irish literary renaissance.

OPEN Easter-Sept., daily 10am-6pm, tel. 091-631436.

ADMISSION £2.50, children 75p, family £5.

DIRECTIONS 1 km off the N18 Galway-Limerick road and 1 km off the Gort-Loughrea road.

STROKESTOWN PARK

Strokestown, County Roscommon

S trokestown Park, with its attendant estate village, was once the centrepiece of a vast 300,000-acre estate owned by the Pakenham Mahon family. The entrance gate, in the form of a Gothic arch, is just off the wide main street which was laid out at the behest of the 2nd Lord Hartland to rival the Vienna Ringstrasse in breadth. The driveway affords a view of the grandiose spread of the Palladian building across acres of parkland where ungrazed grass billows in green waves.

From a distance the house, which has three storeys over a basement, looks deceptively enormous, but the central block has only seven bays, compared to Castletown's thirteen bays, and the rooms in the seventeenth-century section of the house are on a smaller, more intimate scale than their Georgian successors.

The square entrance hall beyond the fanlight doorcase retains its original eighteenth-century panelling, but in other parts of the earlier house the panelling was removed during a burst of Regency redecoration. The faded interiors are poignantly evocative of previous eras and of the 300 or more years of occupation by the Pakenham Mahons. The family were granted nearly 30,000 acres in Roscommon by Charles II, following the Restoration in 1660, in appreciation of their loyalty.

The first incarnation of the house, two storeys over a basement, was begun shortly afterwards. In the next phase of its development, Thomas Mahon, MP for Roscommon, had the wings and a third storey added. His son Maurice Mahon was created 1st Baron Hartland for accepting the 1801 Act of Union. He carried out further improvements and added the bow-ended library - originally intended as a ballroom - at the back of the house. The 2nd Lord Hartland commissioned J. Lynn to add a porch and pilasters to the entrance and had the wide street laid out with 100 good houses for tenants and a Gothic arch to announce the approach to Strokestown Park. It was obviously no coincidence that these grandiose schemes were mirrored in big houses around Ireland at a time when landlords' rents were rising due to increased prices for agricultural produce and increased demand for land.

But disaster was about to strike - both Ireland and the Mahons. Lord Hartland became insane, his heir died childless in 1845 and the estate, run down and populated with 8,000 tenants and thousands owing in rent arrears, was inherited by Major Denis Mahon just as the Famine struck. Evictions by the thousand and emigration by assisted passage to Canada followed, as the Major and his zealous land agent tried to create viable farms on the estate. Major Mahon became a hated figure and was shot in 1847 when it was rumoured that he had hired 'coffin ships' to carry his former tenants across the Atlantic. He had been returning from a Board of Guardians meeting, where he had tried to ensure that the workhouse was kept open to help Famine victims.

Roscommon had a particularly bad record of landlord-tenant relations. Three of the most hated men in Ireland had estates there: Lord Leitrim, who was shot on his way to evict tenants in Donegal; Colonel King-Harmon of Rockingham, whose tenants were made to spread manure from heavy wicker creels carried on their backs as a form of punishment; and Lord Kingston of Kilroan, whose agent was involved in evictions of appalling cruelty. During the 'Boycott' campaign in 1881, one fifth of the thousand incidents occurred in County Roscommon.

Denis Mahon's great-grand-daughter Olive was the last of the Mahons to own Strokestown Park. In the early chapters of her life she led a charmed existence, and her marriage to the heir of the nearby estate of Rockingham, Edward Stafford King-Harmon, was the wedding of the year in 1914. Five months later Edward died in the trenches of the Great War. Olive remarried seven years later, just a month before she inherited Strokestown. Well-liked by local people, she continued to live at Strokestown as times changed radically, eventually becoming bedridden while the house crumbled. In 1979 the house and most of its contents were bought by James Callery, owner of the Westward Group - on the outskirts of Strokestown - who had fallen under the spell of the house and its owner. The arrangement allowed the old lady to remain in her home until her death in 1981, and afterwards a restoration programme was begun.

The interior of the house, with most of its original contents, remains unchanged. The library still has its glorious gold-and-brown Regency wallpaper and Chippendale bookcases, the dining-room also has its Regency furniture and faded red silk damask wallpaper and the former smoking-room is still kitted out with amateur scientist Henry Pakenham Mahon's laboratory equipment. The flagged kitchen - with huge old ranges and a gallery where the housekeeper could supervise proceedings - is located in one of the wings and has become a tea room. The stables, with groin vaulting supported on Doric columns, are in the opposite wing.

Original documents from the estate, including letters from evicted tenants, now form part of a display in the Famine Museum housed in the outbuildings. A reinterpretation of an Edwardian pleasure garden has been created in the four-acre walled garden as an antidote to one of the darkest chapters of Irish history.

OPEN April-Oct., daily 11am-5.30pm; groups by appointment all year, tel. 078-33013.

ADMISSION House only £3, museum only £3, gardens only £2.50; all three £7.50. Restaurant, shops, guided tours.

DIRECTIONS Strokestown is on the N5 Dublin-Ballina road.

PLAIN IRELAND

Laois, Longford, Monaghan, Offaly, Westmeath

The Midlands don't deserve to be bypassed; they have a most rewarding store of interesting houses, historic places and soothing scenery, without a blighting bungalow or a tour bus in sight. I was once sent on a journalistic assignment to write about the least visited parts of Ireland around Cavan and Monaghan, and came back enchanted. The reason they are less discovered is a Catch 22 scenario, as the quiet charm of the central counties is less known about than Kerry and Connemara - if you don't know, you don't go - and writers like William Thackeray, who went from Westport to Ballinasloe and on to Dublin, ignoring the rest of the Midlands in his 1842 sketch book, are partly to blame.

Many guidebooks treat Ireland as though there was a black hole in the middle, but new marketing approaches are breaking the mould, and there are also combined north-south promotions which straddle the previous no-man's-land of the Border.

One of the best holidays I ever had - and certainly the most anecdote-filled - was a kind of four-poster bed tour, involving colourful country houses. Also, research for my previous book, *The Hidden Gardens of Ireland*, taught me that in previous centuries people certainly knew how to pick the most idyllic sites for their homes, so that a tour of country houses is likely to bring you to some of the loveliest locations.

Without such research I would never have experienced some of my favourite visual memories of the Midlands, like lakeside Ballinlough Castle, County Westmeath, looking like an illustration in a book of fairy stories, or Carrigglas Manor - built for Thomas Lefroy, who inspired the character of Mr Darcy in *Pride and Prejudice* - a perfect setting for a Jane Austen novel, or the panoramic view over several counties seen through the *oeil-de-boeuf* windows which pierce the circular wall at Lutyens' sunken garden at Heywood, County Laois.

Central Ireland has some of the most fascinating houses: Charleville Castle, Francis Johnston's Gothic fantasy at Tullamore; Castle Leslie, a late nineteenth-century palazzo overlooking Glaslough Lake; Emo Court, Gandon's great country house. And there are some memorable country houses to stay in, from Hilton Park in County Monaghan to Palladian Roundwood House in County Laois.

There is a certain fine madness abroad in the Midlands: maybe it is the influence of topography on personality, so that being able to see over a great plain gives breadth of vision. Ideas run to extremes. Tullynally Castle in Westmeath turned into the largest castellated mansion in Ireland as the Pakenhams kept on building additions. William, 3rd Earl of Rosse, built what was once the largest telescope in the world at Birr Castle in the 1840s. Baron Belfield built Ireland's largest sham Gothic ruin at Belvedere, Mullingar, although vision was hardly what he had in mind - his Jealous Wall was to block his brother's house from view.

ROUND AND ABOUT

Cavan and Monaghan have - like their neighbouring counties in the Province of Ulster - a landscape of drumlins. These rounded hills are threaded with lakes, like lovely Lough Ramor at Virginia or Cuilcagh Lough, the site of Cuilcagh House, where Dean Swift began writing *Gulliver's Travels*, or Lough Nadreegeel at Ballyjamesduff, the town recalled in the Percy French song. The scenery around Cuilcagh Mountain, where the Shannon rises, is particularly lovely.

Both counties are famous for their lace, and the lace schools of Ireland were an important way of providing employment, especially after the Famine. Each area had its own distinctive style. Carrickmacross lace, the intricate, cobweb lace worked on a net base, was first introduced by Mrs Porter, a rector's wife, inspired by her honeymoon in Italy in 1816. Clones lace was more usually in the Venetian *gros point* style. An abiding interest in lace led me to the Carrickmacross Lace Gallery in the Market Square and to the fascinating St Louis Convent Heritage Centre in Monaghan (the Order ran a very successful lace school), where the nuns are a mine of information. There is also a lace exhibition in Clones, a former garrison town.

Castleblaney is named for Sir Edward Blayney, who received a grant of land there from James I. The town is sited on the edge of beautiful Lough Mucknoe, where Hope Castle (a Victorianised Georgian mansion) gave its name to the ill-fated Hope diamond and is now a reception centre at the Mucknoe Leisure Park. Near Cootehill, named after the Coote family - to whom we are indebted for that expression 'mad as a Coote' - is Bellamont Forest, described by Mark Bence-Jones in *Burke's Guide to Country Houses* as one of the most perfect examples of a Palladian house (by Sir Edward Lovett Pearce, 1730). Cabra Castle (1837) is a rambling Gothic castle, the former seat of the Pratts and now a hotel which retains its country house atmosphere.

Interesting ruins in the area include Drumlane abbey and round tower (fourteenth century) near Milltown, and on an island in Lough Oughter are the ruins of Clough Oughter Castle, an O'Reilly stronghold sacked by Cromwell. The Pig House Collection (sited in a venerable pighouse at Cornafean) houses an exhibition of rural memorabilia dating back to 1700. Brown soda bread enthusiasts shouldn't miss Green's Mill in Cavan, where you can stone-grind flour for your own bread. There is also a restaurant there (tel. 049-62722). And lovers of Patrick Kavanagh's verse will find a literary centre in the old parish church in Iniskeen (tel. 042-78560).

Longford has many literary associations, and this is Goldsmith country. Oliver Goldsmith was born at Pallas near Ballymahon, Pádraic Colum also came from the county, and Edgeworthstown was named for the Edgeworth family, members of which included Richard Lovell, the inventor who installed one of the earliest forms of central heating at neighbouring Tullynally Castle, and his daughter, the novelist, Maria. The western side of the county borders the Shannon complex, with some of the prettiest countryside. The extraordinary 5,000-year-old Corlea Bog Road, an oak road across the bog, was discovered recently near Keenagh, and at Newtowncashel the Cashel museum features a restored nineteenth-century cottage complete with period utensils.

Unspoilt Westmeath is one of my favourite inland counties. There is an interesting drive from attractive Tyrrellspass around Lough Owel, and wonderful views from the top of the Hill of Uisneach and Knockeyon Hill over Lough Derravaragh, where the Children of Lir swam as swans for 300 years. Tullynally and Belvedere are the architectural stars, and the wonderful new gardens at Clonmellon Castle shouldn't be missed.

Nor should the spectacular ruins of Killua Castle, Clonmellon, the eighteenth-century seat of the Chapmans, the last of whom changed his name to Lawrence and was the father of Lawrence of Arabia. Just nearby is the triumphal arch of Rosmead, known as Smiling Bess, all that remains of the classical eighteenth-century mansion at Delvin, burnt during the Troubles, as was Moydrum Castle, an 1814 Gothic revival castle just outside Athlone.

Laois and Offaly were formerly known as Queen's County and King's County respectively and were planted during Elizabeth I's reign. To the south-east the Slieve Bloom Mountains are worth exploring, and to the north-west the Shannon forms the county border. At Shannonbridge there is the great monastic settlement of Clonmacnois, originally founded by St Ciaran in 548. At nearby Banagher, Cloghan Castle, a medieval keep, is open from May to September (Wed.–Sun. 2–6pm).

Emo Court, Charleville Castle and Birr demesne - where the 100 acres of gardens contain a wonderful collection of trees and shrubs and the largely nineteenth-century castle forms a backdrop - make a happy combination as the focus for a tour. Ballaghmore Castle at Borris in Ossory is now open to the public. Mountmellick was founded by the Quakers. Ballyfin House, built for Sir Charles Coote in the 1820s, has a magnificent interior by Sir Richard Morrison and is now a college run by the Patrician Brothers.

Leap Castle, a former O'Carroll stronghold guarding a pass in the Slieve Bloom mountains and dating back to the fourteenth century, has a reputation as one of the most haunted ruins. Human bones have been found in the deep dungeons. The castle, with its Gothic additions, is supposed to be the site of a treasure hoard, hidden by an O'Carroll son-in-law, Captain Jonathan Derby, who was imprisoned and later released half mad and unable to remember its whereabouts.

PLACES TO STAY / EAT

Newly built hotels are a rarity in the countryside, but the area boasts two: the luxurious four-storey Slieve Russell Hotel in Ballyconnell, County Cavan, which can be seen looming like some latterday palace from miles away (tel. 049-26444), and the thoroughly comfortable golf-orientated Nuremore near Kingscourt (tel. 042-61438). The Derragarra Inn at Butlersbridge looks just the kind of enticing pub one should stop at, and you won't be disappointed. The Park Hotel at Virginia, County Cavan, used to be the Marquess of Headfort's 1751 shooting lodge and is now a comfortable country house hotel (tel. 049-47235).

People come from miles around to Crookedwood House, at Crookedwood near Mullingar, a former eighteenth-century rectory which has an award-winning restaurant and also offers accommodation (tel. 044-72165). Nearby at Mornington House, partly dating back to 1710, just beside Lough Derravaragh, you will be spoiled rotten by Warwick and Anne O'Hara (tel. 044-72191). Palladian Roundwood House, Mountrath, County Laois, is the kind of place where people love to go for the weekend to enjoy a wonderful dinner and sit by a roaring fire (tel. 0502-32120). Hilton Park, Clones, County Monaghan, is very memorable - I can recall fabulous dinners and track-stopping breakfasts cooked by Lucy Madden, and using a footstool to climb into a wonderful four-poster bed in this Georgian mansion, which still has some of its original wallpapers (tel. 047-56007). The dower house of Birr Castle, eighteenth-century Tullanisk, where hosts George and Susan Gossip are enthusiastic cooks, is set in a deer park, and game (venison perhaps?) is a speciality on the menu (tel. 0509-20572). Clunagh House at Tullamore is open as a house of architectural and historic merit (12-31 March; 22 Aug.-30 Sept., 9am-1pm) and is also a guest-house, with a charming walled garden under restoration by owners Alison and Noel Badriam (tel. 0506-52357). You can wake up with Gandon - at least, his stableyard - in self-catering accommodation at Carrigglas Manor (tel. 043-45165). Aromatherapy is on offer at relaxing Temple, a Victorian farmhouse at Horseleap, Moate (tel. 0506-35118).

BELVEDERE

Mullingar, County Westmeath

It was one of those rare, blazing June days. Lough Ennell sparkled below the terraces and balustrades of aptly named Belvedere. Inside the grey limestone house there were the twin pleasures of an enchanting prospect and glorious rooms, where fruit and cherubs ran riot in the delicate rococo plasterwork of the ceilings. In short, it seemed a most idyllic spot, perfectly designed to be a romantic hideaway.

And in fact that was just the role intended for the house, which was built by Richard Castle in 1740 for Robert Rochfort, Lord Belfield, and his beautiful young wife, Mary. Designed as a villa rather than a full-time home, it was the kind of architectural solution sought by fashionable folk who wanted an alternative to the constraints of life in a large country house.

Unfortunately for his family, Lord Belfield did not escape nearly far enough and, rather than being an idyllic retreat, Belvedere featured in one of the greatest scandals of the period. The grounds also contain one of the largest physical consequences of a family feud, known as the Jealous Wall.

The Rochforts were established landowners in Westmeath. Robert's father George was MP for the county and the family seat was at Gaulstown Park, just five miles away. In time Robert took over his father's seat and, after the death of his first wife, he married Mary, daughter of Viscount Molesworth, then aged 16 to Robert's 28 years. The couple began to have Belvedere built shortly afterwards. At the time, theirs was considered an ideal match.

Just four years later, Robert was told that his wife was having an affair with his younger brother, Arthur. And, according to a contemporary diarist, Mary, far from denying the liaison, announced that her last child was by Arthur and that she had no pleasure with any other like that she had with him. Arthur was forced to flee the country before Robert carried out his threat to shoot him and Mary was incarcerated in Gaulston, denied company and watched over by servants.

Robert lived a bachelor life at Belvedere, where he entertained lavishly but never forgave the lovers. When Mary escaped after a dozen years of imprisonment, she threw herself on her father's mercy. He refused to give her sanctuary, so that she ended up back in Gaulstown even more strictly imprisoned for another 18 years, with only portraits for company. By the time she was released by her son after Robert's death, her hair was white and her manner strange. When Arthur returned to Ireland his brother had him seized, charged with enormous damages and thrown into the Marshalsea debtors' prison for the rest of his life. Robert's reputation was unscathed and he was created Earl of Belvedere in 1756.

Despite the ugliness of the story, Belvedere is a glorious house. The house is small - just one room deep - and the most important features are the stucco ceilings and wonderful woodwork.

The drawing- and dining-rooms occupy the bow ends of the house. Their ceilings are particularly fine and are thought to be the work of Bartholomew Cramillion, the French stuccodore. In the rococo style, the voluptuous swirls depicting fruit, flowers and cherubs in the dining-room and the goddesses Juno, Minerva and Venus in the drawing-room are offset by the masculine severity of panelled wood

wainscoting. The plasterwork in the hall is scattered with clouds and stars and depicts night. The elaborate terraces and balustrades were added in the Victorian era by the then owner Charles Marley.

Sadly, the contents of the house were auctioned off in 1980 and the house has remained empty since it was acquired by Westmeath County Council, who have opened the gardens and grounds. Happily the council are refurnishing the interiors with appropriate period pieces and the house will be open to the public.

In the grounds at Belvedere the Jealous Wall - a huge sham ruin, the largest of its kind in Ireland - is a monument to Robert's revenge, built to blot out the sight of Tudenham, his brother George's house, with whom he had had a feud. It gives a whole new twist to the meaning of folly.

OPEN House and garden April-Oct., daily 12 noon-6pm, tel. 044-40861.

ADMISSION Information not available.

DIRECTIONS 6 km from Mullingar on the Tullamore road.

CARRIGGLAS MANOR

County Longford

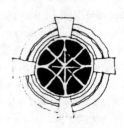

The old entrance gate of Carrigglas may look a little familiar to Dubliners, and this is hardly surprising, since it was designed by James Gandon, architect of the Four Courts, where he used a very similar triumphal archway. Given the gateway, one might expect a classical building, but instead a romantic Gothic Revival house is revealed at a turn in the curving driveway, set in landscaped parkland as fine as any aspiring heroine of a Jane Austen novel might wish.

Jane Austen did in fact have a flirtation with Thomas Lefroy in England, years before he had Carrigglas built. Jane Austen turned the encounter with her distant relation by marriage to good account and used Thomas Lefroy as a model for Mr Darcy in *Pride and Prejudice*. The Kilkenny-based architect, Daniel Robertson, designed the fine Tudor-Gothic home for Thomas Lefroy to replace an earlier, dilapidated house. It was begun in 1837, thirty years after Jane Austen's death, and completed three years later.

Carrigglas's exterior displays all the exuberant rebellion against the predictable symmetry of classicism that was the Gothic revival, with oriel windows here, Gothic tracery there, a soaring stained-glass window, bow windows, crockets and gables and an odd-shaped wing which used to house the kitchen staff.

The restored interior is equally satisfying, for Robinson's fanciful Gothic interiors are matched by the kind of atmosphere and furnishings that only evolve through continuous family occupation for generation upon generation. Beyond the entrance hall lies the drama of the staircase hall, lit by a stained-glass window with the Lefroy coat of arms. The three reception rooms, arranged enfilade along the south garden front, are sunny and welcoming. The splendid ceilings, with Gothic ribbing and a repeating motif of quatrefoils, echo the Gothic tracery on the outside of the building. The drawing-room ceiling still retains its original colour scheme of azure blue, with gilded plasterwork and a rose background to the frieze of foliage and flowers. The bow-windowed library has magnificent Tudor Gothic bookcases and double doors leading from the drawing-room to the blue-grey dining-room where diners at the vast mahogany table come under the watchful gaze of Thomas Lefroy in the wig and gown of the Chief Justice.

The bedrooms, which retain their early Victorian mood, demostrate the rise in consumerism which gathered momentum throughout the nineteenth century, as the increase in carpets, wallpaper, furniture and other manufactured goods and the expanding world markets gave upper-class families more opportunities to exercise fashionable taste.

Without the spending mania and the effect of the Napoleonic Wars which fuelled inflation, there might very well have been a classical mansion to match the Gandon gateway at Carrigglas.

The original manor and estate were left to Trinity College by the Bishops of Ardagh and then leased to the Newcomen family, founders of Newcomen's Bank in the late eighteenth century. Inflation caused the bank (which stands beside Dublin Castle) to crash, precipitating the suicide of the 2nd Viscount Newcomen. Carrigglas was sold when the magnificent stableyard and farm complex had been completed to Gandon's design (1790) - the only example of his agricultural work - but the plans for the house were never executed. Thomas Lefroy, the second generation of a Huguenot family to live in Ireland, leased Carrigglas before buying out the freehold. He was Chief Justice of Ireland from 1852 to 1866.

Carrigglas would never have survived without the commitment of the present generation of Lefroys, Tessa and Jeffry. They gave up a very different way of life based in England when Jeffry was asked to take over the property by a cousin in the 1970s. They subsequently took the courageous decision to open the house to the public, putting it on the map through sheer determination and imagination. Badly needed restoration has been undertaken and an appealing lakeside garden, potager and charming William Robinson inspired woodland gardens have been created. One of the specialities of the house is to offer lunch for groups of 20 plus in the gardens during May, June and September.

There are tea rooms, a gallery and gift shop, a costume and lace museum, and special one day and residential courses in spring and autumn. Self-catering accommodation and private guest accommodation in the house are also on offer.

OPEN May & Sept., Mon. & Fri. 10.30am-3pm; House tours 11am, 12 noon, 2pm. June, July & Aug., Mon., Tues., & Fri. 10.30am-5pm; House tours 11am, 12 noon, 2pm, 3pm. Sun. 2-6pm; House tours 2pm, 3pm, 4pm, 5pm, tel. Tessa Lefroy 043-45165, fax 043-41026.

ADMISSION Garden and museum: Adults £2.50, OAPs/Students £1.50. House additional £2.50. Pre-booked groups (minimum 12) welcome May-Sept. (group rates available). Garden lunches and teas for groups by arrangement. Self-catering accommodation available. Toilets, parking, shop, guided tours, tea room, gallery.

DIRECTIONS Situated 1.6km from Longford by-pass on R194 Ballinalee-Granard road.

EMO COURT

Emo, County Laois

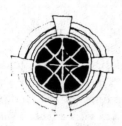

The great country houses of Ireland were magnificent expressions of one-upmanship, designed to reflect the culture and discerning taste of gentlemen who often took a keen amateur interest in architecture. Emo Court is a splendid case in point. It was designed by English architect James Gandon for his friend and patron John Dawson, 1st Earl of Portarlington, who had been largely responsible for bringing Gandon to Dublin to design the Custom House.

Having first engaged Gandon to design the nearby church at Coolbanagher, Dawson later asked the architect to design his first major country house, to replace Dawson Court, which had been built just two generations earlier. The house is on the same heroic scale as the Custom House, with a seven-bay front dominated by a massive two-storey portico, its pediment carried on four Ionic columns. The house has two storeys over a basement, and the addition of an attic floor at each end of the house gives an appearance of towers. The fronts of the attic floors have decorative Coadestone plaques which illustrate - prophetically - the story of the house. Cherubs are portrayed dabbling in the arts and two of them are shown, frozen in time, working with Gandon's plans. As it turned out, it was nearly two centuries later before the house was fully realised in a style befitting architect and patron's original vision.

Just four years after the house was begun, John Dawson fell ill while campaigning during the 1798 Rebellion and died, so work on the house stopped. The 2nd Earl was short of money and fond of gambling (the two being not unconnected) and it was 40 years before any further work was done on the design. Then architect Lewis Vulliamy added the portico to the entrance front and carried out interior work.

The rivalry between the Portarlingtons and their neighbours the Cootes - who had Ballyfin, a house built in the 1820s with remarkably similar features to Emo, and with interiors carried out by Sir Richard Morrison and his son William Vitruvius Morrison - may well have been the spur. The wonderful heart of the house, the central rotunda topped with a copper dome, was not finished until 1860, by William Caldbeck, for the 3rd Earl, after the house had nearly been sold off by the Encumbered Estates Court. By this time, tastes in furnishings had changed, Victorian clutter had taken over and, in some cases, the mood of Georgian interiors had been spoiled by being panelled in oak.

The Dawson family came to Ireland after the Restoration of Charles II. William Dawson held the lucrative post of tax collector for counties Antrim and Down and his son Ephraim, the grandfather of John Dawson, bought the estate - then known as Imoe (the Irish version of the name) - in the early eighteenth century. The Dawson descendants severed their connection with the estate 200 years later and sold Emo for a song in 1930 to the Society of Jesus. Ballyfin was sold to the Patrician Order ten years earlier. The Jesuit Order was undoubtedly the saviour of Emo

during the time it was used as a seminary, but as numbers entering the priesthood declined, due to increasing prosperity and secularisation in Ireland, the house was put on the market and came into the benign hands of Mr Cholmeley-Harrison.

In the beautifully proportioned inner hallway are two apses, which had remained undecorated for 200 years. The new owner had the niches finished as Gandon had intended with a ribbed pattern, cleverly carried out in *trompe-l'oeil* rather than plaster. The detail is symbolic of the restoration work carried out in the rest of the house, with the advice of Sir Albert Richardson and London architects.

Five mahogany doors are arranged symmetrically in the hallway, the central one leading into the breathtaking rotunda, which provide a theatrical prelude to the enfilade of rooms on the garden front. The coffered dome appears to be carried on eight pilasters in Siena marble with gilded Corinthian capitals, the whole being lit from above by the lantern window of the dome. The magnificent inlaid floor had been taken up by the Jesuits in order to install an altar and had to be completely restored.

The former library - now the drawing-room - had been used as a refectory and the capitals of the impressive green Connemara marble columns supporting the screens which divide the room had been used as kneelers. The room, which runs the full depth of the house and has a bow window and magnificent gilded pelmets, has been painted a strong colour, as Georgian rooms often were - in this case a vibrant lime green. The paintings and furniture are in keeping with the period.

In the library the gilded rococo plasterwork ceiling was designed by Vulliamy and matches the marble fireplace which, with its super-abundance of cherubs and grapes, was found in four pieces in the cellar after the Jesuits left. The ornate plasterwork in the olive-green portrait-hung dining-room is also by Vulliamy and the furniture includes two fine Regency console tables.

The house and grounds were taken into state ownership in 1994 and are now in state care. There are plans to open the first floor to the public and, in the longer term, to open the basement.

OPEN Mid June-mid Sept., daily 10am-6pm. Access by guided tour only, tel. 0502-26573.

ADMISSION £2.00, concession £1.50, children £1. Guided tours, toilets, parking.

DIRECTIONS 6 km south of Portlaoise on the main Dublin road.

CASTLE LESLIE

Glaslough, County Monaghan

Castle Leslie is the last interesting gasp of big house building in Ireland. Inspired - at least in parts - by Italian Renaissance style, it was built for John Leslie in 1870 by Sir Charles Lanyon and William Henry Lynn. Picture the consternation of John Leslie, who made the mistake of being absent while the builders were at work and returned to find the exterior of his new home in Lynn's best Belfast brick villa style. 'It is not what I meant,' fumed Leslie.

The rather prosaic exterior of the three storeys over a basement building, with gables and three-sided bow windows in grey stone with brick facings, is redeemed by the magnificent flights of architectural fancy in the interior which were the work of Lanyon in collaboration with John Leslie.

Step into the entrance hall and you are immediately involved in a satisfying drama: a mosaic floor featuring the doves of peace, based on a design at Pompeii; a heavily ornamented chimney piece, coffered ceiling and wall panelling all in mahogany; the walls bristling with weapons and stags' heads.

This dynamic dialogue is kept up throughout the principal rooms,

each providing marvellous changes of mood. The great hall is suitably ornate, with a barrel-vaulted ceiling and a screen supported by Doric columns. The staircase hall, its walls hung with portraits of generations of Leslies, has a gallery with Romanesque arches running around the first floor. The drawing-room, its walls hung with rust-coloured hessian, has a Della Robbia fireplace adorned with the heads of cherubs. The dining-room, with its compart-mentalised ceiling, overlooks the lough, the green of its walls echoing the green (*glas* in Irish) which gives the place its name. The tiled conservatory is a wonderful piece of Victoriana, displaying the technology of the age - an underfloor heating system and curvilinear roof. But the high point of the castle is the cloister, based on Michelangelo's design for Santa Maria degli Angeli in Rome. The long arched gallery which runs behind it has frescos of angels painted by one of the multi-talented Leslies, Sir John Leslie, artist and Royal Academician.

The house has plenty of examples of Victorian technology, including an internal bell system with over 40 bells, the first gas hob in Ireland, a hand-operated lift and - uniquely - centrally-heated rose beds. For a house which is only just over a century old, there are a surprising number of ghost stories attached to Castle Leslie.

The founder of the Leslie dynasty in Ireland was clergyman John Leslie, who became Bishop of Raphoe in County Donegal, where he built an episcopal palace which he successfully defended against the Cromwellians. On the Restoration of Charles II, the octogenarian bishop rode to London to welcome his king and was rewarded for his loyalty with two thousand guineas, having turned down the offer to become Bishop of Canterbury. The reward enabled him to purchase an estate at Glaslough, where the first Leslie residence - a tower house - was built and later incorporated into a gabled mansion.

The Leslies prospered and became amongst the largest land-owners in Ireland, holding over 60,000 acres. Glaslough was built as a model estate village by the Leslies for their tenants. All that now remains in family hands, however, is the walled demesne surrounding the castle. The successor to Sir John the builder was his son - another Sir John. He married Leonie Jermone, whose sister married Lady Randolph Churchill, mother of Winston Churchill. Castle Leslie became the scene of house parties for Edwardian socialites, and guests included the Duke of Connacht and Prince Pierre de Monaco (father of Prince Rainier). Some of the décor dates from this period and the house is full of interesting pieces and memorabilia, including the Iron Duke Wellington's bridle and Winston Churchill's christening robe. The Leslie family motto is 'Grip Fast', dating back to the time when a Leslie forebear helped St Margaret of Scotland to escape by clinging to his saddle, in his role as her protector.

Samantha Leslie, a trained chef and the latest Leslie to take on the challenge of making the castle earn its keep, now runs the house as a restaurant and superior guest-house.

OPEN 30 April-31 Aug., Sun.-Thurs. 2-6pm. Historical tours on the hour, tel. 047-88109.

ADMISSION £3.50, OAPs £2, children £1. Toilet, parking. Accommodation all year round, £48-£58 pp B&B, £58 pp.

DIRECTIONS Just outside the village of Glaslough, 6 km north of Monaghan between the N2 and N12.

TULLYNALLY CASTLE

Castlepollard, County Westmeath

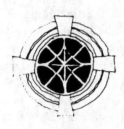

It has been said of the Pakenhams of Tullynally that, if they were not fighting wars, they were writing about them. The family has produced generals in the past and splendid writers in the present, and, perhaps, a genetic disposition to being highly imaginative accounts for the size of Tullynally.

A quarter of a mile long around its exterior, the castle grew, as successive generations and different architects exercised their creative imaginations, until it became the largest castellated house in Ireland.

A castellated gateway announces the castle and at the end of a long avenue its towers, crockets, gables and bewildering array of battlemented buildings come into view in a beautiful parkland setting dotted with venerable oaks. Beyond the forecourt hedge is a magical vista towards Knockeyon Hill and Lough Derravaragh, where the Children of Lir swam as spellbound swans.

At the core of the present building are traces - discernible only in the thickness of the walls - of the castle which was bought by Henry Pakenham in the mid seventeenth century. The architectural history of the castle provides a chronology of changing taste. Several alterations later, the castle had been incorporated into a two-storey mansion with formal baroque gardens complete with canals and cascades. In the late eighteenth century this building was again remodelled, by Graham Myers, to become a three-storey classical building.

No fewer than four architects made fashionable Gothic additions to Pakenham Hall, which became Pakenham Hall Castle as the transformation progressed. Francis Johnston, architect of the spectacular Charleville Forest at Tullamore which helped to fuel the rage for Gothic style, gave the building its first Gothic treatment in 1801, with battlements along the roof of the old Georgian house and four elegant corner towers. James Sheil added a bow to the east front and altered the entrance hall. In 1839 Richard Morrison designed two huge wings, one for the dowager countess, the other for the servants, linking the house to the stableyard. J. Rawson Carroll, architect in the classical manner, added a tower to the stableyard in 1860.

In addition to all this building enthusiasm, Tullynally was also given the benefit of all the latest conveniences. A prototype central heating system was apparently installed here by inventor Richard Lovell Edgeworth (father of the novelist Maria); it was so effective that one of the fireplaces was taken out and replaced with a built-in organ. Turf to fuel the enormous boiler was brought in by the cartload via one of the discreet tunnels which were a feature of the extraordinary lengths taken to hide the servants from sight in great houses. Edgeworth also rigged up a telegraph system between Tullynally and Edgeworthstown.

The octagonal Gothic dining-room has panelled wainscoting and wallpaper with a magnificent Pugin design which was also used in the British Houses of Parliament. There are fine examples of Irish furniture, like the mahogany side table with claw feet and carved with the characteristic grotesque mask. The red drawing-room has an interesting geometric plasterwork ceiling and there are paintings of sea battles in which an ancestor participated. The basement is a splendid museum of the wonders of previous domestic conveniences - including the laundry and drying-room with ingenious drying drawers and rails. Tunnels were also used to segregate the servants, and an underground passage from laundry to drying yard kept the pretty laundry maids out of harm's way from the grooms and stable lads.

The brothers of the second Earl of Longford, Sir Hercules and Sir Edward Pakenham, were both generals during the Peninsular War. Sir Edward was later commander-in-chief of the British army in America and was slain at the battle of New Orleans; his body was shipped back to Ireland in a barrel of rum in order to preserve it. (Needless to say there are stories about the accidental consumption of the rum and discovery of the grisly contents.) The generals' sister Catherine was married to the Duke of Wellington. With a certain irony the family have named the 30 bedrooms at Tullynally after family defeats rather than victories.

More recently the Pakenhams have found the pen far mightier than the sword. The 6th Earl of Longford, Edward Pakenham, is remembered for his involvement with the Gate Theatre. The present Earl of Longford has authored a score of books, including biographies of President de Valera and Jesus Christ. His wife Elizabeth's works include a biography of the Duke of Wellington. Thomas Pakenham and his wife Valerie live at Tullynally and have co-authored *Dublin: A Traveller's Companion* and Thomas Pakenham is perhaps best known for his compelling accounts of the Boer War and the Race for Africa. His siblings are also authors, the best known being Lady Antonia Fraser and Rachel Billington.

The naturalistic pleasure grounds laid out in the eighteenth century with glorious trees, a grotto, walled gardens and an arboretum are also open to the public and there is an ongoing garden restoration scheme.

OPEN 15 June-30 July, 12-27 September, 2-6pm. Groups at other times, tel. 044-61159, fax 044-61856.

ADMISSION Castle and grounds £4, children £2, gardens only £2.50. Gardens open May-Sept., 2-6pm. Guided tours, tea at weekends, toilets, parking, wheelchair access.

DIRECTIONS Just outside Castlepollard on the Granard road.

CHARLEVILLE FOREST

Tullamore, County Offaly

'I am very glad to hear that you have begun your castle for I think that there are few occupations more entertaining than building,' wrote Lady Louisa Conolly of Castletown to Lady 'Tullamoore' [*sic*] in 1800.

The castle in question was Charleville Forest, one of the earliest and most magnificent of Gothic sham castles, designed by Francis Johnston for Charles William Bury, Lord Tullamore (later Viscount Charleville). Begun in 1798, the building kept Lord and Lady Charleville 'entertained' for a further fourteen years and the couple moved in long before the builders moved out.

The result was a splendid extravaganza which launched a vogue for Gothic castles in Ireland and once even featured in an advertisement as Dracula's bank. Charleville Forest would be admirably suited as the setting for some Gothic Transylvanian tale of the supernatural. Approached by a long drive through dense oak woods, the castle rears suddenly and spectacularly before the visitor. A heavy corbelled arch looms over the entrance. To the left a tall tower

rises above the battlements, topped telescope-like with yet another tower; to the right is a massive octagonal tower, its rim menacingly machicolated, as though defenders might need to rain down missiles on attackers below. A lantern tower dominates the centre of the castle and the long, low service wing is battlemented. The cut granite building has sixty rooms, without counting those at basement level, and the attendant buildings include a chapel and stables.

Charles William Bury inherited the proverbial silver spoon at the age of six months when he became heir to the 20,000-acre estate at Tullamoore. The estate had recently been inherited by his father from his brother-in-law John Moore, 1st Lord Tullamoore, plus further estates in Limerick which included the ownership of fourteen towns. John Moore was a descendant of Elizabethan soldier Thomas Moore, who originally received a grant of land which had been confiscated from the O'Molloys during the plantation of Offaly.

The celebrations for young Bury's 21st birthday - which proved rather more spectacular than expected - caused the village of Tullamoore [*sic*] to burn down in 1785. The hot-air balloon, rather than going up, crashed into the barracks chimney and set the thatched roofs of the village on fire. (Bury subsequently made amends, paying out £550 compensation. He also commissioned the Grand Canal to come to the town, bringing prosperity in its wake.)

The interior of Charleville Forest is every bit as extravagantly magnificent as the exterior. It was an age when the aristocracy spent flamboyantly on their country seats, as never before (partly thanks to pocketing compensation when the Act of Union was passed), and Lord Charleville and his ambitious wife Charlotte Maria (*née* Tisdall) were anxious to advance themselves.

The entrance leads directly in to a splendid staircase hall, with a wide staircase rising dramatically between two galleries and under graceful pillars which support a groined ceiling. At the top an ornate double door opens into a room which vies with the ballroom at Slane for the title of the most magnificent Gothic room in Ireland. A double row of giant pendentives hang like exotic stalactites from the fan-vaulted ceiling in a breathtaking room which runs the 120-foot length of the house. The effect and the inspiration are pure Strawberry Hill Gothic.

Next door the dining-room is on an equally grand scale but in a different decorative vein. The ceiling is heavily coffered with a Gothic dado, and a fireplace is a copy of one in Magdalene College Chapel, Oxford. The room has the distinction of being the only room in Ireland to be decorated by William Morris the Arts and Crafts designer, who painted the ceiling in 1860. The morning- and drawing-rooms form a glorious pair, the plasterwork ceilings of stars and trellis picked out in gold leaf.

The second staircase is lavishly decorated, with stairs of carved and grained wood and equally elaborate plasterwork grained in imitation of wood on the walls (not surprisingly, the painters were still at work on this in 1812). The octagonal library, with its confessional-like bookcases and stained-glass windows, still has its original decoration and stencil work.

Bury (created Earl of Charleville in 1806) was a dilettante and amateur architect who was very involved in the design of the castle. He shared with Johnston an interest in geometry and also in more mystical theories. The site for the castle was chosen by finding the point where the grid of ley lines which connect prehistoric sites crossed. In the enchanting little tower boudoir, the vaulted ceiling meets in an eight-pointed star, a geometric device which is supposed to concentrate energy from eight points.

The energy generated, however, was not quite enough to give the Earl and Countess their hearts' desire. As the castle neared completion, they pulled off the social coup of entertaining the Viceroy, the Duke of Richmond, complete with a magnificent dinner for 38 attended by flunkeys in a special uniform of blue and scarlet. Their hospitality was not enough to convince His Excellency to grant Lord Charleville's request for the lucrative position of Postmaster General.

Not surprisingly, Lord Charleville died leaving massive debts. The 2nd Earl went to live in Berlin and Charleville Forest was closed up. The title died with the 5th Earl of Charleville, and his heir, Charles Howard Bury, preferred to live at his other home - Belvedere, County Westmeath - when he inherited in 1912. The furniture was sold off in 1967 and the castle was eventually taken on a repair lease by Michael McMullen, who expended tremendous energy and a lot of lilac-and-pink paint during his solo restoration of the castle.

By one of those extraordinary quirks of fate, the next owners, Mrs B. Vance and Mrs C. Alagna from America, were descendants of a family who had once been evicted by the Bury family. Like many owners of enormous historic houses, they faced a huge challenge in trying to find a compatible use for a castle lying off the regular tourist trail. An extraordinarily imaginative solution has been found.

Charleville is to become a European Campus in a joint venture with the State University of New York, as part of a European orientation course for leadership. Under the title of Quest Campus the venture will be run by two foundations, Campus Trust and Charleville Castle Trust, with an eventual intake of 5,000 students. The principal rooms of the castle will be reserved as reception rooms. The castle will also be the base for a number of brave new ventures based around education networks and communication of knowledge. Strange to tell, one of the prime instigators of the venture sleeps under Johnston's 200-year-old energy-radiating star.

OPEN Details unavailable at present. Fax 0506-23039.

DIRECTIONS The castle is off the main road on the outskirts of Tullamore.

Section Five

WITHIN THE PALE

Kildare, Louth, Meath, Wicklow

The Pale - the area of English influence where the King's writ ran on the east coast - was a shifting concept. The rampart of the English Pale at the end of the fifteenth century stretched from Dundalk over to Naas and down to Dalkey. By the end of the next century it stretched as far west as Athlone and down to Waterford.

Louth, Meath, Kildare and Wicklow encircle Dublin, and the contrast between the prime settled farmland of Kildare and the wildness of the Wicklow mountains, the once traditional territory of the O'Byrnes, O'Tooles and MacMurroghs, couldn't be more extreme. Wicklow - where the mountains and valleys were a perfect hideout for rebels - was always a threat to Dublin. In Meath the Boyne valley gives variety to the gently undulating countryside, while the coast, Carlingford Lough and the Cooley mountains give Louth its interest.

Little Louth is underrated, undeservedly so, and away from the thundering traffic on the Belfast/Dublin motorway there is plenty to intrigue. A visit to the wonderful house and garden at Beaulieu brings the discovery of Baltray and the stretch of coastline north of the mouth of the Boyne, including shell-strewn Termonfeckin beach.

The Cooley Peninsula has a satisfying combination of mountains and sea, plus Ravensdale Forest, the glorious views of the Mournes, and Carlingford - once the border fortress of the Pale - with King John's Castle, a fifteenth-century mint and Taafe's sixteenth-century town house. Then there's the curious resort of Omeath, peopled, it is said, by those who were left behind after Sunday drinking expeditions from the north in the days when the Sabbath was sacrosanct there. Drogheda, one of the most important English towns in the Middle Ages, is forever associated with Cromwell's 1649 atrocities, when 2,000 were slaughtered following the fall of the town. Townley Hall, Francis

Johnston's classical masterpiece four miles away, has a superb staircase and rotunda - should the School of Philosophy and Economic Science ever allow a peek.

The drive from Drogheda to Slane, where St Patrick proclaimed Christianity on the commanding Hill of Slane, is along the pleasing Boyne valley. Slane has a most elegant crossroads, with four classical houses at each corner once occupied by three rival sisters. The Conyngham Arms there has an excellent buffet at lunchtime and Mary McDonnell's Craft Studio in the Newgrange Mall is worth checking out. The site of the battle of the Boyne, which changed the course of Irish history, is nearby. Near Collon is Mellifont, one of the first great Cistercian abbeys, founded in 1142 (open May-October daily), and nearby Monasterboice is also a monastic settlement, celebrated for its high crosses. Collon is associated with the last Speaker of the Irish House of Commons, Anthony Foster of Oriel Court (now an abbey of the Cistercians of Mellifont) - which sprang from a *cottage orné* where his wife played peasant. Alan Chawner's shop in the pretty square at Collon is a great source of antique stripped-pine furniture.

Known as the Royal County for its association with the High Kings of Ireland at Tara (be warned, Tara's fabled halls are now mere mounds!), Meath also has Ireland's answer to the pyramids - the megalithic tombs of Newgrange and Knowth, both near Slane (open all year round). More visually spectacular is the medieval Pale stronghold of Trim.

When you see the medieval outlines of Trim Castle - dating to 1200, the largest Norman fortress in Ireland - and the Yellow Tower, Nagle's and Talbot's castles, you can almost imagine knights and men-at-arms in the streets of the town. The wonderful gardens at Butterstream in Trim - which now has a tea pavilion, in addition to its other attractions - should not be missed (open April-September, 11am-6pm). Laracor, where Dean Swift was rector for thirteen years, is nearby.

Interesting ruins in Meath include early eighteenth-century Arch Hall at Wilkinstown, attributed to Sir Edward Lovett Pearce, and the once superb house Pearce collaborated on with Richard Castle, Summerhill, dating to 1731. Kells (of *Book of Kells* fame) was the site of a monastic settlement founded by St Columcille; a round tower and St Columcille's House, with its incredible corbelled roof, survive. Nearby in the other Blackwater valley is Headfort - once the seat of the Earl of

Bective and now in part a boarding school - with its exquisite staterooms designed by Robert Adams. There is a lighthouse-like folly erected to the Earl's son on top of the nearby Hill of Lloyd.

Kildare is serious horse country, home of the National Stud at Kildare and The Curragh racecourse. The county suffers from being on the way to lots of places, but away from the main arteries there are lovely corners of countryside and some wonderful houses to see. The Liffey valley is a case in point. Take the road along the Strawberry Beds, through Lucan, and try to get a glimpse of Palladian Lucan House (now the Italian Ambassador's residence), about whose design William Chambers, James Wyatt and Michael Stapleton were all consulted. Further along the valley is the pleasant village of Straffan, with the up-market K Club at Straffan House and Lodge Park (the gardens and Steam Museum are open), where the frontage was intended to compete with the façade of father-in-law Earl of Milltown's Russborough.

Castletown House at Celbridge, combined with Furness - surely one of the loveliest of small-scale Palladian houses - reached via winding roads from Kill, makes an ideal short trip. If Carton House at Maynooth, seat of the Dukes of Leinster, were open it would make a fascinating visit. It was remodelled in the mid eighteenth century by Richard Castle for the 20th Duke and Emily, Duchess of Leinster, sister of Louisa Conolly of Castletown. Sheer folly at its Irish best are the fascinating Larchill Arcadian Gardens at Kilcock. A rare survivor of the *ferme ornée* style, the grounds have ten follies set in a 1-kilometre walk through beech avenues (open May-September, 12 noon-6pm).

There are really two Wicklows: east Wicklow - the coastal strip dotted with gorgeous villas, its wooded glens traversed by short, swift rivers - and glorious vales like Avoca and the wilder mountain scenery and natural wonders of west Wicklow, a combination which excited eighteenth- and nineteenth-century imaginations. Deserving its title of the Garden of Ireland, Wicklow also has two of the country's leading gardens - Powerscourt and Mount Usher - and a Garden Festival in May/June. My idea of a wonderful treat would be to set off through Wicklow, starting from the charming estate village of Enniskerry, where there are lots of tempting little cafés and gift shops and where the shell of Powerscourt House (designed by Richard Castle 1731-1740 and gutted by fire in 1974) now houses a shop and excellent lunchtime restaurant.

For fabulous mountain scenery there is a detour over the Sally Gap, passing near the Gothic fantasy of Luggala, beside Lough Tay. There is a wonderful walk (pedestrians only) from Lough Tay to Lough Dan which forms part of the Wicklow Way - from the R759 above Lough Tay head down to Laragh and through the beautiful wooded valley of the Avonmore to Rathdrum and Avondale, home of Charles Stewart Parnell. Painting courses are available June to September at Holly Farm near Rathdrum (daily rate £20, tel. 0404-46912). Just nearby are the ruins of Kilmacurragh (the grounds are open to the public), built for Thomas Acton possibly by William Robinson. Humewood Castle at Kiltegan near Baltinglass combined with the Dwyer McAllister Cottage at Derrynamuck also make a good destination.

The drive over the mountains to Russborough via Valleymount and the Poulaphouca Lake is magic and, if you are visiting Killruddery House at Bray and venturing further south, the Wicklow Fly Fishers and Lady Fishers at Newtownmountkennedy have just the appropriate clothes for country house living, with tempting Harvey's Bistro just beside it (01-281 9203). Further afield, the Vale of Avoca is especially lovely and the Avoca Woollen Mills there offer the combined attractions of knitwear, tweeds, pottery and a restaurant for light meals (tel. 0402-32401; there is another branch at Kilmacanogue, tel. 01-286 7466).

PLACES TO STAY / EAT

Annesbrook at Duleek has a banqueting room built specially for a visit by George IV - in the event he dined outdoors. The Georgian house, set in acres of gardens and woods, also offers relaxed hospitality with fare based on home produce (tel. 041-23293). The possibility of taking a painting or gilding course is just one of the temptations of staying at Loughcrew House. The converted orangery of the 1823 house is said to be cursed, and was burnt three times in 100 years (tel. 049-41356). Mountainstown, an early eigteenth-century house at Castletown, has been in the Pollock family since 1730 and is set in an 800-acre estate (tel. 046-54154).

In Kildare, near The Curragh, is charming Gothic Martinstown House - inspired by Horace Walpole's Strawberry Hill - set in a 170-acre estate and run by Meryl Long (tel. 045-441269). Medieval Kilkea

Castle in Castledermot is particularly associated with the wizard Earl of Kildare and has 1849 interiors combined with spa facilities and innovative Irish cuisine (tel. 0503-45156). Also in Castledermot, Kilkea Lodge Farm has been in the Green family for 250 years; it is also a riding centre (tel. 0503-45112).

Whaley Abbey (1760) near Rathdrum was once the country home of the notorious rakehell Buck Whaley. Far from hellish now, it is thoroughly cosy, informal and a favourite with the cast of the television programme *Ballykissangel* (tel. 0404-46529). The wonderfully hospitable Cullys welcome guests in to their home at the Manor, Manor Kilbride near Blessington, a rambling 1835 house set in glorious grounds. One of my firm favourites, both for the atmosphere of this old coaching inn and for its traditional fare, is Hunter's Hotel, Rathnew (tel. 0404-40106). The Glenview Hotel, revamped in 1993, serves excellent dinners in the delicious nouvelle cuisine style (tel. 01-287 3399). Sited in an old schoolhouse, Mitchell's in Laragh, County Wicklow, have an original and reasonably priced menu for lunch and dinner. Tinakilly House (1870), built for Captain Robert Halpin of transatlantic cable fame, with a staircase copied from a ship, is a place to dine in style (tel. 0404-69274).

On the north side of Wicklow, Rathsallagh House at Dunlavin is the stables - in the Queen Anne style - of a house that was burnt down in the 1798 Rebellion and offers thoroughly luxurious country house living and dining (tel. 045-403112).

HAMWOOD

Dunboyne, County Meath

Seven generations of Hamiltons have lived at Hamwood, a Palladian house built and completed in 1769 for Charles Hamilton, who later became land agent to Lord Leinster. The house is on a modest scale with two little wings, the front door rather unusually - if a little inconveniently - being at the end of one. Both have ceilings lined with Russian pine from Memel, giving the place the feel of a rustic retreat, which is exactly what Hamwood was.

History often hangs on the unexpected and the Hamiltons certainly came to Ireland in unusual circumstances. Among the plots to secure the throne for Elizabeth I was Bothwell's plan to kidnap Mary Queen of Scots and force her into marriage. The Hamiltons joined forces with the Gordon clan to rescue her but were defeated and fled in two ships, one of which ended up in Ireland and another in Sweden.

The grandfather of Charles Hamilton, the builder of Dunboyne, settled in the north and his second son, Alexander, worked as a land agent, became wealthy and left his five sons land worth £50,000. The boys were educated at Finglas in County Dublin (their father had their heads shaved and gave them wigs in case their hair might be pulled). Maybe their schooldays gave them a liking for Leinster, for, on inheriting, they all sold up and moved south. The youngest son, Charles, bought land near Dunboyne and first tried his hand as a wine merchant. The story of the Hamilton family is delightfully outlined in the diaries of Caroline Hamilton, wife of Charles's son - another Charles. 'The trade of a wine merchant in those days when so much claret was drunk was very lucrative and respectable', wrote Caroline. Charles was apprenticed before setting up a wine store, 'but being a very sober, moral, industrious man, he did not like the necessity imposed upon him of entertaining, like other wine merchants, his less sober customers and he withdrew to live on his own means at Mount Venus near Marlay'.

Charles fell in love with pretty Miss Chetwood when she was on a visit from England. They married and, with a growing family to support, Charles became a land agent, initially for the Archbishop of Dublin and Lord Lansdowne. The couple sold Mount Venus and built their home at Hamwood at a cost of £2,500.

When Lord Leinster's agent was killed by rebels in the 1798 uprising, Charles became agent in his stead, nearly meeting the same fate. He was seized by rebels and taken to Dunboyne, where he was saved by the intervention of blacksmith Reilly, who argued that Charles Hamilton would do more for their cause alive than dead. Descendants of the same Reillys still work as blacksmiths in Dunboyne and continued to work for the Hamiltons in the days when there were still horses.

In the next generation Charles's son Charles went to Trinity, was called to the Bar and married a fellow classmate's sister, Caroline Tighe of the Tighes of Rossanna, County Wicklow. Caroline laid out the gardens at Hamwood, discussing ideas and visiting with the Ladies of Llangollen, Eleanor Butler and Sarah Ponsonby, who had close family connections. (Mrs Tighe helped the cousins in their scandalous flight to Plas Newydd in Wales.)

Hamwood was generally used as a summer house and there are descriptions of the family making the journey to their former town house at 40 Dominick Street with cartloads of silver, plate and chattels, and a cow to give fresh milk bringing up the rear. Fresh fruit and vegetables from the four-acre walled garden at Hamwood were brought to town twice weekly.

Memorabilia at Hamwood afford all kinds of glimpses into the lives of previous generations of Hamiltons. The drawing-room is arranged just as it appears in Victorian photographs taken by the grandfather of the present Charles Hamilton. The walls of the principal bedroom and hallway are hung with the paintings of talented aunts Eva and Letitia, showing the former glories of the herbaceous borders at Hamwood and the sunlit scenes of a more leisurely age. Portraits of earlier Hamilton relatives stare down from the dining-room walls - including little William Tighe, dressed as a girl in the customary eighteenth-century manner to prevent the fairies stealing him away to become a changeling. And the lithographs of Ireland collected by Caroline Hamilton -

one poking fun at the notion that temperance is fit only for servants - provide a wry commentary on contemporary Irish life. Over the years the house, with its fine collection of eighteenth-century furniture, has inevitably had some alterations made to it. The twelve-pane windows were replaced with Victorian sashes and the old kitchen and the basement are no longer in use.

Hamwood is still a family home. Major Charles Hamilton and his wife Anne have a fund of information about their family, their home and its contents. Their garden, which features a serpentine rockery, is also open.

OPEN 1 Feb.-31 March, Mon.-Fri. 10am-2pm; 1 May-31 Aug., Mon.-Fri. 2-6pm; and on the third Sunday of each month, 2-6pm. Groups by arrangement, tel. 01-825 5219.

ADMISSION £2 for house, £2 for garden. Guided tours, parking, toilets.

DIRECTIONS 3 km from Dunboyne on the Maynooth road.

FURNESS

Naas, County Kildare

Richard Nevill caused Furness to be built at around the same time as Russborough House began its ten-year journey towards magnificent completion. The desire to keep up with the Leesons may have influenced Nevill to build beyond his means. The Nevills, an Anglo-Norman family originally from Wexford, owned 1,400 acres, not a very large estate by the standards of the time, and Furness is rather grander than was warranted by their holding.

The first Richard Nevill at Furness, who had the good fortune to marry an heiress from the Ash family, purchased lands cheaply which were originally held by a monastery. His son, another Richard, built Furness and was succeeded by two further Richards. Richards two and four - at a time when low standards in high places were generally much lower than now - were dismissed as members of the Irish parliament for cheating the public purse (as opposed to the widespread practice of private cheating).

Whether or not Furness was the cause of their financial need, it is a most appealing house, with all the harmony and symmetry of the Palladian style, but on a modest scale. Two rather benign, curly-headed lions guard a doorway flanked by pairs of Ionic pillars. The design, attributed to architect Francis Bindon, features a central block just three bays wide, with the pillared doorcase - surmounted by a pedimented window, topped by a lunette window - forming a pleasing diminishing composition. On either side of the central block, two links - given interest by rusticated doorways flanked by lunette windows - reach out to two-storey pavilions, while the addition of an extra storey above one of the links gives an endearing lop-sided air. And in a typically Palladian device, the front elevation of the house is lengthened still further by two quadrants which join the outbuildings to the pavilions. The back of the house has five bays, with a bow front on the dining-room wing.

Beyond the front door lies an impressive hall, stretching the whole width of the house, with a broad staircase of handsome Spanish chestnut at one end and a beautifully detailed pearwood chimney piece at the other. An archway joins the two sections of the room. The Doric frieze in the hall finds a contrast in the Vitruvian scroll decorating the staircase. An anteroom forms the link between drawing-room and dining-room at the garden front of the house.

A two-storey extension was built above and behind one of the links by Richard Nevill (Richard mark four) around 1780, principally to house a generous dining-room. This later addition of a designated dining-room is very typical. Previously, dining-tables tended to be moved around the house as the need dictated, and guests spent a great deal of time standing. Increased notions of comfort, the possibility of seating guests - the better to admire the prospect of demesnes landscaped in the new romantic manner - and of course keeping up with the Joneses (or the Leesons) all played a part in the rise of the dining-room. The same Richard also engaged Michael Stapleton to design the splendid classical plasterwork for the drawing-room ceiling and landscaped the demesne.

Scandals or not, the Nevills were accounted good landlords, even instituting a prize (something almost unheard of) for the tenant who planted the most trees. They built cabins - again relatively unusual - for their tenants and assisted those building stone cottages. But this may not have been totally philanthropic, as higher rents could then be charged - and Furness, together with the Slane and Castletown estates, charged at 20 shillings an acre, among the highest rents in the country at that point. Behind the house is Furness church, rebuilt in 1200, on the site of a much earlier holy place where there is a Bronze Age stone and a burial stone dating to 600. The Nevills allowed local people to worship there in penal times.

In the mid eighteenth century the house was sold to the Beaumont family and was bought in 1897 by Nicholas Synnott, at which stage it was in a dilapidated condition. The house was restored at that point and is now the home of Patrick Guinness.

OPEN Aug.-Sept., daily 10am-2pm; other times by appointment, fax 045-866815.

ADMISSION £5, children £4. Toilets, parking, guided tours on the hour.

DIRECTIONS Turn off the N7 at Kill village, turn right, then left, and fork right again. Furness is 2 km from the village.

FRANCIS LEDWIDGE COTTAGE

Slane, County Meath

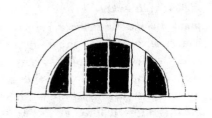

J ust outside the village of Slane on the road to Drogheda is a modest cottage overlooking the bosomy slopes of the Boyne valley. The cottage is a celebration of the short life of poet Francis Ledwidge and opens a door on rural life in Ireland at the turn of the last century. His home and the countryside around it were both Frank's lodestone and his inspiration. He would write from the battlefront of Gallipoli and France, where he lost his life at the age of 30, of the way he longed just for a few hours to walk familiar paths and fields.

Cottage Number 1116, dating to 1886, was one of the thousands built in Ireland around this time by Rural District Councils to house farm labourers. With two windows either side of the door, a slate roof and the brick facings and quoins picked out in maroon paint, it has the simplicity of a child's drawing. It was here that Francis Ledwidge, the eighth child of Patrick and Anne Ledwidge, was born in 1887 shortly after his parents had been allocated the cottage at Janeville.

The cottage probably represented a huge improvement over the family's previous accommodation. There were four small rooms: a kitchen, bedroom, parlour, an outside toilet, and a room which must, with such a large family, have served as a second bedroom. Family life revolved around the kitchen, where cooking was done over an open fire using a crane to suspend pots. The family's few possessions would have extended to a kettle, a three-legged pot and a couple of skillets, a dresser to hold delft and provisions, a table, a few chairs, and a settle bed which served as a seat by day and a bed at night. Each of the other rooms had a fireplace. The bedroom held just an iron bedstead and chair and the other rooms are now filled with memorabilia about the poet's life. A half-acre garden at the back of the cottage and a pigsty helped the family to provide their own food; water came from the nearest pump or well. Bread, tea and potatoes would have been staples.

Work on farms, which relied on manual labour, was back-breakingly hard. Patrick Ledwidge died when Francis was four years old and his new brother Joseph just three months. Anne Ledwidge managed to sustain her family on just eight shillings outdoor relief and any money she could earn from labouring in the fields. But she instilled in her children a sense of pride in a lineage drawn from poets and soldiers, entertained them at the end of the day with stories and kept them all at school, seeing education as the key to a decent job. But her hopes for her eldest son Patrick were short-lived: he qualified as a book-keeper and got a well paid job in Dublin, only to be sent home suffering from tuberculosis which was rife in those day and nearly always, as in Patrick's case, fatal.

Francis Ledwidge was a natural poet in every sense. He began writing instinctively from an early age, drawing on the imagery of the land, of plants and wild life to express the profoundest emotions and the wonder of the countryside. He wrote of the death of a neighbour's child who had been a familiar sight as he herded cows.

The moon leans on one silver horn
Above the silhouettes of morn
And from their nest sills finches whistle,
Or stooping pluck the down thistle.
How is the morn so gay and fair
Without his whistling in its air?

Frank left school at 14; he worked in a series of labouring jobs, before getting work in the Beauparc copper mine where he was one of the instigators of a strike for better pay and conditions (Irish workers were the worst paid in Europe), and lost his job. His prospects seemed to be improving when he became secretary of the Meath Labour Union and began writing for the local newspaper, the *Drogheda Independent*. The paper also published his poems. Through his contact with Lord Dunsany his poetry was brought to the attention of the publishers of his first book of poetry *Songs of the Field* (1915) and the *Saturday Review*.

But even the quietest of rural lives can get caught up with national and international issues. The Irish question and the third Home Rule Bill prompted the formation of the Ulster Volunteer Force in the North to fight for Ulster's exclusion from Home Rule, and the formation of Irish Volunteers in the south to oppose any dilution of the Bill. Frank joined the Volunteers. Crisis and confrontation loomed, but what was to become one of the most intractable political problems of the twentieth century was temporarily defused by the outbreak of the First World War. The Irish Volunteers, in the wake of an impassioned speech by John Redmond, became national volunteers and joined up with the British army in their thousands. Despite his disagreement with Redmond, Frank Ledwidge enlisted with the Royal Inniskilling Fusiliers in 1914. His decision may have been influenced by being jilted by the love of his life, Ellie Vaughey. Frank Ledwidge died in Ypres in 1917.

Relatives of the Ledwidge family lived in the Janeville cottage until 1980 when it was advertised for sale. A local committee was formed, funds raised and the cottage was bought, restored and a garden created there around a trysting stone which once stood near Ellie Vaughey's home on the Hill of Slane.

OPEN Daily daily 10am-1pm; and 2-6 pm, tel. 041-24544.

ADMISSION £2.

DIRECTIONS On the Drogheda road just outside Slane.

HUMEWOOD

Kiltegan, County Wicklow

The landscape of south-west Wicklow is glorious: to the east is the drama of the mountains, the plains of Kildare and Carlow stretch into a blue infinity and in the middle ground are pleasing low hills, lakes and woods. It is the kind of countryside where the desire for some grand architectural statement grows with every turn of the road and in Humewood that expectation is satisfied.

The castle, built on a palatial scale between 1867 and 1870, was originally intended as 'an occasional resort for the summer shooting season' for the Right Honourable Hume Dick, MP for Wicklow. The fairytale outline of turrets, battlements, gables and chimneys dominated by a massive central tower can be glimpsed from the

Kiltegan-Baltinglass road. The Gothic gateway at the end of the estate village, the long avenue and the magnificent beech trees screening the house only serve to increase anticipation for a closer view of the cut granite, castellated mansion.

Humewood is one of the last of the great country houses to be built in Ireland, a final fling of the Victorian vogue for sham castles in the Scottish baronial style: an extravaganza made possible not by rent rolls but by new wealth from a rising mercantile class. The Hume ancestors - from a Scottish shipbuilding family - came to Ireland in the early eighteenth century and bought land stretching from Kiltegan to Tallaght. Their earlier Georgian house on the site of Humewood was originally called Butlerswood and withstood a siege during the 1798 Rebellion. Three generations of Humes, William Hume, his son William Hoare Hume and his son William Wentworth Fitzwilliam Hume, were MPs for Wicklow. William III inherited a fortune from his mother, Charlotte Dick, daughter of a wealthy Dublin merchant, and on the strength of his inheritance added his mother's family name to his and commissioned architect William White to design the Gothic revival building.

White might have done well to heed his contemporary, Edward Godwin (architect of Dromore, County Down, and Glenbeigh Towers, County Kerry), who advised him, after problems with damp and insolvent clients, 'When offered an Irish commission refuse it.' While most buildings overrun estimates, White's design overshot the budget of £15,000 by a spectacular £10,000. Hume Dick refused to pay the builder, where-upon the builder sued both Dick and White and won. White's career was ruined by the episode and Humewood stands as a lone, magnificent testimony to the architect's quirky talent.

Beyond the entrance is an almost cathedral-like staircase hall, lit by stained-glass windows, with a sandstone groin vaulted ceiling. In the principal rooms White's genius results in interiors which are both romantic and opulent. The drawing-room has a coffered ceiling with magnificent painted panels, featuring roses, thistles and shamrocks, to symbolise the family connections with England, Scotland and Ireland, between the gilded beams. An inviting archway lined with White's intricate Gothic woodwork leads off into one of the turrets and the ornate carved chimney piece is of different coloured Irish marbles. The dining-room is in similar style and even the original dining-table was designed by White. The cosy, oak-panelled library, with Gothic bookcases and overmantel mirror also designed by White, is on a more intimate scale. The banqueting hall, two storeys high in the style of a medieval great hall complete with panelling and a minstrels' gallery, is breathtaking and capable of holding over 100 guests. The house, unusually for a revival castle, has a basement, and was designed by White - mindful of the Fenian rising - with defensive features.

The last of the Humes, 'Mimi' Hume-Weygand, granddaughter of the builder, owned Humewood until her death in 1992. Married into a distinguished French family (her father-in-law General Maxime Weygand was the commander of the French army at the fall of France in 1940), she divided her time between Humewood and France. Madame Weygand entertained in style at Humewood and her Saturday lunch parties, which always included members of the diplomatic corps and sometimes celebrities like John Boorman and David Bowie, were legendary. After her husband's death

Madame Weygand spent less time in Wicklow and only a few of the rooms were used.

Fate most definitely played a part in the arrival of a new owner for Humewood. Various celebrities were rumoured to be on the point of buying but were evidently daunted by the 60,000 square foot house, by then in a poor state of repair. Businesswoman Renata Coleman, despite her resistance to going to inspect 'a Victorian monstrosity', fell in love with the house at first sight but baulked at the amount of work involved. But when the prospective purchase by a development company fell through, Renata decided that the place was meant to be hers and it became her labour of love.

Now six years and an enormous amount of work later, White's original vision for the house has been realised once again. Heavy curtains and flock wallpapers were stripped away, walls were painted in cool, clear colours and clutter removed so that the glorious detailing of the house comes into its own again. A whole new dimension has been added in the imaginative redecoration of the 13 bedrooms, each with a different theme. Among the most spectacular are the blue-and-gold Marie Antoinette suite; the star suite with its Napoleonic furniture; and two chinoiserie rooms which take their themes from Chinese lacquered furniture found by Mrs Coleman on business trips to the Far East, and to an astounding Chinese imperial bed (with room for half a dozen concubines) found by Renata in hundreds of pieces in Austria.

Hume Dick's original intentions for the castle are being realised too on a far grander scale than he ever imagined: Humewood has become a magnificent sporting and country retreat, offering shooting, polo, riding from the Gothic stables, and trout and pike fishing on the lakes in the landscaped grounds. The castle will not be a hotel but an owner-occupied home offering hospitality to people from all over the world.

OPEN Open all year for accommodation. Room tariffs from £140 per room. Viewing by appointment, tel. 0508-73215.

ADMISSION £3, OAPs £1.50. Toilets, parking, guided tours, tea rooms.

DIRECTIONS On the outskirts of Kiltegan, signposted from Baltinglass.

AVONDALE

Rathdrum, County Wicklow

Avondale is known first and foremost as the lifelong home of the great nationalist leader, Charles Stewart Parnell. And the house and beautiful demesne in the wooded valley of the Avonmore River provide some clues to the contradictions in the life of one of Ireland's most powerful men.

It may seem ironic that the champion of land reform came from the Protestant landlord class. In many respects Parnell was a typical country gentleman and yet he succeeded in uniting nationalist Ireland and drawing together the three burning issues of agrarianism, nationalism and constitutionalism. Many of the influences that shaped his political vision were to be found in his family and at Avondale.

Avondale came into the Parnell family through inheritance. It was built for barrister and Wicklow MP Samuel Hayes in 1779, and passed to William Parnell Hayes, Charles Stewart Parnell's grandfather. There was a strong vein of liberal thinking in the Parnell family; Charles's great-grandfather Sir John Parnell supported Catholic representation, his son Henry (Charles's great-uncle) favoured Repeal of the Penal Laws and Catholic Emancipation, while his grandfather William wrote influential papers analysing the causes of Catholic discontent. Perhaps Parnell's American mother, Delia Tudor Stewart, whose family took part in the Boston Tea Party and who was anti-English, was the greatest influence of all, contributing to Parnell's belief that the English should be 'stood up to'.

The Parnells and some of their Wicklow neighbours, like the Tighes and Fitzwilliams, were improving landlords. The sawmill at Avondale, for instance, was a project designed to provide local employment.

Life at Avondale - although the family were in reduced circumstances - was in the comfortable late Victorian tradition, staffed by a plentiful supply of cheap servant power. 'Upstairs' life revolved around the study, drawing-room and dining-room, and there was socialising with other nearby Ascendancy families and tennis and cricket matches. Although the house – probably designed by James Wyatt, the architect of Castle Coole – has rather a severe box-like exterior, relieved only by a small Doric porch and small stone panels carved with swags, the interior is much more rewarding. The front door opens directly into a dramatic two-storey hallway with neo-Gothic plaster-work featuring trefoils and oak leaves, the dining-room has splendid neo-classical plasterwork and the bow-windowed drawing-room has a Bossi fireplace.

Quite a number of pieces of furniture are original to the house, including an extraordinary Wooton desk in the study which belonged to Parnell's maternal grandfather, Admiral Charles Stewart, and a splendid curved mahogany sideboard specially designed in 1835 to fit an alcove in the dining-room. But Coillte Teoranta (the Irish Forestry Board), which owns the estate, has done a splendid job of refurnishing the principal rooms and Parnell's bedroom in the style of the mid 1800s. A restaurant and other facilities are now situated in the basement.

Even without the Parnell connection, Avondale makes an enchanting place to visit. Situated just on the outskirts of Rathdrum - a town which holds a special place in my affections, since I was married in the now vanished sweetie shop cum registrar's office there - the estate is a forest paradise. Set in a curve of the swift-flowing Avonmore in the Vale of Clara, the 500-acre estate became the base for a forestry school in 1904. Walks run through groves of lofty conifers, the beeches - which were planted over 200 years ago by Samuel Hayes - still stand and there is an arboretum of rare trees.

OPEN May-Sept., daily 10am-6pm; Oct.-April, daily 11am-5pm. Last admissions 1 hour before closing, tel. 0404-46111.

ADMISSION £3, concession £2, family £6, parking £2 per car. Audio-visual aids, restaurant, toilets, picnic areas, gift shop, walks.

DIRECTIONS Rathdrum is off the N11 on the R752. Avondale is signposted 1.6 km from there.

KILLRUDDERY

Bray, County Wicklow

Houses are generally more venerable than the gardens surrounding them, but at Killruddery the reverse appears to be the case. Against the rugged hills of the Little Sugar Loaf and Bray Head is the 300-year-old baroque garden where nature has been tamed into sublime formality. The exterior of the house is Tudor revival, an accomplished concoction of mullioned windows, Elizabethan chimneys, and gables topped with finials, executed in grey Wicklow granite to the design of father and son, Sir Richard Morrison and William Vitruvius Morrison. The building was commenced for John Cambre Brabazon, 10th Earl of Meath, in 1820 and completed nine years later, at a cost of £20,000.

Under the Tudor mantle, however, is a seventeenth-century house, built by the 2nd Earl of Meath on land granted to William Brabazon, 1st Earl of Meath, in 1627. There is a charming naïve painting of the house, which was built in 1651. Two generations later, Captain Edward Brabazon - perhaps following the example of the Duke of Ormonde, who returned from exile after the Restoration and introduced the French baroque style to Ireland - had the formal gardens created by a Versailles-trained Frenchman named Bonet.

The Brabazons are of Norman stock - Jacques de Brabançon was one of William the Conqueror's knights. His descendant, Sir William Brabazon, was appointed Receiver General and Vice-Treasurer of Ireland in 1534.

The 10th Earl of Meath was considering 'improvements' in 1814, when he commissioned Francis Johnston for a new design. However, Lord Meath and his family went on an extended European tour (they returned four years later armed with Italian marbles and fireplaces for Killruddery) and in the end the commission went to Johnston's rivals, the Morrisons. It was a period when the owners of country estates vied with each other in building and rebuilding their seats. The new Killruddery was so vast that, when dry rot was discovered in the 1950s, the opportunity was taken to reduce the house by demolishing the north wing, great hall and dining-room.

Nevertheless, the remaining interiors are fascinating, embellished with sumptuous plasterwork and with original furniture. The entrance is now through a small lobby with a display of china leading into the darkly panelled hall, which is lit by a stained-glass window depicting William the Conqueror with de Brabançon as his standard bearer and dominated by a centrally placed staircase. The clock above the stairs is a curiosity, created by the 13th Earl from a bed warmer and a bicycle chain.

The drawing-room is on a heroic scale. Pairs of Ionic scagliola columns appear to support one side of the coved and compartmented ceiling - filled with a design of wreath-filled octagons - and the plasterwork is signed and dated, 'Simon Gilligan 1824'.

The delightful small drawing-room, now used as a dining-room, has an exquisite vaulted ceiling, with a cat's cradle of garlands inset with stars, doves and musical instruments, and with a frieze of plasterwork drapery. The library has handsome eighteenth-century bookcases. A great cruciform conservatory designed by William Burn in 1852 is used as a statue gallery to display the fine Italian statues brought back by the 10th Earl.

The house is still the home of the Earls of Meath and the baroque gardens with their twin canals, sylvan theatre and circular pool are also open to the public.

OPEN May, June & Sept., daily 1-5pm. Gardens April-Sept., daily 1-5pm, tel. 01-286 3405.

ADMISSION House and garden £4, OAPs £2.50; garden only £2. Groups at other dates and times by arrangement. Toilets, parking, wheelchair access.

DIRECTIONS On the outskirts of Bray.

BEAU PARC

Slane, County Meath

Beau Parc lives up to its name admirably. A long driveway winds through fine trees, enormous old rhododendron bushes and the greenest of undulating parkland, arriving eventually at the welcoming façade of the house. Two quadrants stretch out to unite the house with small wings. The scale and proportion are pleasing and the central block, faced in silver-grey ashlar, has five bays and three storeys and the wings have two. A harmonious diminishing scale is also used in the classical arrangement of a tripartite doorway which is topped by a Venetian window and, above that again, the half circle of a Diocletian window.

Most breathtaking of all at Beau Parc is the view - revealed only from inside the house - of the River Boyne hundreds of feet below, framed by the tops of trees.

The house was built for Gustavus Lambart MP in 1755 and is one of the very few designed by the amateur architect and man of many parts, Nathaniel Clements. By the age of 22 Clements was already an MP and rose rapidly to become Paymaster General. He speculated in property in Dublin and was a business associate of Luke Gardiner, who owned the land on the north side of Dublin where the new capital was taking shape. The Lambart family became established in County Meath during the seventeenth century and the family returned five generations of MPs up until the 1801 Act of Union.

Inside the house there are two portraits of Fanny Lambart (*née* Conyngham) which explain the link between Beau Parc and the adjoining estate of Slane. One shows a smiling Fanny, with Beau Parc in the background, which used to hang at Slane. This was evidently a thank you portrait, for her father - the 2nd Marquess Conyngham of Slane - who bought Beau Parc from the financially embarrassed Lambarts for his favourite daughter as a wedding gift when she married into the family. Fanny Lambart became Oliver Lambart's grandmother. The other portrait shows Fanny in a severe Victorian riding habit with Slane Castle in the background, looking every inch the proud Conyngham.

From his family home at Slane, the Earl of Mount Charles used to visit his relatives at Beau Parc and worked in the gardens there as a teenager. Later, when he had taken over his inheritance at Slane and was working as a representative for Sotheby's, he would sell pieces of furniture for Oliver Lambart - little realising that in fact he was dispersing part of his inheritance. Quite unbeknown to Henry, Oliver Lambart had decided to make him his heir. When Oliver Lambart died in 1986, Henry Mount Charles inherited Beau Parc, re-establishing the link between the property and Slane.

Elizabeth, Countess of Fingall, in her memoirs, *Seventy Years Young*, paints a charming picture of the Victorian Misses Lambart at the Vice-Regal ball in Dublin Castle: 'The Lambarts of Beau Parc in Meath, seven sisters of them and all good lookers, and they had such slender waists, all of seventeen or eighteen inches, that some wit christened the white house on the Boyne from which they came Waistland.'

Large old houses may be a privilege but they are also a liability to own. Henry Mount Charles can never, in his worst imaginings, have expected to have to carry out two major restorations of eighteenth-century houses within a decade. First Beau Parc was found to be riddled with dry rot and the whole building had to be stripped back to basics, then came the disastrous fire at uninsured Slane in 1991.

Beau Parc is now all it should be, the rooms painted in strong eighteenth-century colours, the plasterwork beautifully restored. The front door opens directly on to a square entrance hall with a flagged floor and heavy baroque detailing which would have been used as a reception room. A portrait of Elizabeth Marchioness Conyngham, mistress of George IV, has pride of place on the wall. The blue drawing-room affords a magnificent view of the Boyne from the bow window at the centre of the garden front. The dining-room and a second drawing-room are on either side, and beyond the staircase hall is a study dominated by a wonderful chinoiserie cupboard. A long corridor with Gothic vaulting runs the length of the first floor. Bedrooms, furnished in the period, are ranged either side and the views from them are matchless.

OPEN 1-20 March, 1 May-9 June, 9am-1pm.

ADMISSION £3.

DIRECTIONS Ask in Slane - it's tricky!

DWYER MCALLISTER COTTAGE

Derrynamuck, County Wicklow

T he golden light of a September afternoon was softening the silhouette of the mountains rimming the Glen of Imaal, the cry of a lone kestrel emphasising the wild isolation in the heart of the Wicklow Mountains. As I climbed a boreen past a farm and trickling spring to a thatched cottage guarded by a berry-laden rowan tree, this seemed the most peaceful spot, remote from the influence of the outside world.

Yet within a matter of minutes I was plunged back 200 years to a freezing winter night in February 1799 when gunfire rang out, with the chill of fear, the cries of death and blood as red as the rowan berries spilt in the snow. For this is the cottage where Michael Dwyer, one of the leaders of the ill-fated

1798 Rebellion, escaped with his life, thanks to the heroic action of his companion Sam McAllister. The rebellion, aimed at ending English rule of Ireland and inspired by the politics of the French and American revolutions, was led by Wolfe Tone and Lord Edward FitzGerald, who enlisted French help in their cause. The story that follows was related so vividly by Padraic Hoxey, great-grandson of the Patrick Hoxey of the farm at the foot of the boreen who gave shelter to some of Dwyer's gang, that I could almost smell the reek of gunpowder.

An informer had betrayed the whereabouts of Dwyer and a handful of his companions, bringing Captain Roderick McDonald over the mountains from Hacketstown at the head of a force of soldiers from the Highland Regiment. The soldiers first took the two cottages lower down the mountainside, capturing some of Dwyer's men, then they surrounded the third cottage, which belonged to Miley Connell, and demanded that Dwyer surrender. He refused, and in the ensuing gunfire his companions John Savage and Patrick Costello were shot dead, and Sam McAllister, a Presbyterian from the Glens of Antrim, was wounded. McAllister reckoned that he was finished and sacrificed himself by stepping out of the cottage door into a hail of bullets in order to draw the soldiers' fire. While they were reloading Dwyer escaped, miraculously missed by a bullet when he slipped on ice in his flight to the safety of the bog.

Dwyer, who was born in the Glen of Imaal, knew the territory like the back of his hand and took refuge in another property owned by a cousin, Thaddeus Dwyer. Once again he was saved when Mrs Dwyer saw the soldiers approaching across the snow, allowing Dwyer to escape out the back of the farm. The pursuing troops fired on him as he leaped the little Slaney River. Dwyer's bare feet were cut; seeing the bloodstains in the snow, the soldiers mistakenly imagined that he was wounded and gave up the chase - while Dwyer escaped into the Hollywood valley.

Four years later Dwyer gave himself up to Colonel William Hoare Hume of nearby Humewood Castle, who Dwyer believed to be an honourable man, surrendering on condition that he and his family be allowed passage to America. The authorities did not respect the terms and Dwyer was incarcerated in Kilmainham for 18 months.

Eventually he was transported to Botany Bay with his wife, cousin and seven others. After a 168-day voyage aboard the *Tellicherry*, the Dwyers settled in Australia at Cabra, where Michael was granted 100 acres. Great-grandfather Hoxey was held on suspicion of harbouring rebels but later released on foot of a surety and bond given by his Protestant neighbours.

To this day the Military Road, built to help British forces rout out the rebels, remains the only road to cross the central Wicklow massif, a monument to the men of the '98 Rebellion.

Miley Connell's cottage was subsequently burnt down, rebuilt, let and eventually fell into disrepair before it was declared a national monument in 1948. Thomas Hoxey and Patrick Hoxey (father of Padraic) were both involved in the work and the cottage is now in the care of the OPW. A good example of an eighteenth-century cottage in the vernacular style, it is one of the all too few small dwellings open to the public. The cottage is built of local stone and clay mortar and is whitewashed inside and out. All the materials are local, put together with now forgotten traditional skills. The roof timbers are of oak and ash lined with turf for insulation; the thatch is of oaten and wheaten straw, and the smoke hood over the fire is ingeniously made of clay and wattle. The floor, typically, was of beaten earth and slabs, and cooking was characteristically over an open turf fire with a crane to hold pots over the heat. Possessions in such a home would have been few: a dresser for the display of delft and for storage, a three-legged pot for baking bread, stools, a table, a bed and a couple of sugán armchairs for the man and woman of the house to take the place of honour on either side of the hearth. But however remote and traditional, the cottage was not immune to the French and American events which convulsed Ireland 200 years ago.

OPEN Mid June–mid Sept., 2-6 pm.

ADMISSION Free of charge.

DIRECTIONS Signposted from the Blessington–Baltinglass road; look for the turning to the left after the Tollhouse pub going south and follow signs.

CASTLETOWN

Celbridge, County Kildare

Castletown House was once described to me as Ireland's answer to the Parthenon, and it is the first and the greatest of the country houses in the Palladian style. Despite its magnificence, the house has an intimacy about it, perhaps because its interiors still reflect the warm personality of Lady Louisa Conolly, who directed their creation. Castletown also gives the lie to the notion that all big houses belonged to the Anglo-Irish Ascendancy.

The house was built for Speaker William Conolly, the richest man in Ireland at that time, who began life as the son of Protestant innkeepers in Donegal, studied law and went on to make a vast fortune through buying and selling land forfeited by Jacobite supporters in the wake of the battle of the Boyne. He became collector and receiver of revenue for the government, and MP for Donegal. He favoured nationalism and eventually became Speaker of the Irish House of Commons. The building of a home to reflect his wealth and influence began in 1722. The central block was designed by Italian architect Alessandro Galilei in

the style of an Italian palazzo, but he did not stay in Ireland to oversee the design, which was completed by Edward Lovett Pearce, who added the graceful colonnaded wings and pavilions.

An avenue of limes approaches Castletown at right angles, so that visitors come suddenly upon the pale golden façade. Its thirteen-bay front, with three storeys over a basement, faces a serene stretch of the River Liffey and the arms of the colonnades topped with a string of urns reach out to embrace the formal grounds. The classical Palladian style, inspired by Italian Andrea Palladio, was also essentially practical. Farm buildings and domestic offices were concealed behind colonnades and in pavilions, with the principal residence in the central block.

William Conolly died in 1729, his estate passed first to his nephew, and then to his great-nephew, Thomas Conolly, in 1754. Four years later, at the age of 24, Thomas married fifteen-year-old Louisa Lennox, daughter of the Duke of Richmond, who had been brought up by her sister Emily, Countess of

Kildare, at the neighbouring estate of Carton. While the exterior of the young couple's Irish country home was complete, Castletown's unfinished interior offered Louisa endless scope for what she and her sisters called 'business'. 'Decoration, landscaping and building occupied Louisa for 25 years', writes Stella Tillyard in *Aristocrats*, her wonderfully evocative account of the four Lennox sisters, Caroline, Emily, Louisa and Sarah. Louisa's letters, accounts and diaries provide a fascinating insight into life at Castletown.

After several years of to-ing and fro-ing between England and Ireland, the Conollys made Castletown their main home from 1761, when Tom was elected MP for Derry. Tom's life revolved around his racehorses and hunting, Louisa's around the supervision of the house and entertaining guests.

When the house was empty, Louisa moved in the decorators, employing the most talented practitioners of the day. The dining-room to the left of the hall was reconstructed from two smaller rooms to the design of Sir William Chambers, and Dublin carver Richard Cranfield - who was probably responsible for the frames of three pier glasses which are original to the dining-room - was paid considerable sums of money for carving and gilding. The staircase hall was given a magnificent cantilevered Portland stone staircase, built under the direction of Simon Vierpyl, and was decorated by the Lafrancini brothers in the baroque style with shells, masks and cornucopias. Louisa evidently disputed their bill and wrote to her sister Emily: 'Mr Conolly and I are excessively diverted at Francini's impertinence.'

The main reception rooms, arranged enfilade on the north side of the house, were also completed to the published styles of Sir William Chambers, who never actually worked in Ireland but had his designs supervised by his associate Vierpyl. In the red drawing-room, with its damask-lined walls, the pier glasses and chimney piece are also typical of his designs. Of particular interest are the mahogany bureau, with its numerous drawers and compartments, specially made for Lady Louisa in the 1760s, and the Chinese Chippendale chairs, which she considered extravagant at one-and-a-half guineas each. The green drawing-room served as the main state room for receiving important visitors. Items of furniture like the pier glasses and the pier tables (copies of the originals) were specially designed to co-ordinate with the plasterwork and repeat its Greek key pattern. The silk wallcovering has been copied from a fragment of the original and was specially woven by Prelle of Lyons.

Two of the rooms in the house were Louisa's special creations: the delightful print room next to the state bedroom (originally used, in the French manner, for receiving guests at the morning levée) is a unique surviving example of the eighteenth-century rage for decorating rooms with monochrome or 'grisaille' prints. The Long Gallery on the first floor was her other masterpiece.

Measuring 80 feet by 23, the Long Gallery must be one of the most impressive rooms in Ireland. Louisa had it redecorated in the Pompeian style with painted panels and motifs by English artists Thomas Ryder and Charles Ruben Riley. Three chandeliers from Venice were made to order and were intended to co-ordinate with the exact shade of azure blue of the walls (much to Louisa's dismay, they didn't), and the four large sheets of mirror glass survived the perilous journey from France intact. There is a discreet reference to Louisa's loneliness as a young bride in the copy of an engraving, 'La Nouvelle Epouse', which she had painted in the Long Gallery.

The room, which was elegantly furnished by Louisa, is glowingly described by Lady Caroline Dawson after a visit: 'What struck me most was the gallery, I daresay 150 feet long, furnished in the most delightful manner with fine glasses, books, musical instruments, a billiard table, that it is the warmest most comfortable looking place I ever saw.' Tom Conolly's income was more than adequate - at £25,000 a year - to meet the cost of refurbishment.

The Conolly family and their descendants the Conolly-Carews remained at Castletown until 1965, when the house was sold. It lay empty for two years until rescued by Desmond Guinness of the Irish Georgian Society, which undertook initial restoration work. The house was then opened to the public. In 1979 the Castletown Foundation was set up to own, manage and restore the house, and in 1994 it was transferred to the care of the Irish state. It is now managed by the Department of the Arts, Heritage, the Gaeltacht and the Islands, through Dúchas - The Heritage Service.

OPEN Apr. & May, Sun. & Bank holidays. June, daily.

ADMISSION £2.50, groups & OAPs £1.75, children and students £1, family £6, tel. 01-628 8252.

DIRECTIONS Signposted from Celbridge.

SLANE CASTLE

Slane, County Meath

W hen I went to see Slane Castle one raw April day, an enormous daffodil-yellow crane stood in front of the castle like a strange engine of war with its head over the mock battlements. The object of the exercise, however, was not destruction but a dramatic chapter in the restoration of the castle involving the installation of a new roof.

In November 1991 the castle fell to the worst enemy of old buildings - fire. The damage caused was extensive but, in one sense, providential, for the advanced spread of dry rot was discovered.

Miraculously, the famous circular ballroom, with its fabulous Gothic ceiling and colourful association with George IV, although damaged, survived the fire. The two-storey room was designed by Thomas Hopper in honour of the King's 1821 visit to Slane and - much more importantly, from the royal perspective - to his mistress, Elizabeth Marchioness Conyngham, one of the great beauties of the day. The fire in the family drawing-room, ready for lighting with sticks and newspaper, escaped the fire too.

Henry, Earl of Mount Charles, who has undertaken the daunting task of restoring the castle out of his own funds, has left the fire set. It appeals to his sense of humour.

The present castle at Slane is the third version of the building on the strategic site, which commands a height above the River Boyne. The first was the fortress of the Norman Fleming family, whose lands were confiscated following their support of the Jacobite cause and later acquired by the Conynghams - probably by General Henry Conyngham in 1703 - who later built a house on the foundations of the earlier castle in the early eighteenth century.

The next reconstruction of Slane was begun in 1785 for William Burton Conyngham, MP and Teller of the Exchequer. He was a complex man, a patron of the arts with strong views of his own on architecture, who consulted a number of architects, among them Capability Brown - who designed the charming Gothic stableyard and grounds - James Gandon and Francis Johnston. In the end James Wyatt got the main commission and turned the house into a Gothic revival castle with four flanking towers, a battlemented parapet and other medieval touches.

The interior of the castle was completed by Francis Johnston for William's nephew - who inherited in 1796 and became the 1st Marquess Conyngham - and his wife Elizabeth, who became the last mistress of George IV in her fifties. The Marchioness was once described unkindly by Princess Lieven as 'having not an idea in her head, not a word to say for herself: nothing but a hand to accept pearls and diamonds with and an enormous balcony to wear them on'. The last part may have been true, and the portrait of her by Hugh Douglas Hamilton shows a generous embonpoint, but her influence on the King was generally sensible and she was in favour of Catholic Emancipation in Ireland. George IV was devoted to her, and her position at court was such that she was known as the Vice Queen. The unusually straight road between Slane and Dublin is supposed to have been built to speed the King's journey to his favourite.

When I visited, the walls of the ballroom were bare and the breathtaking lace-like intricacy of the Gothic ceiling and the fan vaulting of the alcoves were somehow all the more hauntingly beautiful, still stained with smoke, and with the different coloured sections of restored plasterwork showing the wonderful skill of contemporary craftsmen.

The restoration of the 40-foot square great hall by Francis Johnston was also nearing completion. The Conyngham motto on the coat of arms, 'Over Fork Over', is a reference to a Scottish ancestor who was instrumental in helping King Malcolm escape from Macbeth by forking hay over him.

The drawing-room - with its Georgian frieze and Gothic alcoves - will eventually be reopened to the public. However, the corner tower - which was completely gutted by fire, its walls blackened, floors gone and open to the sky - may well be left as an insight for visitors into the grim challenge facing Henry Mount Charles and the restoration team.

The castle will reopen on a time-scale dictated by the flow of money available for restoration work. One day, too, Henry Mount Charles is determined that Slane Castle will become a family home again - and the fire in the first-floor drawing-room can be symbolically lit.

OPEN Unlikely to open during 1999. Check (tel. 041-24207) for update.

BEAULIEU

Drogheda, County Louth

Beaulieu is a glorious survivor of the Restoration period - a rare example of the earliest unfortified houses to be built in Ireland. Although it stands at the mouth of the Boyne, just a few miles from the site of the battle of the Boyne, Beaulieu remained untouched.

Previously held by the Anglo-Norman Plunkett family, the land on the river estuary was forfeited for the Plunketts' part in the 1641 uprising and was subsequently purchased by Sir Henry Tichborne, a prominent Royalist commander during the Civil War. Tichborne had held Drogheda against Sir Phelim O'Neill as the Ulster leader of the rebellion marched south.

These were uncertain years for a king's man. Oliver Cromwell landed in Ireland in August 1649, storming Drogheda and massacring 2,000 in September. Following this reign of terror, parts of Louth were designated for redistribution to adventurers, a means of repaying them for monies advanced to finance the Roundhead army. Sir Henry had lived at the Plunkett castle and it wasn't until 1661, the year following the Restoration, that

his son Sir William Tichborne began to build Beaulieu. His family's tenure of the property was confirmed in the 1662 Act of Settlement and the house was completed in 1667, the year that Sir Henry died. Descendants of the Tichbornes have lived there ever since and Mrs Nesbit Waddington is the ninth generation in residence.

Beaulieu is hidden away on a side road near Baltray. The welcoming façade is revealed suddenly, facing the road at the end of a short driveway. The steeply pitched roof is pierced by attic dormers and carries two central moulded chimney stacks. The projecting eaves are borne by a heavy modillion cornice. The seven-bay front is rendered, and dressed in rosy brick imported from Holland, and the front door is surmounted by a curved pediment with exuberantly carved festoons.

The house marks the important transition from defensive to domestic architecture. The modern poky concept of a hall bears absolutely no resemblance to Beaulieu's most impressive feature. Immediately beyond the oak front door is the most breathtaking room, two storeys high, its walls hung with a fascinating collection of paintings. The height of the room is balanced by the scale of the massive chimney piece and overmantel and the room is wonderfully lit by both internal and external windows at second-floor level. The arches above the doorways were adorned in the early eighteenth century with magnificent woodcarving - bristling with weapons and musical instruments, celebrating the achievements of the family - by Sir Henry Tichborne, first and last Lord Ferrard, the grandson of Sir Henry Tichborne I.

The hall was designed as an impressive reception room and is hung, in the manner of the day, with portraits of family, friends and enemies, royalty and landscapes. Two paintings are of special historic interest. One by Van der Hagen over the hall chimney piece shows Drogheda with its walls intact. The other, by Van der Wyck, shows King William, mounted as he was at the battle of the Boyne on a brown charger.

On either side of the hall lie the dining-room and drawing-room. The latter is an exquisite room with original panelling and the heavy bolection moulded cornice typical of the period. The ceiling is inset with a delightful painting, garlanded with plaster leaves and flowers, where cherubs fly through the clouds, giving the illusion of greater height. The small panelled study or library and the later staircase were added by Lord Ferrard, probably to the design of John Curle, architect of Castle Coole. The staircase hall is, like the hall, designed to impress and also features exquisite woodcarving.

Lord Ferrard was the last of the male line to inherit Beaulieu and since then the house has always passed through the female line. Looking out across the garden, with its watch tower and nearby family church, to the broad Boyne estuary, it is easy to see why Sir William Tichborne chose the name Beaulieu ('beautiful place') for his home. The garden is open May to November, Mon.-Thurs. 9am-1pm, except bank holidays and August.

OPEN House open 5 May-16 Sept., except bank holidays and Aug., 9am-1pm; special interest groups by appointment, tel. 041-38557

ADMISSION £4, children £2.

DIRECTIONS Beaulieu is a few miles from Drogheda, just outside Baltray.

Section Six

DUBLINIA

Dublin is extraordinarily blessed in its setting: for all the world like a
northern Naples, with the sweep of Dublin Bay held in the arms of
Killiney and Howth and the Sugar Loaf as Ireland's answer to Vesuvius.
To the south the hazy blue swell of the Dublin mountains marks the
playground for the city; to the west the expanses of the Phoenix Park are
its green lungs and the Liffey is the dull silver ribbon which holds its
history together.

The face Dublin presents to the world is Georgian, with gracious
squares and wide streets of uniform terraces in mellow brick which give
the magnificent stone public buildings all the more impact. Despite the
depredations of developers, the heart of the city, delineated by two
canals - the Grand and the Royal - is fairly intact. But Dublin (literally
'black pool') was originally a Viking town, established by a mix of
Norwegians and Danes during the second half of the ninth century. The
remains of the main Viking settlement on the hill by Christ Church
Cathedral are now buried under the concrete bunker of Dublin
Corporation's civic offices.

The centre of Dublin is quite compact and the majority of buildings
of architectural merit are within easy walking distance of each other.
There is an architectural feast to be had in Trinity College alone, where
the 1759 Provost's House is one of the most fabulous houses in the city
(not open to ordinary visitors, alas). The splendid former Parliament
House, now the Bank of Ireland, is just opposite Trinity College. Dublin
Castle and the City Hall - formerly the Royal Exchange (1769) - are a
five-minute walk up Dame Street. The Custom House by James
Gandon is just down the river.

There is an intimacy and ease of access about the city which is very
beguiling. I used to bicycle to work from what was once the old village
of Harold's Cross down to Abbey Street on the north side of the Liffey
imagining myself passing through layers of history. The route passed
some Dutch 'Billies' - curvy gable-fronted houses built in the late

seventeenth century of the bricks that were introduced by King William
- and wonderful Marsh's Library, built in 1701 by Archbishop Narcissus
Marsh. Then on to St Patrick's Cathedral, where Swift was Dean, built
in 1191 on the site of a fifth-century church, and through Christ Church
Place, where, during the excavation of the Viking site, I saw the close-
packed wattle walls of the traders' streets, the cobblers' still littered with
scraps of leather. Off to the left was the view of High Street, where
there are remains of the medieval walls of the city, and Dublin Castle is
on the site of the castle which King John ordered to be built in 1204 to
strengthen the Anglo-Norman hold on Dublin after Strongbow, Earl of
Pembroke, took the city in 1170. Christ Church Cathedral itself was
originally founded by Norse King Sitric in 1038 and rebuilt by the
Normans after 1170. Between the castle and the Liffey some of the
medieval streets are remembered in names like Fishamble Street and
Winetavern Street. Thomas Read in Parliament Street, the oldest shop
in Dublin, used to be a swordsmiths, no doubt supplying blades for the
notorious duels of the eighteenth century. The name of Abbey Street
recalls St Mary's Abbey, founded by the Benedictines in 1139, the most
powerful of the abbeys which ring Dublin.

It was terribly tempting to make detours on that bicycle ride, to
discover more about fascinating buildings like the house belonging to the
Sick and Indigent Roomkeepers' Society and Tailors Hall in Back Lane,
built for the Tailors' Guild in 1706 – just the tip of the iceberg of history.

The present character of Dublin only began to take shape after the
Restoration of Charles II, when the Earl of Ormonde returned from
exile in France, inspired by European architecture, to become Viceroy.
He gave the city its first great classical building – the Royal Hospital
Kilmainham (by Sir William Robinson, 1680), inspired by Les Invalides
in Paris – set aside the Phoenix Park as a deer park, and had the first of
the quays built beside the Liffey. St Stephen's Green was also laid out at
this time for the recreation of Dublin citizens.

After a century of war, the battle of the Boyne in 1690 established
peace, prosperity and a new Ascendancy – composed of Old English,
Old Irish who had given up Catholicism in the face of the Penal Laws,
English grantees, and those newly rich from land speculation and trade.
People wanted town houses to be close to the source of power. The city
began to expand rapidly from 1730, fuelled with money from the
landowning classes, new aspirations to style and a mood of

enlightenment. Major public buildings were undertaken, like Parliament Buildings (1729), and great town houses were built, like Leinster House (1745) and Charlemont House (now the Hugh Lane Municipal Gallery, 1762). The Wide and Convenient Streets Commission was established in 1757 to oversee the development of the city and grand streets and squares were laid out, mainly developed by the Gardiners on the north side of the city and the Fitzwilliams on the south side. Henrietta Street, Sackville Street, Mountjoy Square and Merrion and Fitzwilliam Squares took shape. Behind the plain façades of Georgian houses, with their characteristic doorways and fanlights and symmetrical twelve-pane windows, the elegant proportions of the rooms and the exuberant stuccowork gave interiors their impact.

In 1801 the passing of the Act of Union, abolishing the Irish parliament, took away the *raison d'être* for Dublin's elegant town houses. From then on the importance of the city waned. Development continued but never in the same cohesive way - many of the finest Victorian buildings in Dublin are institutions or public buildings like the Shelbourne Hotel or Heuston Station. The advent of the railway and public transport encouraged a move to the healthier suburbs and further afield to the villas of south County Dublin and County Wicklow. The Victorian and Edwardian terraces and squares kept the tone set by Georgian Dublin, with regular façades and front doors approached by granite steps.

By the start of the twentieth century the once magnificent town houses on the north side of Dublin had become teeming tenements, their rooms subdivided. Houses on squares and once gracious streets were converted into offices; some fell to developers and others became mere reproduction façades. The few remaining great estates of County Dublin have become islands surrounded by suburbia. But now that the tide of conservation has turned, appreciation of Dublin's great legacy can be seen in projects like the magnificent restoration of number 85 St Stephen's Green, in the re-creation of a typical Dublin eighteenth-century home at number 29 Lower Fitzwilliam Street and in the acquisition by Fingal County Council of properties like Newbridge and Ardgillan.

There are many different Dublins to be explored - medieval, Restoration and Georgian Dublin, the literary Dublin of James Joyce and O'Casey, religious Dublin, the Dublin of benefactors, official Dublin and, of course, the open houses of Dublin; and not forgetting the pubs.

On the literary trail there is the Shaw birthplace - the modest terraced house at 33 Synge Street, wonderfully evocative of a 'shabby genteel' Victorian upbringing - and the Dublin Writers Museum, in a striking house with a magnificent first-floor salon at 18/19 Parnell Square (open all year, Monday-Saturday, 10am-5pm; June, July and August open to 6pm; Sunday 11am-5pm). The first-floor drawing-room of number 82 Merrion Square is decorated just as it was when William Butler Yeats lived there.

One could found a tour on Joyce alone, following not only the odyssey of *Ulysses* but Joyce's own life: Belvedere House with its wonderful Adam interiors in Great Denmark Street, where he was a pupil (which is still a school); Newman House at numbers 85 and 86 St Stephen's Green (two of the finest Georgian buildings; number 85 is now magnificently restored), where Joyce was a BA student; and the Joyce Tower, the setting for the opening of *Ulysses*, now a Joyce Museum (open April-October, Monday-Saturday, 10am-5pm; Sunday 2-4pm). The door of number 7 Eccles Street, the fictional home of Leopold and Molly Bloom, is in the James Joyce Centre at 35 North Great George's Street (open all year, Monday-Saturday, 9.30am-5pm; Sunday 12.30-5pm). One of my favourite memories was the Bloomsday privilege of hearing the passage from Joyce's *A Portrait of the Artist as a Young Man* describing the family row over Parnell at Christmas dinner read in the very house it describes. 1 Martello Terrace in Bray is open from 2-4pm on Tuesdays and Thursdays. Number 20 Lower Dominick Street - built by Robert West in 1775, with one of the most magnificent plasterwork interiors - was once lived in by Sean O'Casey and is now the headquarters of the National Youth Federation.

Dublin's benefactors financed their buildings in all kinds of ways. Dr Bartholomew Mosse was responsible for the 1750 Rotunda Lying-In Hospital for Dublin's poor (before London had its first maternity hospital), designed by Richard Castle. The chapel has wonderfully appropriate plasterwork by Bartholomew Cramillion featuring Faith, Hope and Charity amid bands of plump cherubs. The attached Assembly Rooms, which were intended to finance the hospital, became a fashionable fundraising venue, and events included the first performance of Handel's oratorio 'Judas Maccabaeus'. The hospital is still very much in use.

The Iveagh Market in Francis Street and the striking redbrick Iveagh buildings just beside Christ Church Place, designed to house and help

Dublin's poor, were financed out of Guinness fortunes by the 1st Earl of Iveagh. A little ironically, the Iveagh Market is being redeveloped as a yuppie shopping experience and the Iveagh baths are to become an up-market health club. Dr Richard Steevens left his fortune to his twin sister Grizel and for the building of a hospital after her death. Grizel decided to keep an eye on things while she was still in the land of the living and Dr Steevens's Hospital (now the headquarters of the Eastern Health Board) was begun in 1721 to the design of Thomas Burgh.

Sometimes the least known of houses are the most rewarding. Henrietta Street (just behind the Law Society) was the grandest of all the Dublin streets, and number 12 is now being gradually restored, an ongoing process with all the fascination of an archaeological dig. Less known than it deserves to be perhaps, being slightly off the beaten track, is the Marino Casino, for me one of the most breathtaking pieces of architecture in Dublin. This miniature palace was built for the 1st Earl of Charlemont, designed by Sir William Chambers: a most perfect expression of the Age of Enlightenment. Drimnagh Castle, once in danger of demolition, dates back in part to the sixteenth century and has a wonderful great hall (which can be booked for festive events). It is the only castle left with a river-fed moat.

Visiting the houses of God, particularly Dublin's early churches, can be uplifting in the architectural sense. The chapel in the Royal Hospital Kilmainham has the most magnificent Carolinian ceiling, decorated with secular-looking cabbages, carrots and pumpkins. The way into Werburgh's Church, just beside Dublin Castle, is mysteriously through the door into number 8 Church Street. The baroque style church may have been designed by Thomas Burgh in 1716. The interior, dating from 1759, is original and the wonderful carving by Richard Stewart is still in place; ditto a royal coat of arms above the Viceroy's pew. Idealistic Lord Edward FitzGerald, one of the leaders of the 1798 Rebellion, is buried here.

Also on my church crawl is St Mary's of Mary Street, designed by Sir William Robinson, which has an elegant gallery. It has now become a wallpaper shop, with rolls of colourful paper in place of a congregation. St Michan's, across the Liffey in Church Street, is even more venerable. It is a seventeenth-century church on the site of an eleventh-century one, where Handel is supposed to have played the organ. Mummified crusaders, naturally preserved by the dry, limestone environment, lie on stony beds in the vaults.

There are still precious few open houses in Dublin. There is as yet no breathtaking display of period Irish furniture in the city, and some of the most wonderful interiors which might - given an imaginative scheme - be more accessible are out of bounds to all but the most well-heeled of special-interest groups.

PLACES TO STAY/EAT

Dublin has been dubbed the fun capital of Europe for its vibrant night life, lively arts scene, pub culture and young profile, and has become a very popular destination. For that reason it can be difficult to get accommodation in the high season and it is best to make advance bookings for top restaurants.

Genuine pubs - where the Irish look isn't newly minted - are getting increasingly hard to find. Old reliables where you can get a decent pint include Doheny and Nesbitt's, and Toner's - both on Merrion Row. Also Ryan's on Parkgate Street (with snugs complete with bolts on the doors dating from the time when soldiers from the nearby Collins Barracks entertained ladies there), the Stag's Head on the corner of Dame Lane and Dame Court (full of mirrors and mahogany) and Mulligan's in Poolbeg Street. Outside Dublin, on the edge of the mountains at Glencullen, Johnny Fox's dates back to 1798 and promises plenty of *craic* and good food, with the emphasis on seafood and entertainment. It is also a historic pub, where Daniel O'Connell held one of the first meetings of the Catholic Association. Two interesting new pubs with great atmosphere and lunchtime dishes like dressed crab are Thomas Read - on the corner of Parliament Street and Dame Street - and the Harbour Master's Bar, beside the harbour in the Financial Services Centre.

Dublin is also now a café society and there is a wonderful choice of establishments offering really good coffee and snacks. Café Java branches and Café en Seine (which, as the name suggests, has a startlingly Left Bank interior and is also a pub) are among newcomers, but the originals are Bewley's 'lofty clattery cafés' on Grafton and Westmoreland Streets.

There is a veritable cornucopia of restaurants to choose from. Stars of the foodie firmament include Patrick Guilbaud's - venerated for wonderful food and the place to take the current partner for an anniversary treat - now situated in Upper Merrion Street, opposite Government Buildings. Also on Merrion Street is relative newcomer, Lloyds, a brasserie-style restaurant. Peacock Alley in South William Street is where vertically presented food has all the panache of a Phillip Treacy hat, and the Tea Room is one of my favourites, situated in a lofty Arts and Crafts style dining-room in the beautifully restored Clarence Hotel.

For great atmosphere and prices that are not in the stratosphere, there are Roly's Bistro in Ballsbridge and any of the Fitzers restaurants (the one in the Royal Dublin Society, Ballsbridge, has a stunning décor, or there is La Stampa on Dame Street with its fabulous former ballroom setting). On the north side, 101 Talbot Street is cheerful and informal, with an Italian menu, and Chapter One, beside the Dublin Writers Museum on Parnell Square, has a special pre-theatre menu and beautifully presented imaginative fare.

For budget eateries look no further than Temple Bar, between the Quays and Dame Street, which has become Dublin's answer to the Left Bank (there is a thoroughly tempting food market there on Saturday mornings), or Powerscourt Town House, originally the Dublin residence of Lord Powerscourt and now a shopping and restaurant centre. For the best ray and chips in town, Leo Burdock's - on the corner of Werburgh Street and Christchurch Place - is the place to go.

Beside the Grand Canal is Thornton's: classy, with a Michelin star, it is a serious contender as the best restaurant in Dublin. Further afield, in Glasthule, Morel's has a thoroughly modern, stylish approach to food with Mediterranean leanings, and, in Dalkey, PD's Woodhouse is delightfully informal, great for barbecue-style dishes and seafood. On the northside the Red Bank in Skerries and the Old Schoolhouse in Swords are established favourites.

New small hotels have been springing up around the centre of Dublin - given the city's appalling traffic situation it makes a good deal of sense to stay either near the centre or on the DART line. Among the options are: the U2-owned, beautifully refurbished Clarence Hotel on the quays (tel. 01-670 9000); Bewley's Hotel on Fleet Street (owned by the same group as the famous cafés); Longfield's, situated in two eighteenth-century town houses in Lower Fitzwilliam Street and named for former owner, Viscount Longueville (tel. 01-676 1367). On Upper Fitzwilliam Street is cosy Fitzwilliam, situated in a typical Georgian terrace (tel. 01-660 0048). The Davenport (in the top price range), just off Merrion Square, incorporates the neo-classical façade of Merrion Hall, a former church (tel. 01-607 3500).

Still within walking distance of the centre is the stylish new Mount Herbert on Herbert Road, Ballsbridge (tel. 01-668 4321). Near the DART line in Dalkey is Moytura House, designed by John Loftus Robinson - one of the Hidden Ireland group (tel. 01-285 2371). Staunton's on the Green deserves points for the restoration of a landmark building beside the Department of Foreign Affairs with a view over St Stephen's Green and the Iveagh gardens (tel. 01-478 2300).

THE SHAW HOUSE

33 Synge Street, Dublin

There are precious few modest houses of the kind that people can easily relate to in this book. However, this is not through any desire to exclude them, but simply because very few are open to the public. That Shaw's birthplace and home for the first ten formative years of his life can now be seen at all is due to a happy chance and to the determination and imagination of two people.

In the mid 1980s Frances and Michael MacCarthy were looking for a house and discovered one for sale in Synge Street. To Frances' great delight the house was next door to Shaw's birthplace.

However, number 33 was in a bad way; weeds grew from the roof, windows were missing and only two rooms were occupied by the reclusive owner. When it became apparent that the house was to be sold the MacCarthys started a campaign to save the house. The house was eventually bought privately by the trust, restored through Dublin Tourism, backed by EU funding, and opened to the public in 1993.

Go down the area steps and into the dimly-lit green-and-brown basement kitchen and you are immediately cocooned in the world where Shaw spent a great deal of time as a child - near the warmth of the range, listening to the stories told by the cook, the maid and the odd-job man, and to the Dublin patterns of speech which were to stay with him for the rest of his long life, most of which was spent in London. Upstairs in the second-floor drawing-room, dominated by a grand piano, was another world - the world of music, which would lay the foundations for Shaw's early career as a music critic.

In 1838, when the single-fronted house was built, there were still only eleven houses in the street, and the surrounding Portobello area would have been considered 'shabby genteel'. Number 33 became the first home of Lucinda Elizabeth (*née* Curly) and her husband George Carr Shaw in 1852. The couple were ill-matched. Lucinda was a talented mezzo-soprano, a young, lively woman who saw in her marriage to an established older man, with a career in the civil service, the means of escaping from her parents, but things never turn out as expected. Carr Shaw was made redundant and bought a half share in a grain mill in Dolphin's Barn which collapsed. From then on he was regarded as a loser and developed a drink problem. It was a loveless house, and the nature of Lucinda's relationship with her impresario, George Vandeleur Lee - who might well have been a model for Svengali - was the subject of speculation.

The Shaws had three children: two daughters, Lucinda Frances, known as Lucy, born in 1853, and Agnes Eleanor (known as Yuppy), born in 1855, and their son George, who was born in 1856. Whatever his other failings, Carr Shaw was very fond of his children and, while his wife went out visiting her friends, he stayed at home and wrote poems and stories for his children, and his story-telling undoubtedly influenced young Sonny (as George was known); another influence was a seafaring uncle who returned home with many spicy tales.

The restored and refurnished house captures beautifully the stuffy Victorian atmosphere of the period: the green-and-red dining-room cum parlour beside the front door where the family ate, young George's austere room in the small back return off the half landing, his sisters' room overlooking the back garden and his parents room above that, filled with the clutter so beloved of Victorians.

The sunny first-floor drawing-room which runs the full width of the house was used for entertaining. The 1840 Broadwood piano took pride of place, surrounded by comfortable seats, and it was here that Vanderleur Lee conducted rehearsals for the amateur musical society and Mrs Shaw and Lucy, who had a fine voice, would entertain the assembled company. Even in such a modest house the upstairs-downstairs division prevailed. There was a maid's room in the basement and the Shaws employed a variety of live-out servants, from nurse to governess to laundress.

OPEN May-Oct., Mon.-Sat. 10am-5pm; Sun. 11.30am-6pm. Closed 1-2pm, tel. 01-475 0854.

ADMISSION £2.50, children £1.30, family £7.50. Tape-guided tour.

DIRECTIONS Synge Street is off the South Circular Road between Harcourt Street and Heytesbury Street.

KNOCKNAGIN

Balbriggan, County Dublin

Ireland is full of forgotten ruins and abandoned homes which only reveal elements of their past to those who care enough to research them. Not alone houses but whole villages and roads can turn to rubble and be swallowed up by undergrowth.

When Richard and Patsy Berney first glimpsed Knocknagin House from the overgrown driveway it was teetering on the brink of dereliction. Trunks of ivy as thick as a man's arm grew on the walls of the room known locally - and, it seemed, ironically - as the ballroom. Ivy also festooned the front of the house, the floors were rotten and damp and rats were at work. Only details like the unusual French windows, complete with external shutters, and the seventeenth-century staircase remained to suggest that this was a building with an interesting past.

What to others might have seemed a nightmare was for Richard and Patsy the dream house they had spent years searching for and, incredibly, the owner was willing to sell. The couple sold everything they had and spent their first three months there living in a caravan as Knocknagin House was reduced to a skeleton. They used direct labour, as no builder was prepared to take on the project, and their morale reached its lowest point when they could stand in the hallway and see stars where two floors and a roof used to be.

Pieces of the history of the three-storey house began to emerge. The oldest part of the house, with its triangular pediment, dated to around 1680. Much later, in the nineteenth century, Knocknagin was owned by a member of the Catholic gentry named Myles O'Reilly, leader of the Irish Brigade in the Papal Wars against Garibaldi. It was O'Reilly who gave the house its continental air, perhaps inspired by his travels abroad, adding wings to the house and dropping and widening the sills to create French windows, complete with external shutters. In rescuing Knocknagin the owners have tried to reinterpret O'Reilly's bold vision for the house, conserving what was best rather than restoring every detail: sweeping away gloomy back passages and a rickety return which had been added at a later date.

Four years on, Knocknagin now has the air of a modest French manor, with an enfilade of rooms - study, dining-room and kitchen - on either side of the flagged hallway. The 'ballroom' - which it transpired really had been used for fundraising dances by O'Reilly - has become an enviable drawing-room with a coved ceiling and French doors leading out onto the paths of a formal garden which Patsy discovered beneath the undergrowth.

But Knocknagin has turned out to be far more than the house itself. The remains of a village - complete with a shop and bakery - and an ancient walled road, thought to have led from the vanished fishing village of Newhaven to Balnascadden, have emerged in the jungle clearance. So too has a culverted stream, a very early outdoor privy built over the stream, an old walled fruit garden and box upon box of broken crockery and old glass bottles. Patsy and Richard intend to reinstate the orchard to the north of the house that was shown on the Ordnance Survey map of 1868 and to restore the two-storey thatched cottage beside their entrance gate. Already Patsy has created a garden full of old-fashioned herbaceous plants in the shelter of a walled farm enclosure. There are plans too to recreate other gardens and orchards in this peaceful setting where the River Devlin ambles to meet the sea.

The Berneys' enthusiasm for the place - which has become part consuming passion, part historical dig - is infectious. Knocknagin is a place where work is still very much in progress, representing a happy marriage of rediscovered past and present.

OPEN May & Sept., 9am-2pm; or by appointment, tel. 01-841 4560.

ADMISSION Adults £3.50, children £1.50.

DIRECTIONS 2 miles north of Balbriggan on the N1, on the left from Dublin.

NEWMAN HOUSE

85/86 St Stephen's Green, Dublin

The twists and turns of history make for some very strange bedfellows. Richard 'Burn Chapel' Whaley, the second owner of number 85 and a vehement anti-Catholic, could hardly have envisaged that the Catholic Church might one day acquire his small palace, dedicated to entertainment, in order to found a university there. Nor could Cardinal Newman, first rector of the University of Ireland, have foreseen that James Joyce, another anti-cleric, would feature the physics theatre of his former Alma Mater as the setting for a passage in *A Portrait of the Artist as a Young Man*.

At the time when Richard Whaley purchased number 85 and the adjoining site on the south side of St Stephen's Green, Dublin was on its way to establishing its reputation as the second city of the English speaking world. Parliament House (now the Bank of Ireland) rivalled any English public building. Splendid town houses like Tyrone House (1744) set the tone for a period when the wealthy built town houses for entertaining and to impress.

Number 85, commissioned by Drogheda landowner Captain Hugh Montgomery in 1738 and attributed to Richard Castle, seems to have been designed almost exclusively with those functions in mind. The dignified panelled entrance hall leads to a sumptuous staircase hall and is adjoined by the Apollo room, one of the most beautiful examples of plasterwork in Ireland, executed by the Lafrancini brothers Paul and Philip. Apollo occupies pride of place above the mantelpiece, with his nine muses, to provide inspiration for every branch of the arts from music to astronomy, stationed around the walls. Upstairs, the restored saloon, running the full width of the building, prompts a strong desire to lie flat on the floor, the better to admire the pairs of gods and putti in frozen play amid the baroque splendour of the ceiling. The scene represents the theme of Good Government and Prudent Economy, and six pairs of gods exercise their dominion over the prudent management of the elements in the centre of the ceiling.

The room with tall Gothic windows at the back of the house, which later served as the University of Ireland's physics theatre, was a later addition. There were only a few small bedrooms and a rather poky kitchen in the basement, so that the servants would have had to sleep in odd corners around the house.

Richard Whaley began building number 86 in 1765, having found number 85 too small, perhaps on account of the seven children his eighteen-year-old second wife rapidly produced for him. The couple are said to have met when Anne was walking past the house with her father, the Reverend Bernard Ward, and asked a man who she believed to be the agent if she could view the house. When she said that she would love to live there, Whaley revealed his identity and said that she could do so if she would become his wife.

The house, with its exuberant plasterwork by its architect Richard West, was built 30 years later and represents the next chapter in the history of Dublin's Georgian architecture. The most remarkable feature of the building is the staircase hall, adorned with West's signature of beaked predatory birds.

Tantalisingly little is known about the colourful eighteenth-century personalities associated with the two houses. Young Anne's second son Thomas became the infamous eccentric 'Buck Whaley', a member of the Hell Fire Club. Number 85 was left to Bernard Ward and, through that connection, the house became the home of the Earl and Countess of Clanwilliam from 1785, when it became known as Clanwilliam House.

Number 86 was purchased by the Catholic Church in 1853, after the hierarchy had taken the decision to set up a university for Catholics in Dublin. With the expansion of the university, number 85 was bought in 1865 and Newman House took its name from the first rector of the university, the great theologian John Henry Newman. The bishop's room on the first floor of number 86 still retains its Victorian ecclesiastical feel, with ponderous furniture and portraits of stern-faced clerics on the flock-wallpapered walls.

The third floor, with its class-rooms and spartan lecturers' bedsitting-rooms, has changed little since James Joyce studied there. The poet Gerard Manley Hopkins came to the university as Professor of Classics in 1884 and, seeing his austere room, where his coal was rationed to one-and-a-half buckets a day, one can appreciate the conditions which induced the sombre mood of his collection of poems known as *The Terrible Sonnets*. The poet died of typhoid fever in Newman House.

In 1968 the university moved to its new home on the modern Belfield campus and in 1991 an ambitious, ongoing restoration project was begun, under the supervision of architect David Sheehan.

OPEN June, July & August, Tues.-Fri. 12 noon-5pm; Sat. 2-5pm; Sun. 11am-2pm, tel. 01-706 7422.

ADMISSION £2, concession £1. Guided tours, toilets.

DIRECTIONS Situated on the south side of St Stephen's Green.

THE MARINO CASINO

Dublin

One of the greatest architectural treats in the country is, paradoxically, one of the least well known. While just a mile and a half away thousands of visitors flock to Trinity College to see the *Book of Kells*, the Casino is bypassed unseen on the route to the airport, its extraordinary impact masked by trees and buildings.

A miniature masterpiece, the Casino is, on one level, an elaborate architectural trick. What appears from a distance to be a monumental one-roomed cube turns out, on closer inspection, to be an opulent joke, three storeys high, its tiny but exquisitely formed rooms fitted into the space with all the ingenuity of a Rubik's Cube.

Visiting the Casino on one of those rare cloudless days when the sea and mountains turn an indefinable

blue - the exact blue chosen for the Casino's azure-and-gilt dining-room - was an unforgettable experience. The Casino seemed almost to float in the golden light, offering views of Dublin Bay which confirm its role as a belvedere. But the Casino was much more than the centrepiece of the ornamental estate surrounding Marino House (now long gone). It was the embodiment of James Caulfeild, 1st Earl of Charlemont's ideals, inspired by classical civilisation and expressed in architectural symbolism. The Earl used to hold court, reclining on a couch like some latterday Roman emperor, in the Casino's stateroom while supplicants waited in the anteroom outside.

The foundations for Charlemont's passion for neo-classical architecture were laid in the four years he spent in Italy with his tutor, between the age of 18 and 22, as part of a protracted Grand Tour. In addition to amassing a magnificent art collection, Charlemont also became friends with William Chambers - who later designed the Casino - sculptors Simon Vierpyl and Joseph Wilton, and the artist Giovanni

Cipriani, all of whom became involved in his architectural schemes.

On his return from Italy, the Earl was offered Donneycarney House by his stepfather to house his growing collection of pictures and sculpture. James Caulfeild engaged his friend Chambers to enlarge and improve the house - which was renamed Marino - but rather than spend a great deal on the house the Earl concentrated instead on the ornamentation of his demesne, with the Casino in the form of a Roman temple as its principal feature. Almost uniquely, the demesne was without walls - a practical expression of the Earl's liberal views - allowing the public to enjoy the grounds. A true son of the Age of Enlightenment, Charlemont saw himself as wedded to Ireland, committed to its development and culture. He became the first commander-in-chief of the Irish Volunteers, earning him the nickname the Volunteer Earl.

Originally designed by Chambers as a pavilion for Harewood House in England, the Casino was commenced in 1758. However, Chambers did not supervise the building work, being tremendously busy with his British practice, and the role fell instead to Simon Vierpyl. Building work continued for over two-and-a-half decades and the final cost was estimated at £20,000.

The exterior of the Casino has a monumental sculptural quality. The graceful detailing and many ingenious architectural tricks disguise the secrets of the mini-palace which is fitted ingeniously inside. Raised on a plinth of steps guarded at the corners by smiling lions, the principal floors are cruciform in plan with twelve Doric columns supporting the heavy pediment and balustrade. The detailing of the stonework is exquisitely carved, from the frieze of ox skulls and shields to the four gods - Bacchus, Ceres, Apollo and Venus - atop each elevation.

The windows, reaching nearly the full height of the building, give the impression of a single-storey building, but if you look closely at the east window you can see that behind it there are two floors. The massive panelled front door is the biggest leg-pull of all, for the central panel opens as a modest-sized door. The sudden change of scale only adds to the sense of having stepped, like Alice in Wonderland, into a world where the scale is miniature but at the same time everything is wonderfully grand.

Beyond lies the glorious saloon, which has a breathtaking coved ceiling, where the decorative feature of diminishing lozenges is used to give the illusion of greater height. At the centre is a panel with

Apollo's head, set in a sunburst. The blue ceiling surround – the blue used to pick out the acanthus leaves of the frieze – unites the ceiling with the azure walls and offsets the elaborately inlaid floor. There is only a single door in the saloon, suggesting that the space within the ground floor has been exhausted, but concealed beyond Gibbsian doors are two miniature flanking rooms.

Known as the zodiac room and the china closet, these are apparently a his and hers arrangement. The exquisite Lilliputian china closet was originally intended as a bedroom and has a coved ceiling, ornamented with glorious plasterwork featuring agricultural devices, and an elaborately inlaid floor. The zodiac room takes its name from the star signs capering around the rim of a drum set into the ceiling – another device to give a greater illusion of space.

The first floor is dominated by the opulent state room, decorated in gilt and aquamarine. A screen of Doric pillars divides the room: in one half the Earl of Charlemont lay enthroned on his bed, in the other is a reception area with an inlaid floor and a chimney piece in a severe classical design. The state room is flanked by a waiting-room for those wishing to call on the Earl, and a simple bedchamber. The roof, which acted as a viewing platform in fine weather, is reached by a staircase with chinoiserie rails. In the basement the vaulted kitchen with its open fire and copper pans seems almost contemporary in its functional simplicity. By the end of the nineteenth century the Charlemont estate was in decline and after the sale of the estate the Casino fell into disrepair, was taken into State care in 1930 and partially restored, and underwent a major restoration between 1974 and 1984.

OPEN Feb.-April & Nov., Sun. & Wed. 12 noon-4pm; May & Oct., daily 10am-5pm; June-Sept., daily 9.30am-6.30pm (guided tour only), tel. 01-833 1618.

ADMISSION £2, concession £1.50, children £1, family £5. Parking, toilets.

DIRECTIONS Off Casino Park, on Malahide Road, just after the junction with Griffith Avenue.

29 Lower Fitzwilliam Street

Dublin

There is nothing new about the current boom in Dublin house prices. When wine merchant and paper manufacturer David Beatty bought number 29 Lower Fitzwilliam Street from developer and apothecary John Usher, he paid £320 for the house (four storeys and a basement). Twelve years later his widow Olivia Beatty sold it to the banker Mr Ponsonby Shaw for £700. When the house was given to the nation by the Electricity Supply Board in 1991 to celebrate Dublin's year as cultural capital of Europe, it was then worth £1 million. It is probably now worth double that figure.

In the late eighteenth century, Dublin was expanding rapidly on the south side of the city. The Commission for Wide and Convenient Streets was established in 1757, with powers to make new streets in the cramped older quarters of the capital.

The houses depended for their impact on imposing doorcases surmounted by fanlights and on the graceful plasterwork of the entrance hall and principal rooms. Chandeliers, the then extremely expensive wallpapers and window drapes provided the other main decorative features at the turn of the century. The saloon and drawing-room, where guests were received, were always on the first floor, above the noise and smells of the street.

Georgian houses were - literally - an exercise in vertical living. Anyone wishing to return to that lively era would probably not wish to return as a maid of all work. At number 29, the skivvy toiled up and down 87 steps from the bottom to the top of the house carrying turf and imported 'sea' coal from the cellars under the pavement, water - which had been delivered by cart to a tank in the basement - up to the bedrooms, and meals from the basement kitchen to the first-floor dining-room.

Number 29 provides an insight into the comfortable lifestyle of a middle-class Dublin family. Mrs Beatty was widowed shortly after her husband had bought the house in 1794. She had a housekeeper, a maid of all work to help look after her three children and a stable lad to care for her coach and horses. Mrs Beatty reigned upstairs, spending her morning in her third-floor parlour or sulking room, where she breakfasted, wrote letters and embroidered, before going calling or receiving visitors in the afternoon.

The servants' world was the dimly-lit basement, where the day started with raking out and stoking the range. The basement holds examples of the ingenious domestic technology of the age, from washing dollies to bread hasteners to goffering irons.

Number 29 represents a more enlightened approach to the past, but Dublin's legacy of Georgian architecture was not always appreciated. From the 1950s, as Ireland began to emerge from the economic doldrums, speculative builders favoured knocking down what were seen as relics of Ascendancy rule in favour of modern office buildings. The ESB's head office at the far end of the street is a sad reminder of former attitudes.

The exhibition of home life between 1790 and 1820 at number 29 is jointly presented by the ESB and the National Museum, and the reinterpretation of the house was undertaken in consultation with a team of experts, including architect John O'Connell. David Skinner was consulted for wallpapers, Fergus O'Farrell for colour schemes and Sulcar Mouldings of Killarney. Some of the furniture is on loan from the National Museum, other pieces have been lent by private individuals, and paintings have been loaned by the Royal Hibernian Academy. The result is a house furnished in the style of the period 1790 to 1820 with all the period details - like the whiskey rail and petticoat mirror in the front hall (one for bibulous gents, the other for ladies to check for trailing undergarments).

OPEN Tues.-Sat. 10am-5pm; Sun. 2-5pm, tel. 01-702 6165.

ADMISSION £2.50, concession £1. Guided tours, tea room, gift shop, toilets.

DIRECTIONS On the corner of Merrion Square and Fitzwilliam Street.

12 HENRIETTA STREET

Dublin

'Where can we see inside a Georgian house in Dublin?' visitors ask. Tantalised by glimpses of glorious plasterwork beyond the windows of elegant squares, and by imposing doorcases in run-down streets, tourists are curious to know what goes on behind those prim façades. While many of the magnificent public buildings dating from the Hanoverian period (1714-1837) are on view, precious few private houses open their doors to visitors.

The streets and squares, which were laid out mainly between 1730 and 1801 when the Act of Union came into effect (abolishing the Irish parliament), suffered a variety of fates as their fortunes gradually declined and affluent society moved out to the suburbs. Some of the Georgian houses on the north side of the city became teeming tenements, remembered in Sean O'Casey's *Juno and the Paycock* and James Plunkett's *Strumpet City*. Many have been demolished, others fell prey to speculators, and most of the surviving houses are now offices or flats or are owned by institutions. True, there are the Dublin Writers Museum in Parnell Square and the Joyce Centre in North Great George's Street, but neither is furnished as a home; and the excellent 29 Lower Fitzwilliam Street is a reconstruction.

Some of the grandest and earliest of Dublin's Georgian houses are in a small backwater on the north side of the city, with a triumphal arch leading to the King's Inns at the end of the cul de sac. On a palatial scale, the houses in Henrietta Street were built for gentlemen of rank and designed with a very specific purpose. As Dublin grew in importance in the first half of the eighteenth century, it was essential for people of consequence to have a town house in addition to their country seats, in order to be close to the centre of power. The houses were designed for entertaining, for receiving contacts in impressive reception rooms which relied for their impact on magnificent plasterwork, the noble proportions of the rooms and the use of mahogany and other valuable woods. The street was laid out around 1721 when Luke Gardiner, the developer of much of Georgian north Dublin, bought the land which had once been part of St Mary's Abbey. The street was named after the Viceroy's wife, Henrietta, Duchess of Grafton.

Henrietta Street has survived mainly through being 'cocooned in poverty' as Desmond Guinness so aptly puts it in the introduction to his book *Georgian Dublin*. Number 12 Henrietta Street, like its immediate fellows, looks as though it might be empty from the outside. When I visited the house a year and a half before this book was published, the scene inside the front door could have come straight from *Juno and the Paycock*. Bare boards, walls grimy and pitted with knocks from bicycles and sacks of coal, daylight visible through the planks in the landing, banisters wound with wire netting - all contributed to the impression of dereliction.

Until the 1980s number 12 was still a tenement home to ten families. But when it was built in 1730 it was designed as a town house for the first Viscount Mountjoy by Edward Lovett Pearce. In the first-floor

saloon, the grandeur of the house becomes fully apparent. Double mahogany doors divide the two rooms which run the depth of the house; there is an elegant frieze of urns, and the cornice has an egg-and-dart design; the marble fireplace is original to the house. Almost empty and still carrying the marks of the division and subdivision that occurred when landlords packed families into smaller and smaller spaces, the rooms speak more eloquently of the past than any pristine interior.

They also represent an opportunity to understand everything from the use of paint colour and materials to the alterations that have taken place over the years. 'It is like an archaelogical dig,' says the present owner Ian Lumley. Investigation reveals here a patch of red paint dating to 1800, there green paint from 1780, and wood graining, a paint technique sometimes used to disguise humble woods. Lumley adds that it is a mistake to assume that houses remained unaltered after they were built. The house was originally built as a pair to number 11, and at a later stage it was altered and lost a floor so that it is now a three-bay, three-storey over a basement house. The present plasterwork was carried out by Charles Thorpe in the 1780s after the house had passed back to

Gardiner. There are only three bedrooms in number 12 and servants would either have lived out or slept in the basement. There would have been a small formal garden between the house and the stables at the back of the house.

Numbers 9 and 10 on the opposite side of Henrietta Street were also designed by Pearce, for Thomas Carter, Master of the Rolls, and for Luke Gardiner, respectively, and neighbours included arch-bishops, bishops, peers and MPs. After the Act of Union there were lawyers and MPs in the street but by the end of the century each of the rooms was let to a different family. Number 12 is undergoing restoration as time and funds allow and there are plans to use the saloon for receptions.

OPEN 1 May-30 June, Mon.-Sun. 2-6pm. Group tours by appointment, tel. 01-873 4964.

ADMISSION £2.50.

DIRECTIONS Henrietta Street is off the west side of Bolton Street.

DRIMNAGH CASTLE

Long Mile Road, Dublin

There couldn't have been a better place to go for a Sunday outing with a four-year-old godson, armed for the occasion with breastplate and sword and full of glee at all the things a genuine castle can offer, from murder holes to moats. The small door in the great wooden gate set in the curtain wall creaked open in a satisfactorily spooky manner and our small knight was given a great welcome and the promise of knights to remember within.

The castle is tucked away in an unlikely spot behind the Christian Brothers' School on the Long Mile Road. Amazingly, it is still surrounded by a deep moat, fed by the River Camac, and is probably the only castle left in Ireland to have its original moat. The core of Drimnagh Castle dates back to the early thirteenth century and was built by the Norman Barnewall family on extensive lands granted to them by King John which included Terenure and Ballyfermot.

Such grants were systematic and part of the wider plan to secure the Anglo-Norman hold on Ireland, and particularly the rich land to the west and north of Dublin within the 'Pale' (the area where the English monarch's rule applied), by placing strong barons or knights on the land with a responsibility to build castles and keep men at arms. The Anglo-Norman adventurers who overran Ireland in the wake of Strongbow's 1170 invasion used their superior strength to sequester the best land. The Irish warriors armed with slings and stones were outmatched by the Normans with their chainmail armour, their archers and military strategies. The wood and earth of motte and bailey castles which the Normans used to defend their new territory was rapidly replaced by stone castles – the great castle at Trim dating from 1200 is one of the earliest – and villages grew in their protective shadow.

Of course, things did not work out quite as planned, the Anglo-

Normans intermarried with the Irish, adopted many of their customs and became Hiberno-Normans. They rebelled on occasion and in 1641 the 'Old English' joined forces with the 'Old Irish' to form the Catholic Confederacy. However, the Normans were a tenacious lot: the legacy of Norman names and straight sharp noses still persists and a few are still on their original lands.

Dubliners are lucky to have a castle on their doorstep and if it had not been for the concern of local conservationists Drimnagh might be just another ruin. The Barnewalls' tenure lasted for 400 years. The last people to live there were the Hatch family, who ran a dairy farm. In 1954 the bachelor Hatch brothers donated the property to the Catholic Church; the Christian Brothers took over and lived in the castle while a new school and accommodation were built. After they moved out in 1958 the castle declined and nearly thirty years later was in danger of demolition. A plan was put forward by conservationists in 1986 for the restoration of the castle, a committee was set up and an imaginative FÁS scheme with an international training exchange programme was set in motion. Five years later, the castle, restored using traditional methods of craftsmanship, was opened to the public.

The oldest part of the limestone castle is the rectangular keep, dating to the early thirteenth century. Typically this would have been surrounded by a bawn or walled enclosure with towers at the corners. The adjoining battlemented tower with lookout posts is sixteenth century, the drawbridge was replaced by a stone bridge in the 1780s and the wing was built in the last century.

The entrance to the castle proper is via a narrow door with a murder hole above it for pouring boiling liquid or hurling projectiles on attackers. The door opens directly into the undercroft, a low dark room lit by arrow slits with a vaulted ceiling of lime-washed wattles. Spiral stone stairs lead up to the splendid great hall, two storeys high, with a magnificent oak-beamed roof copied from the one at Dunsoghly Castle, another Pale castle, dating from the fifteenth century. The ends of the supporting beams have been carved with delightful heads, commemorating some of the key individuals involved with the project, carved in the manner of medieval characters. Peter Pearson, the conservationist, is portrayed as a crusader!

Here the Barnewalls would have sat at meat before a great log fire, its smoke escaping through a central hole in the roof, known as a *fumerelle,* which was adorned with the Barnewall Falcon. The chandeliers were donated from the film *Excalibur* and the reproductions of medieval floor tiles were copied from St Andrew's Church, Swords. The buffet for displaying silver vessels and the great stone fireplace are probably from the seventeenth century. The bawn of the castle has been turned into a seventeenth century parterre and there is also a collection of rare breeds of ducks, hens and geese at the castle. The castle is for hire (a wedding feast in the great hall would be memorable)

and Christmas carols by a roaring fire are an annual event.

OPEN April-Oct., Wed., Sat. & Sun. 12 noon-5pm, or by arrangement.

ADMISSION £1.50, concession £1, children 50p. Toilets, parking, herbs for sale, guided tours, tel. 01-450 2530.

DIRECTIONS 5 km from the city centre on the Longmile Road, Dublin 12.

MALAHIDE CASTLE

Malahide, County Dublin

Malahide is described as the most distinguished of all Irish castles by Mark Bence-Jones in *Burke's Guide to Country Houses*, the bible of big houses in Ireland. It is certainly the castle with the longest (virtually) continuous occupation by one family. The Norman Talbot family owned Malahide for almost 800 years, from 1174, when Richard Talbot was granted the lands by Henry II, until 1976. It also has the only surviving medieval banqueting hall.

Every so often a character emerges among the previous inhabitants of open houses who I would really like to have met. Milo Talbot, 7th Baron Malahide, seems just such an individual. He intended Malahide, together with its unique collection of historic contents, to be donated as the official residence for the Irish Taoiseach. (There is currently no official residence.) It was not to be. Milo Talbot died unexpectedly in 1973 before any decision was taken, and the Irish government insisted on collecting death duties rather than Malahide, effectively forcing the sale of the contents of the castle.

Dublin County Council acquired the castle in 1976. Some of the furniture was bought back by Bord Fáilte and the National Gallery acquired 35 portraits from Malahide's wonderful collection. Important pieces of Irish furniture have also been added to the contents.

The exterior of Malahide has a Georgian Gothic appearance, cloaking the castle's early medieval heart. Reached by a spiral stone staircase from the hall is the oak room, its panelling elaborately carved with biblical scenes and now darkened to black. Over the fireplace a Flemish carving depicting the coronation of the Virgin is said to have vanished during the years of the Cromwellian regime when the Talbots lost Malahide to Miles Corbet, a signatory to the death warrant of Charles I. Following the

Restoration, Corbet was hung, drawn and quartered for regicide and the Talbots, unlike many other Catholic landowners, had their property restored to them. The family remained Catholics until the late eighteenth century and probably used the oak room as a chapel during penal times.

The great banqueting hall dates from the reign of Edward IV and had a minstrels' gallery added in the nineteenth century. Among the portraits of the Talbots and their allies hangs a picture of the battle of the Boyne from the National Gallery. The Talbots were staunch Jacobites and, according to family legend, fourteen male members of the family breakfasted in the great hall on the morning of the battle and none returned.

The library has the most magnificent seventeenth-century Flemish wall hangings in leather, painted with stylised exotic flowers. Two particularly spectacular rooms are the Georgian drawing-rooms, both painted an unusual orangey red which proves a successful foil for the collection of portraits lining the walls. These rooms are situated in the west side of the castle, which was rebuilt in 1760 when the earlier seventeenth-century section was burnt, and have rococo plasterwork featuring the signature birds of stuccodore Robert West.

Among the familiar Irish personalities in the collection of paintings are Jonathan Swift by Charles Jervas, his love Hester van Homrigh by P. Hussey, Wolfe Tone, the Liberator Daniel O'Connell by G. Mulvaney, and Carolan the blind harper by F. Bindon.

The gardens created by Milo Talbot are also open and the Cyril Fry model railway exhibition is housed in the castle yard.

OPEN April-Oct., Mon.-Sat. 10am-5pm; Sun. & bank holidays 11am-6pm; Nov. & March, 2-5pm, tel. 01-846 2184.

ADMISSION Adults £3, children £1.65, family £8.25, group rates available. Shop, tea room, guided tours, toilets, parking.

DIRECTIONS Malahide is 14 km north of Dublin via the Malahide Road.

ARDGILLAN CASTLE
Balbriggan, County Dublin

The Reverend Robert Taylor had wonderful vision in his choice of a site for his new home, which was completed in 1738. Aptly named Mount Prospect, the house was sited at the top of a heavily wooded hillside with a magnificent view across the sea to the Mourne and Cooley mountains.

Thousands of visitors now enjoy the same prospect, thanks to the imagination of Fingal County Council, which acquired a necklace of old estates around the outskirts of Dublin - including nearby Newbridge House and Malahide Castle - with the twin aims of conservation and recreation.

The story of the Taylor family's origins in Ireland is an interesting illustration of social mobility in the seventeenth century. Thomas Taylor came to Ireland for professional reasons, to work on the enormous undertaking of the Down Survey under Dr William Petty. The survey was to be a key factor in Cromwell's plantation policy under which land was to be redistributed to his soldiers, in lieu of back pay, and to the adventurers who had advanced him money (the total debt amounting to a then staggering £3.5 m).

But many of the soldiers and adventurers had no desire to try the risky business of farming. Thomas Taylor saw his opportunity to capitalise on the situation and bought Irish land cheaply from ex-soldiers and adventurers, amassing an estate of 21,000 acres. He continued to prosper following the Restoration, holding a number of public appointments culminating in Treasurer of War. His son, another Thomas, consolidated the family fortunes, and Thomas's son Robert followed a career in the Church. Robert bought the lands at Ardgillan, directing the building of the classical bow-fronted mansion with two flanking wings himself and paying his labourers 1p a day.

In most houses one personality looms larger than most, and at

Ardgillan the diaries of Marianne Harriet St Leger, who married clergyman Henry Edward Taylor in 1807 at the respective ages of 27 and 39, bring the upper-class lifestyle of the period vividly to life. The couple made many changes to the house, changing the name to Ardgillan Castle, giving it the fashionable Gothic treatment, adding battlements to the wings and an additional storey and crenellations to the bow front to give it the appearance of a round tower.

Marianne was a lively character, fond of travel, theatre, sea bathing and horse riding. Her diaries record the life at Ardgillan, the births of her seven children, and visits to concerts and plays.

The Taylors travelled frequently and spent part of each year in England. They took their daughters on the Grand Tour of Europe. The family were part of the Dublin Castle set and took part in the social life which revolved around the Viceroy, including 'bringing out' their daughters during the 'season'. Henry Edward died on one of their continental trips at the age of 82. After she was widowed Marianne continued to live at Argillan until her death in 1859. Her son Edward, an MP for Dublin from 1841, was a Tory government Whip for seventeen years. He inherited his uncle's property, Dowdstown, and

his brother Robert inherited Ardgillan, but the two exchanged inheritances and Edward carried out a number of improvements to the house and grounds of Ardgillan. By the time his son Edward Richard inherited in 1883 the whole pattern of land ownership had begun to change - through successive Land Acts - and a considerable portion of the Taylor lands were sold. Many of the Protestant Ascendancy left, the number of Protestants falling by over forty per cent between 1911 and 1926. Richard and Gwen Taylor were the last of the family to live at Ardgillan. They returned from Singapore intending to sell the house and return to the East but were overtaken by the events of the Second World War. Ardgillan was eventually sold in 1962 and became the holiday home of a German family until 1982, when the property was purchased by Dublin County Council.

The castle has now been restored, and furnished with loans of eighteenth- and nineteenth-century furniture. The house still retains something of its Victorian atmosphere.

The battlemented silhouette of Ardgillan looks like a castle, but in reality the house is a manor - with two storeys over a basement - wearing a Gothic cloak. The central three-bay block has a three-storey tower in the centre, and the wings, with towers at either end, have pointed Gothic arches over the windows. The entrance is now at the side of the castle, so the impact of stepping through the front door into the spacious Gothic hall divided by two Gothic arches is lost. The gold drawing-room has elaborate stencil work and adjoining it is a small conservatory. The dining-room has intricately carved oak panelling by the Italian brothers Guardocici, dated 1889, featuring the Taylor family crest. The library shelves also date from this period and cost £57 10s from Pim Brothers of Exchequer Street.

The gardens at Ardgillan, including the rose garden, green-house and four contrasting gardens within the walled garden, have been beautifully restored and re-created.

OPEN April-Sept., Tues.-Sun. & public holidays 11am-6pm; Oct.-March, Wed.-Sun. 11am-4.30pm. Gardens open all year, 10am-5pm, tel. 01-849 2212.

ADMISSION £2.75, concession £1.75, family £6.50. Tea room, guided tour, toilets, wheelchair access, parking.

DIRECTIONS Signposted from the N1 via Balrothery.

RATHFARNHAM CASTLE

Rathfarnham, County Dublin

For years the sight of the shabby top of Rathfarnham Castle used to prompt in me a mixture of curiosity about the building and concern for its future. Now the exterior is pristine, frosted with limewash, and the interior, bare save for glorious plasterwork, speaks eloquently of a previous age of elegance.

The fortified house was built in the sixteenth century for Adam Loftus, on lands confiscated from Milo de Bret following the Desmond Rebellion of 1583. Loftus was an ambitious Yorkshireman who started his career as chaplain to the Earl of Sussex and went on to become Bishop of Armagh, first Provost of Trinity College, Archbishop of Dublin and, finally, Lord Chancellor of Ireland.

In its day, the rectangular castle with four flanker towers was the grandest house in Dublin, with eighteen hearths listed in the hearth roll of 1664. Later, the building was made grander still, but not before a great deal of family scandal and intrigue had occurred. The castle passed through the Loftus line to Viscount Lisburn, who was killed during the siege of Limerick while fighting for William of Orange. His daughter Lucia, who was married to the Duke of Wharton, inherited the castle, but her son the Marquess of Wharton incurred such massive gambling debts that it had to be sold.

The property was sold back to a cadet branch of the Loftus family, to Nicholas, 2nd Earl of Ely. The 1st Earl had been extremely cruel to Nicholas, holding him as a semi-prisoner. Understandably, the lad was traumatised, making him a bit odd, and when Nicholas's father died his mother's family, the Rochfords, tried to have Nicholas declared insane. His uncle, Colonel Henry Loftus, successfully defended the unfortunate young man and when Nicholas died two years later he left the Colonel his estate in gratitude. Now extremely wealthy,

Colonel Henry determined to employ the best talent money could buy to enhance his home.

First William Chambers (architect of the Casino Marino) was engaged and he was involved in the addition of a dining-room and ballroom. Perhaps the two did not hit it off, for next Colonel Loftus commissioned James 'Athenian' Stuart, who designed a suite of the most exquisite neo-classical rooms on the first floor and a picture gallery on the ground floor. The rooms are the only example of Stuart's work in Ireland, apart from the Temple of the Winds at Mount Stewart; all his major commissions were in England. 'Athenian' Stuart was one of the first architects to popularise design inspired by classical Greek - as opposed to Roman - architecture. He got his sobriquet from his influential volumes, *The Antiquities of Athens*.

When Henry Loftus died the estate passed to his nephew, Charles Tottenham, who assumed the name of Loftus and became the 1st Marquess of Ely in 1801. But by 1837 the castle lay empty and the 2nd Marquess of Ely was planning to demolish it and sell off the land in lots. Instead, it was bought by Francis Blackburne, another Lord Chancellor of Ireland and also Vice Provost of Trinity. Latterly the house was in the hands of the Jesuits, who used the ballroom as a chapel, built a robust wooden staircase and put paintings of religious subjects in the panels of the gallery ceiling where once there may have been paintings by Angelica Kauffman. The castle has been in the care of the Office of Public Works since 1987 and is now open to the public, with the restoration work partly completed.

The front door leads directly into a low-ceilinged hall flagged in limestone. The walls are adorned with six medallions of classical heads - among them Cleopatra with an asp and Lucrezia with a dagger - and divided with a half-screen of pairs of Corinthian pillars.

Upstairs, the ballroom is monumental in its scale and execution. The Venetian window is flanked by pairs of Corinthian pillars and the room is partially divided by a screen of matching pillars. Off the ballroom is a charming little octagonal room, probably used as a cabinet or library, the plasterwork featuring a design of bows, arrows and quivers. The room is supposed to be haunted by the young woman whose body was found entombed in a cupboard there - possibly after two young men shut her in and then mutually destructed in a duel. The intrepid Mrs Blackburne had the corpse's silk dress made into cushions.

The greatest joy at Rathfarnham is the enfilade suite of small rooms, the earliest adorned with wonderfully crisp rococo plasterwork of roses and garlands. The other two are to the design of Athenian Stuart. One is in gilt and white with a central star and circles filled with classical martial symbols, its coffered surround filled with flowers and lozenges. The other is in strong golden shades with painted panels inset in the design of circles and squares.

The ongoing restoration of the castle by the OPW, under the aegis of Dúchas - The Heritage Service, with the attendant insights into the successive layers of the building's architectural history, has provided enough fascinating data to keep architects, archaeologists and art historians busy for years to come.

OPEN Mid April-end Oct., daily 10am–5pm, tel. 01-493 9462.

ADMISSION £1.50, children 60p, family £4. Tea room, hot and cold lunches, toilets, parking.

DIRECTIONS Just beside Rathfarnham village.

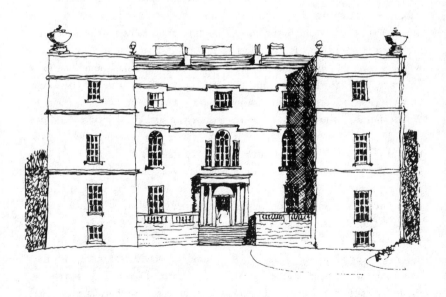

NEWBRIDGE HOUSE

Donabate, County Dublin

To visit Newbridge is to see a Georgian country house at its best. The house is approached by a long curving drive through the original landscaped parkland, probably laid out by Charles Frizell in the mid eighteenth century, inviting - as it was always intended to - admiration of the pleasing façade in its harmonious setting of trees and pasture.

Unlike so many historic houses where the contents have been auctioned, robbing the homes of much of their character and meaning, Newbridge is complete with its original eighteenth-century furniture. In 1986 the house and its contents passed directly from the Cobbe family, who had lived there for 250 years, into the care and ownership of Fingal County Council. And thanks to a unique arrangement, the Cobbes still use their ancestral home on occasion, giving the house that special, indefinable feeling that comes with continuous occupation.

Charles Cobbe started out modestly enough in Ireland, arriving in 1717 to take up the post of chaplain to his cousin the 2nd Duke of Bolton and Lord Lieutenant of

Ireland. However, he rose rapidly through the ecclesiastic ranks, becoming Bishop of Kildare in 1732 and Archbishop of Dublin in 1746. Three years after becoming a bishop, he asked his good friend, leading architect George Semple, to design a fitting residence for him on land he had purchased in the previous decade at Newbridge.

Newbridge presents a most welcoming aspect, due partly to the warm rose colour of the ashlar facing and to the regularity of the architectural features, which give the house a doll's-house like appearance. The bishop's classical house was on a relatively modest scale - two storeys over a basement, with a tripartite doorway, flanked by two windows on either side and approached by a wide, shallow flight of steps. The house was not considered quite grand enough by the bishop's daughter-in-law Lady Betty Beresford, sister of the 1st Marquess of Waterford. (Considering the grandeur of Curraghmore, the Earl of Waterford's seat at Portlaw, she may have felt a bit upstaged by her sister.) A large wing was added to the back of the house after the bishop's death in 1765, chiefly to accommodate the spectacular drawing-room, which also doubled as a gallery for her husband Thomas's growing collection of old masters.

The drawing-room reflects the changing taste of successive generations: whereas the earlier bishop's rooms are panelled with heavier, dignified detailing, the drawing-room ceiling has lively rococo plasterwork by Richard Williams, its elaborate curlicues a counterbalance to the richness of the paintings and furnishings. The room was redecorated in 1828 with crimson damask wallpaper, matching curtains and a red carpet.

The handsome entrance hall is flagged in black-and-white stone and dominated by the pedimented chimney piece, which carries the Cobbe family coat of arms - a device of two swans and the motto *Moriens Cano* ('Dying, I Sing'). Typically for the period, the entrance hall, which was used for receiving callers, has very little furniture and the architraves have shoulders characteristic of the early Georgian period. The library, formerly the drawing-room, has a baroque ceiling with plasterwork depicting the four seasons dating from the earlier period.

If ever there was a room where one would long to have been a fly on the wall in the past, the Cobbes' museum of curiosities must be a contender. Started by an imaginative member of the family in the 1790s, the room contains display cases full of all manner of memorabilia from the Cobbes' travels. The room was used to entertain visitors while the Cobbes recalled the colourful adventures connected with the different objects, ranging from Indian daggers to a stuffed crocodile.

A visit to Newbridge now offers a wonderfully complete insight into the self-sufficient lifestyle of a big house. The kitchen and laundry have been restored and are equipped with all the domestic implements, from wooden scales to knife polishers. The outbuildings, walled garden and farmyard - complete with animals - also afford a picture of the hive of eighteenth-century rural industry.

OPEN Tues.-Fri. 10am-5pm; Sat. 11am-6pm; Sun. & bank holidays 2-6pm, tel. 01-843 6534.

ADMISSION £2.85, children £1.55, family £7.75. Guided tours, tea room, shop, toilets, parking.

DIRECTIONS Turn off the M1 for Donabate beyond Swords. Newbridge is signposted from the main road.

SIX OF THE NINE COUNTIES

Antrim, Armagh, Derry, Donegal, Down, Fermanagh

T he old Kingdom of Ulster was literally a place apart. The province originally included not only Derry, Antrim, Down, Armagh, Tyrone and Fermanagh, but counties Donegal, Cavan and Monaghan as well. Physically cut off from the rest of the island by lakes, bogs and dense forests - until these were exploited for timber in the seventeenth century - Ulster had only three access routes: from Ballyshannon, Enniskillen and through the Moyry Pass below Newry. The Gaelic way of life persisted there longer than in the rest of Ireland, until after the final defeat of the Gaelic order in 1601.

The effects of the plantation of Ulster that followed the Flight of the Earls have reverberated ever since, and different patterns of settlement and styles of architecture can be clearly seen. Plantation happened differently in different parts of the country. A small private settlement by Scottish adventurers Hamilton and Montgomery in 1606 brought thousands of Presbyterian Scots in its wake, who rapidly spread out into Down and Antrim and other counties. With just 13 miles between Ireland and Scotland, the Scots had been settling in Ireland for centuries.

In James I's 1610 plantation, County Derry was settled by the wealthy City of London Guilds (hence Londonderry), and counties Donegal, Armagh, Tyrone, Fermanagh and Cavan were settled by high-ranking undertakers, servitors (generally soldiers allocated smaller estates) and the Irish. Now part of southern Ireland, but connected by only the narrowest strip of coast near Ballyshannon, County Donegal in particular has more in common historically and architecturally with the other northern counties.

There are fewer grand houses in the north. Most of the properties open to the public are under the aegis of the excellent National Trust, and those that are - like magnificent neo-classical Castle Coole, Ardress, the tall-roofed plantation house, and The Argory, frozen in an 1890s time warp - are memorable. There is a heritage scheme like the one in the south, which encourages private houses to open to the public, but so far very few houses are involved. Tourism and conservation are extremely well organised in all seven counties, so that there is a huge amount to see and do.

Part of the fascination of the north is the sheer variety offered, in an area no bigger than Yorkshire. To the south-east there is the dramatic eruption of the volcanic Mourne mountains, dominated by Slieve Donard, which contrasts with a demure landscape of rounded drumlin hills (one area is aptly known as the Basket of Eggs). There is an inland sea, in the shape of Lough Neagh, source of that great local delicacy - eels. Totally different again is island-dotted Strangford Lough, with the arm of the Ards peninsula stretched lovingly around it (anyone who has seen the film *December Bride* will know just how beguiling the scenery is).

To the north are the Glens of Antrim, nine in all, each with a different story attached to its name, contrasting with dazzling silver beaches like White Park Bay and Portstewart Strand. The incredible basalt columns of the Giant's Causeway in County Antrim are one of the eight wonders of the world and the Fermanagh lakelands are one of the relatively undiscovered delights of the north. There is the added dimension of water travel, especially exciting since the Erne and Shannon complexes were joined so that it is now possible to sail from near Ballyshannon down to Limerick, by river, lake and canal.

A northern upbringing has given me a store of childhood memories connected with heritage. There were bicycle trips to the Giant's Ring - Ireland's answer to Stonehenge - a 600-foot circle of standing stones near Shaw's Bridge in Belfast, steamy encounters with Turner's magnificent Palm House in Belfast's Botanical Gardens, and I even lived for a while in the medieval fishing port of Ardglass near Jordan's Tower, the home of merchant Simon Jordan, one of several castles there. My paternal grandmother was a great one for poking about in old houses (an enthusiasm I seem to have inherited) and I remember picnic trips to the bluebell wood of the Saintfield House (1750) demesne in County Down and to the derelict Adamesque rooms of ruined Mount Panther (1770) at Dundrum.

ROUND AND ABOUT

Given the small scale of Ulster, it is possible to see a great deal in a short space of time. Starting from the border, there is the option of turning east at Newry for enchanting Derrymore, a sophisticated example of the *cottage orné* style. Nearby Bessbrook is an interesting Victorian model village, but also sadly the site of a British army base. At Mullaghbawn Folk Museum there is a reproduction of a traditional thatched farmhouse.

Armagh was St Patrick's choice for his principal church in the fifth century. Built of 'Armagh marble', the city was the birthplace of eighteenth-century architect Francis Johnston, who was responsible for many of the principal buildings. It is also the home of the famous Observatory. In the Archbishop's Palace stables there is an exhibition reproducing life in 1776. Outside the city is Navan fort, base of the Kings of Ulster for 800 years.

In County Tyrone there is another estate village at Caledon, near Caledon House, one of the finest Georgian houses in Ireland, designed by Thomas Cooley in 1779 (not open, alas). The park there was laid out by Dean Swift's friend, the Earl of Orrery. Gosford Forest Park, with a mock Norman castle and walled garden, also has associations with Dean Swift. The Argory is in a pretty stretch of countryside overlooking yet another Blackwater River.

Armagh is known as the Orchard of Ireland. The Orange Order was founded in 1795 at Loughgall in the heart of apple country (there is a display centre in the high street) and nearby Ardress, at Moy, has an idyllic setting among apple orchards.

In Mourne Country drives to the Silent Valley lakes and along by Carlingford Lough, via Rostrevor, around the foot of the mountains are recommended. Tollymore Forest Park is a fine ornamental estate, created by Lord Clanbrassil, with Gothic follies - including one to the memory of his friend the Marquess de Monthermer.

Heading for the Fermanagh lakelands, the hinterland of the Erne complex has some wonderful scenery and the two rival stately homes, Florence Court and Castle Coole. One of the best ways to explore - and to see places like Devenish Island, with its abbey and perfect twelfth-century round tower, the park at Castle Archdale (1773, now a ruin), and Crom ornamental demesne, laid out in 1838 and the setting for

Crom Castle (1611) and a Tudor revival mansion - is by boat (there are some wonderful self-catering former estate houses there). Places of architectural interest and ruins in Fermanagh include: Enniskillen Castle, once a Gaelic stronghold; Castle Balfour, a 1618 plantation castle in Main Street in Lisnaskea; Tully Castle, a fortified 1610 castle near Derrygonnelly; and Harry Avery's Castle. The Ulster American Folk Park near Omagh is beautifully done and shows the 1813 birthplace of Thomas Mellon, who emigrated to Pittsburgh and became the richest man in the world, and the eighteenth-century home of Rocky Mountain pioneer Robert Campbell.

The birthplace of US President Woodrow Wilson is near Strabane and the Wilson family are happy to show callers around. In County Derry the seventeenth-century manor house, Springhill, near the plantation town of Moneymore, is one of my favourites, for its air of serenity and relative simplicity. The lovely Sperrin mountains, stretching from Strabane to Limavady, were the childhood territory of poet Seamus Heaney.

In Antrim the ruins of Dunluce Castle, precariously perched on a rocky clifftop (so precariously that the kitchens fell off into the sea), has to be the most spectacular sight in the north. It was built between the fourteenth and seventeenth centuries by the McDonnells. Running a close second for me, though, is the Mussenden Temple, built in 1785 on the edge of the cliffs, to serve as a library for the eccentric Bishop of Derry, Frederick Hervey. The Temple is in the care of the National Trust and is open April to September, 12 noon-6pm. The bishop also became Earl of Bristol and travelled so much that the Bristol hotels were named after him, while the Temple was named after a cousin, Mrs Mussenden, of whom the bishop was very fond. His nearby palace, Downhill Castle (1770s, by architect Michael Shanahan), is in ruins.

In humble contrast is the Hezlett House, a seventeenth-century thatched former rectory. It is furnished in Victorian style (open afternoons April-September), and is situated on the A2 north-west of Coleraine. Near Ballymoney is Leslie Hill, a 1760 house (two other Leslie houses feature in this book) which is open to groups by appointment and is set in an estate with lakes, gardens and rare ornamental breeds of beast and fowl (open April-September, 2-6pm, tel. 08012656-66803). At the other end of the county the Irish Linen Centre, in Market Square at Lisburn, gives an insight into the industry that helped to fuel Belfast's Victorian prosperity (open summer-September, Monday-Saturday 9.30am-5.30pm; Sunday 2-5.30pm, tel. 0801846-663377).

For years the Troubles overshadowed the fascination of Derry city - with its beautiful position on the Foyle and its historic walls. Beside the Foyle, just where the infamous boom was sited during the Siege of Derry, is Regency Brook Hall, where the arboretum is open by appointment to groups (tel. 0801504-351297).

Whenever I am away from Ireland I get, not so much homesick, as Donegal sick, especially for the hillscapes and seascapes of the Fanad peninsula. There are some of the loveliest (and emptiest) beaches in the world in Donegal - the miles-long Portsalon strand facing the cliffs and mountains of Inishowen, the double sickle bays at Melmore, some of the most spectacularly wild scenery around Horn Head, Rosguill and Glencolumbkille. There are also satisfying mountains like the Derryveagh and Bluestack ranges. The combination of house and gardens and the National Park make Glenveagh Castle and nearby St Columb's the perfect place for an outing. Also in the area are the Lurgyvale traditional thatched 150-year-old cottages.

En route from the north to Glenveagh, just outside Lifford on the Letterfrack Road, there is seventeenth-century Cavancor House, where James II dined during the siege of Derry. The house is also the birthplace of US President James Knox Polk and there is a tea room and craft shop there (open Tuesday-Saturday afternoons, Sunday 2-6pm, tel. 074-41141). History is very visible in Donegal, in its plantation villages and castles and dramatic ruins like Doe Castle - the Mac Suibhne fortress built beside the sea at Creeslough. There is also Dunfanaghy Workhouse (1845), where there is a Famine exhibition (open all year, tel. 074-36540), or the ancient ringfort, Grianan of Aileach - on top of Greenan mountain, near Burt on the Inishowen peninsula - and the pre-Christian monuments at Glencolumbkille, the retreat of St Columcille.

The county is known for its tweeds; McNutt's at Downing's and Magee's in Donegal town are recommended, and Ardara is also a happy hunting ground for tweeds and knitwear. Donegal has done a great deal to develop visitor attractions in a sympathetic way and these range from the award-winning Lakeside Centre at Dunlevy, once the home of the famous weaver Manus Ferry, to the Folk Village at Glencolumbkille.

An alternative place to start a tour of the north would be from County Down and Belfast, touring through the Mournes (some of the best scenery is beside Carlingford Lough and around the Silent Valley). Dundrum is one of the finest Norman castles in the north, dating from 1177 (open April-September, Tuesday-Saturday 10am-7pm; Sunday 2-7pm). On the Lecale peninsula - where Downpatrick has many associations with St Patrick, including the Struell Wells - there are also the ruins of Inch Abbey, founded by John de Courcy in the 1180s on an island in the Quoile River.

The Ards peninsula is fascinating and offers a trio of houses, Castle Ward, Mount Stewart and Ballywalter Park, with the excitement of a voyage between them across Strangford Lough, sailing between the attractive villages of Strangford and Portaferry. At Grey Abbey there are the ruins of a Cistercian abbey founded by Affreca, wife of John de Courcy.

Belfast has become a fun place to shop and to eat and has a fine legacy of Victorian buildings. Not to be missed is the wonderfully ornate Crown Liquor Saloon in Victoria Street, the Palm House and tropical ravine in the Botanic Gardens. Just outside of Belfast there is the Ulster Folk and Transport Museum, Hillsborough - ten miles south of Belfast, with its market house, Georgian town houses and 1650 fort - and Carrickfergus, with John de Courcy's great castle.

PLACES TO STAY / EAT

At country guest-house Tempo Manor, near Enniskillen, I was tantalised. Sarah Langham was out when I called by chance, but I could glimpse fascinating Victorian interiors, overlooking beautifully landscaped lakes and gardens. The 1863 house is in Victorian Jacobean style and the park is believed to be the setting for Maria Edgeworth's *Castle Rackrent* (tel. 0801365-541450).

Cookery these days is about fashions. Franco's, on the old waterfront, Queen Elizabeth Road, Enniskillen, is a happy mix of Irish and Italian (tel. 0801365-324424). At Streeve Hill in the grounds of Drenagh, an 1837 mansion by Charles Lanyon, Peter and June Welsh are continuing the tradition of hospitality that they established at Drenagh. A gourmet dinner and views of parkland and the Sperrin Mountains are part of the charm (tel. 08015047-66563).

On the Antrim coast at Ramour you will find all kinds of foodie delights, from fresh asparagus in season to truffle oil, featuring on the international menu, near the harbour at Portrush (tel. 0801265-824313). Views of the Mourne mountains, a lush secret Japanese garden, a cross-country riding course and gourmet cooking are just part of what makes David and Sally Corbett's creeper-clad Georgian mansion, Tyrella House, near Downpatrick in County Down, appealing (tel. 0801396-851422). The Northern Ireland Tourist Board have an excellent guide to self-catering accommodation, which ranges from a remote converted shepherd's cottage to a converted eighteenth-century barn. Send an SAE for a free copy to NISCA, Carlton Cottages, Belleek BT93 3FX.

Focusing on Belfast, foodies should not leave without lunching or dining at Michelin-starred Roscoffs in Shaftesbury Square, for the kind of truly original dishes that you tell your friends about for months afterwards (tel. 0801232-331532). Nick's Warehouse, near St Anne's Cathedral, has a great atmosphere and equally good food, cooked by Nick and Cathy Price (tel. 0801232-439690). There are interesting pubs tucked away in Belfast's characteristic 'entries', or laneways. Among the oldest are seventeenth-century White's Tavern in Winecellar Entry.

In Mourne country, friends recommend Mario's Italian Restaurant in Newcastle (opposite the Harbour Bar), The Briars Country House on Tullymore Road (tel. 08013967-24347) and Maple Leaf Cottage, Bryansford, for teas and evening casseroles.

Quite the most wonderful dinner and wine I have ever enjoyed was at the Egon Ronay listed Castlegrove Country House (eighteenth-century) on Lough Swilly; a new accommodation wing has recently been added (tel. 074-51118). Informal, lively and original, the Yellow Bittern in Rathmullan is another favourite (An Bonnán Buí, tel. 074-58453). Rathmullan House Hotel has an incomparable setting just beside the shore, where the Earls and their 99 followers took flight in 1607.

In south Donegal on the shores of Lough Eske is a unique 120-year-old garden, where rare rhododendrons create 60-foot high canopies of bloom. In their midst is Ardnamona, a Victorian fishing lodge now run as a Hidden Ireland guest-house by Kieran and Amabel Clarke (tel. 073-22650). In north Donegal you can dine on the terrace and look out over Portsalon strand to Inishowen, surrounded by a beautiful garden, at John and Kay Deane's purpose-built award-winning guest-house (tel. 074-59548).

BALLYWALTER PARK

Newtownards, County Down

The fate of houses often hangs on chance - never more extraordinary than in the case of Ballywalter Park. If the poet John Betjeman had not come to tea with the 4th Baron Dunleath, while on a visit to Belfast, Ballywalter Park might well have been condemned to be dismantled as an undeserving Victorian white elephant.

Thanks to the poet's great enthusiasm for the building, one of the finest examples of the mid nineteenth-century Italianate palazzo style in Ireland was saved. Ballywalter Park was designed by leading architect Charles Lanyon around 1846 for linen tycoon Andrew Mulholland and has a magnificent setting on the Ards peninsula. The main block incorporates an earlier 1810 house called Springvale, which

had belonged to a family called Matthews.

The front of the house has three storeys over a basement, the central block balanced by single-storey wings, their windows framed by Corinthian pediments. The *porte-cochère* is flanked by tripartite windows and supported by pairs of Doric columns. The back of the house has six bays, while the wings have projecting bays. Beyond the north wing is a later addition containing a billiard room and terminating in Lanyon's magnificent domed conservatory - which so entranced Betjeman. This is executed in stone, its long windows flanked by Corinthian columns.

The palazzo style was a new architectural fashion at the time: an appropriate choice for the *nouveaux riches* in that it did not attempt to ape existing aristocratic houses, being neither classical nor - like revival castles - baronial. It also belonged to the new era of comfort and convenience and was built specifically with the needs of family and guests, and the army of servants required to service them, in mind.

Beyond the mahogany panelled entrance hall is the sumptuous great hall, which dominates the centre of the building. Two storeys high and sixty feet long, the hall is lit from above by two ornate glass domes. The gallery is carried on Doric columns and the first storey is adorned with porphyry pilasters and niches with classical statuary. The staircase, which is of white marble with an ironwork balustrade, rises at one end of the hall behind a screen of columns. The other end of the room was used as a saloon and a picture gallery at first-floor level. The principal rooms are arranged around the great hall. The library, with magnificent pedimented mahogany bookcases installed by Andrew Mulholland's son, the 1st Lord Dunleath, and the bow-ended music room, with its collection of keyboard instruments and elaborately coved and coffered ceiling, occupy one wing.

It was a house designed for entertaining, and house parties were frequent occurrences. The 2nd Lord Dunleath, Andrew Mulholland's grandson, having added an extra service wing for an indoor staff of up to twenty, further extended the building in order to put up a visiting team during his cricket week. In the mid 1890s Ballywalter had its own electric house - the first of its kind in the north - complete with its own steam engine powered generator.

The fortune that built Ballywalter Park came from two apparently unrelated events. One was the invention of mechanised linen spinning, the other was the advent of the American Civil War, which cut off raw cotton supplies and created a boom in Belfast's linen industry.

The early history of the Mulholland family is a little obscure, but records show that Andrew Mulholland's father started up a cotton spinning business which was continued by his sons. Their mill was destroyed by fire in 1828 and they later switched to linen, introducing power spinning to Ireland for the first time using a new wet spinning technique. Profits soon exceeded their wildest dreams and the brothers' mill became the biggest of its kind. The Mulhollands' growing fortunes went hand in hand with social advancement and civic responsibility. Andrew Mulholland became Lord Mayor of Belfast in 1845. Andrew's heir, John, wisely diversified the family interests. He became an MP for Downpatrick and was created Baron Dunleath in 1892.

This century has seen many changes in the style of life at Ballywalter Park. At the turn of the century there were some forty staff; now there is virtually none. The 3rd Baron Dunleath had been in favour of reducing the house to its pre-palazzo size by removing the top storey and demolishing the conservatory and additions. Fortunately, he got no further than halving the size of the Cricketers Wing before Betjeman persuaded him that the house would, within a few decades, become a mecca for architectural enthusiasts.

His son, the 4th Baron, waged battles - which he won - against dry rot, which insidiously broke out with horrible regularity. Then, in 1974, a major fire threatened to engulf the house, but, though the damage was immense, that too failed to destoy Ballywalter Park. The 4th Baron restored the hall and state rooms, but died in 1993, shortly after work on the ballroom was completed.

Now a major refurbishment programme is underway to breathe new life throughout the mansion. Charity functions and film location work have, to an extent, replaced the glittering Edwardian house parties, as the Lord Dunleath of today, the 6th Baron, adjusts the role of his vast architectural treat to modern life. However, although the house is open - by appointment - to the public, it remains in private ownership, a living entity, and wonderfully preserved. In addition, the recently modernised listed gate lodge, only 100 metres from the beach, is available for self-catering holiday lets throughout the year.

OPEN By appointment only, tel. 08012477-58264.

ADMISSION £3.

DIRECTIONS Go from Newtownards towards Portaferry, turn left at Greyabbey. At end of main street turn right, after 1 km turn right again, immediately before gate lodge, into Ballyatwood Road. Gates on left after 500 yards.

THE ARGORY

Moy, County Armagh

The lion mask glaring above the shallow fanlight of The Argory's imposing front door suggests that this is a house with a difference. And so it is. From the high drama of the entrance hall to the insight afforded into comfortable Victorian lifestyles, aided by the ingenuity of a burgeoning industrial age, The Argory is fascinating.

Although the classical grey ashlar block house was completed around 1824, the interior of the house - which was home to four generations of the McGeough Bond family - reflects the cosy family life of upper middle-class Victorians. Complete in every detail - from the acetylene lighting system to the billiard table, with its original baize covering and accessories - the house seems as though frozen in time a century and a half ago.

It seems evident that, when Walter McGeough Bond commissioned Arthur and John Williamson of Dublin to design The Argory (the name is thought to be anglicised from the Irish for the 'hill of the garden'), he wanted the very latest in everything for his new

home. The entrance hall is a stunning period piece, dominated by a cantilever staircase with 161 brass uprights (still polished by hand). The walls are painted in a *trompe-l'oeil* Siena marble design and a classical urn on a cast-iron plinth occupies the centre of the black-and-white floor. This feature is in fact an ingeniously disguised heating stove, with a descending flue to carry the smoke away under the floor. The hanging light-fitting was another modern convenience in its day, designed first for oil and later adapted to acetylene in 1906.

Upstairs, in the extensive first-floor lobby, is further evidence of Walter McGeough's passion for the new-fangled, in the shape of a cabinet barrel organ, specially commissioned for the house. The organ, built by James Bishop, came complete with mechanical barrels, and provided the music both for family prayers and for entertainment.

The Argory's drawing-room and dining-room both demonstrate the change in taste which took place in the Victorian era. Previously, furniture had been fairly minimal.

The drawing-room at The Argory is chock-a-block with possessions, from the rosewood grand piano to a desk-cum-needlework table, while the dining-room, with its heavy mahogany furniture, has several ingenious expanding side tables and a warming cabinet: a precursor of the hostess trolley.

The Victorian passion for collecting and for souvenirs is evident throughout the house: a cabinet filled with a fossil collection, watercolours of New Zealand, Tasmanian and European scenes by Mary Nicholas - Lady Bond's mother - and lances carried by Captain Shelton's regiment in the Crimean War. Everyday items also abound: a 1937 copy of the *Belfast Newsletter*, a workbasket, a 1930s gramophone, and Lady Bond's 1920s shoes - adding to the lived-in feel of the house.

Family portraits tell the story of four generations. Walter McGeough Bond built The Argory on land he inherited which was purchased by his great-grandfather, Joshua McGeough (through the foreclosure of a mortgage), in the first half of the eighteenth century. Pictures of Walter McGeough Bond's six children by his second wife hang in the billiard room. The second of the children, Ralph Shelton McGeough Bond, known as Captain Shelton, had a distinguished military career and inherited the house.

Shelton had no children and was succeeded by his nephew, Judge Walter Adrian MacGeough Bond (the spelling of the family name changed at this point, from 'Mc' to 'Mac'), who had already inherited the other family property at Drumsill. He was knighted in 1916 for his services as vice president of the Court of Appeal in 1945. Walter MacGeough Bond's presence lingers. It almost seems as though he might reappear, and add to the pile of letters waiting to be posted beside his desk in the study - the only main room he really used towards the end of his life. He donated The Argory, its contents and endowment funds to the National Trust in 1979, lived in the north wing until his death in 1986 and is buried in the grounds.

OPEN April, May & Sept., Sat., Sun. & bank holidays 2-6pm; June-Aug., daily except Tues. 2-6pm, tel. 00 44 18687 84753.

ADMISSION Adults £2.50, children £1.25. Tea room, shop, toilets, wheelchair access.

DIRECTIONS Take exit 14 from the M1 and follow signs for 5 km to Derrycaw Road. Coaches take exit 13.

ARDRESS

Annaghmore, County Armagh

Orchards of apple trees beside the driveway were laden with ripening fruit when I visited Ardress. The setting for the house and mellow brick farmyard, on top of a drumlin with the Tall River meandering through the home pastures, is beguiling. The house itself, with a sham façade - a simple plantation house at its core - and a grandiose neo-classical drawing-room along-side modest panelled rooms, is an architectural conundrum.

The story of Ardress goes to the heart of the troubled history of Ulster and to a chain of events which began with the Flight of the Earls in 1607, among them Ulster's principal chieftains - Hugh O'Neill, Earl of Tyrone, and Rory O'Donnell, Earl of Tyrconnell. Their withdrawal and the confiscation of their lands was followed by the systematic plantation of Donegal, Tyrone, Derry, Cavan, Armagh and Fermanagh. The Clarke family who built the house in the late seventeenth century came to Ulster in the retinue of Sir Anthony Cope, who was granted lands in Armagh and built a fort at Ardrea. The Clarkes built a modest home, two storeys high over a basement, each floor divided into three. A decade or two later, two wings were added, only one of which survives.

When Sarah Clarke, heiress to Ardress, and her successful architect husband George Ensor decided to make it their main home twenty years after their marriage in 1760, they did not rebuild the house but doubled its size by adding a block, which included a drawing-room with plasterwork by Michael Stapleton, to rival any of the fine houses. His brother John worked as assistant to leading architect Richard Castle, or Cassels. The brothers came originally from Coventry, and George was involved as Clerk of the Works to the Surveyor General in the development of Dublin.

Stapleton would have been a colleague of Ensor's, which explains his undertaking a commission in such a modest house.

In the next generation another George Ensor gave the house its present appearance, adding a wing to one side and a curious sham wing to the other - so that the house looks much wider than it really is - and making it appear more rakishly grand still by adding an undulating parapet topped with urns. The two main rooms from this period were the first-floor library and the dining-room beneath. George Ensor II made good use of the library. A very serious man, who read law and wrote a number of books, including *The Principles of Morality* (1801) and *A Defence of the Irish and the Means of Their Redemption*, he was also against the 1800 Act of Union. The estate passed to a third George Ensor and to two further generations, before the National Trust purchased the house from Captain Charles Ensor in 1960.

The interior of the house offers a quick march through the architectural styles of succeeding centuries. The parlour and the hall and inner hall are typical of the intimate seventeenth-century scale, with panelling, a sturdy brass-bound front door lock and flagged floors. The oak roof timbers in this section are still original and are one of the few surviving examples of the butt-and-purlin system which was introduced to Ireland by the planters. In contrast, the cool elegance of the Stapleton drawing-room, with its classical allusions in the medallions around the walls and mischievous putti stepping out of line, is on a much grander scale.

The house has been filled with period Irish furniture by the National Trust and someone has expended a great deal of energy and enthusiasm on the enchanting farmyard, where there is a display of old farm implements. It is a working farm, stocked with rare old breeds like Plymouth speckled hens and saddleback pigs. There is a potato house, a fowl house, a walled orchard garden, a charming garden featuring old roses and a Tall River walk.

OPEN April, May & Sept., weekends & bank holidays only; June-Aug., daily except Tues. 12 noon-4pm, tel. 0044-1762-851236.

ADMISSION £2.30, children £1.15, family £5.75. Toilets, wheelchair access.

DIRECTIONS Signposted from Loughgall, intersection number 13 on the M1.

ST COLUMB'S

Church Hill, County Donegal

A friend rang the painter Sir Derek Hill recently to invite him somewhere. Derek declined: 'I have to go to the Palace,' he confessed. Derek Hill now lives in London, is wonderfully sociable, gives Prince Charles painting lessons and knows absolutely everyone.

Another side of a life full of variety and contrasts is reflected in his former home, St Columb's, near the remote village of Church Hill in County Donegal. The rust-red former glebe house overlooking Gartan Lough was Derek Hill's home for nearly forty years. Many of his best-known paintings are of the intimate landscape of small fields and hills in this particularly lovely corner of Donegal, and some of his most compelling portraits are of local people.

Originally known as Gartan Glebe, the house was built in 1828 as the rectory for St Columba's (Church of Ireland) and later became a small fishing and shooting hotel for fifty years. Derek first came to the area as a guest of Henry McIlhenny, owner of nearby Glenveagh Castle. Several years later he heard that St Columb's was for

sale and bought the property in 1953. He also took up the position of Art Director at the British School in Rome. From 1954 St Columb's became his home, although he still travelled widely, and that year, in the company of Freya Stark, went on a journey to Anatolia, the first of many trips in pursuit of his interest in Islamic art.

St Columb's is typical of dozens of rectories built in the Georgian period, with a square, almost doll's-house like appearance, a three-bay front, with a fanlight over the doorcase and a half basement. Throughout the house are re-minders of various episodes in the painter's life and objects gathered with the unerring eye of the collector. A sketch by costume designer Oliver Messel provides a clue to Hill's early career, which began with study of stage design in Munich and later Paris, Vienna and Russia. The stairway is hung with a gallery of paintings by the many artists he knew and whose work he collected, including Louis le Brocquy, Italian artists like Renato Guttoso and Dalla Zorza.

The small entrance hall of St Columb's, with its vivid blue walls, immediately signals the highly decorative theme of the house. The walls are hung with Chinese paintings of warriors collected by Hill in Peking, which sets the oriental theme for both the hall and the small morning-room, where Chinese prints are happily married with pieces of bamboo furniture collected in Donegal.

The contents of the green dining-room and lilac drawing-room are a delightfully eclectic mix, ranging from prie-dieu Victorian chairs to Irish Belleek china. Derek Hill shared a passion for the work of Victorian animal painter Sir Edwin Landseer with McIlhenny, and organised a major exhibition of Landseer's work in 1961. Four paintings by the artist hang in the dining-room.

Pieces of Derek Hill's collection of Wemyss ware - the delightful rose-strewn cottage ware made in the Fife Pottery in Scotland up to the 1930s - are scattered throughout the house. For me, one of the most intriguing rooms is the kitchen: its old-fashioned dresser painted in primary colours, its shelves bright with a collection of plates, from spongeware to Staffordshire pieces. The walls are hung with the fascinating paintings of the Tory Island primitives.

The kitchen was Gracie McDermott's domain. A natural cook, Gracie had worked at St Columb's when it was a hotel and became Derek's housekeeper, catering for the guests he loved to entertain, including celebrities like Yehudi Menuhin, who joined a céilí in the kitchen. Derek's portrait of Gracie hangs by the kitchen window. The upstairs rooms are full of patterns and textures. In the Morris bedroom the wallpaper, carpet and curtains are all from William Morris's company.

In 1981 Derek Hill followed the example of his friend Henry McIlhenny of Glenveagh Castle and donated his home, its contents and the garden to the Irish nation. The Glebe Gallery in the former stableyard now houses the Derek Hill collection and hosts touring exhibitions.

OPEN Daily except Fri. 11am-6pm; Sun. 1-6.30pm, tel. 074-37071.

ADMISSION £2. Parking, toilets, tea room.

DIRECTIONS 2 km beyond Church Hill on the Losset road.

DONEGAL CASTLE

Donegal Town, County Donegal

D onegal town always seemed to me exotically different from other provincial towns. There was the distinctive Diamond in the centre, the mark of a plantation settlement, and there was the mysterious honey-coloured stone façade of ruined Donegal Castle. The castle seemed all the more intriguing since it incorporated two clashing traditions: the Gaelic tower house built for the first Red Hugh O'Donnell around 1474, and the manor house built for Elizabethan planter Sir Basil Brooke in 1623.

The two buildings, joined in an L shape, make two very different statements: one tall and defensive with devices to repel attackers - from murder holes to musket loops to machicolated towers to arrow slit windows; the other a serene

Jacobean manor house, an aspiration for more tranquil times with style and comfort the main considerations.

The O'Donnells were powerful, independent chieftains, and the four-storey tower house, built on the site of an earlier castle overlooking the River Eske, would have been their chief stronghold and a major symbol of their lordship over south-west Donegal. The massive square keep is typical of the tower houses built both by the descendants of the Anglo-Normans and the Gaelic chiefs from the second half of the fifteenth century. These towers were the successors to castles after the gap in major building that occurred from the first part of the fourteenth century due to the Great European Famine, the Black Death and invasion.

Square, four to six storeys high, usually with a single chamber on each floor and often with corner towers containing stairs or a *garderobe* (a combined privy and closet for clothes where urea fumes were supposed to have a 'dry cleaning effect'), they were the typical residence of gentry in the fifteenth and sixteenth centuries. The first floor was used as a hall for communal living and dining and the upper floor for private chambers.

The tower house was also the home of Red Hugh O'Donnell II, proclaimed The O'Donnell in 1592, last chief of Tyrconnell and ally of Hugh O'Neill, Earl of Tyrone, who rebelled against Elizabeth Tudor in defence of the Irish way of life and whose defeat by Mountjoy at Kinsale in 1601 spelled the end of the old Gaelic order. Hugh O'Donnell died in Spain the year following Kinsale and his heir Rory O'Donnell sailed with O'Neill in the Flight of the Earls in 1607, partially destroying his castle before he left.

The stage was set for the 1610 plantation of the Earl's territories, counties Donegal, Tyrone, Derry and Armagh. The O'Donnell lands were forfeited and Captain Basil Brooke was given a grant of lands which included the Borough of Donegal and Donegal Castle in 1611. Having arrived with the English army in 1598, Brooke was later appointed a servitor of the Ulster plantation.

Captain Brooke subsequently modified the castle, incorporating it into his new manor house, adding gables to match the gabled front of the house, installing fine fireplaces, mullioned windows and a bow window. Chimney stacks and corner turrets were also added to the castle and the complex was protected by a walled bawn with a tower at one corner and a gatehouse at another. The property remained in the Brooke family for several generations before becoming derelict in the eighteenth century. Eventually the then owner, the Earl of Aran, placed it under the guardianship of the Office of Public Works in 1898.

In 1996 Donegal Castle was reopened after a major eight-year restoration programme funded by the EU. The interior of the castle is now furnished as it would have been in the seventeenth century, with period pieces, Persian rugs and French tapestries. In the great hall barrels of wine, boars' heads and stuffed pheasants set the mood for feasting. Of particular interest is the seventeenth-century secular sculpture and an elaborate chimney piece with the Brooke and Leicester coat of arms. There is an interpretative exhibition which links life at Donegal Castle, the O'Donnells and the Brookes with the march of history.

OPEN June-Sept., 9.30am-6.30pm daily, tel. 073-22405.

ADMISSION £2, OAPs £1.50, children £1. Family ticket £5. Guided tours, car park, toilets

DIRECTIONS In the centre of Donegal town.

GLENVEAGH CASTLE

County Donegal

Set in bleak isolated splendour beside the brooding waters of Lough Beagh, Glenveagh Castle looks like the feudal stronghold of some medieval baron. But, like a mini Balmoral, the castle is Victorian, the final fling in the fashion for remote highland sporting retreats. Despite its lack of antiquity, the castle has a colourful history, combining elements of Irish tragedy and American glamour.

Built by land speculator John George Adair in 1870 to the design of his cousin John Townsend Trench, the castle was a crown for his achievements and a home for his new bride, wealthy American widow Cornelia Adair. The story of John Adair's relationship with the locality is anything but romantic, however, and he was involved in an infamous land eviction, the last in Ireland. He made his fortune in buying up bankrupt estates via the Encumbered Estates Court after the Famine, before establishing his Donegal estate. He then embarked on a plan to introduce black-faced sheep on the mountains - land where tenants had previously grazed their cattle - resulting in bad blood, which escalated to the point that

Adair imagined a local conspiracy and tragically evicted 47 families, despite a national outcry.

No sooner was the castle completed than the couple began to spend most of their time in America, where Adair had interests in ranching and brokerage. After his death in 1885, his widow returned to Glenveagh and enhanced the stark castle by planting shelter belts and developing the grounds. She also entertained in the grand manner.

The castle's American connections continued with Henry McIlhenny, the last private owner. In a sense, McIlhenny was coming back to his roots: his grandfather had emigrated from Donegal and made a fortune, through his invention of the gas meter and business concerns in commodities and utilities. When the family businesses were sold off, Henry McIlhenny was able to pursue his parents' interest in fine arts as a full-time career, studying fine art at Harvard before joining the Philadelphia Museum as curator of Modern Art. His widowed mother, Frances, rented Glenveagh in the 1930s, and both mother and son fell in love with the wild beauty of the place. McIlhenny purchased the Glenveagh estate, with the castle as a setting for his growing art collection, in 1937.

From 1947, after serving with the Pacific fleet during World War Two, McIlhenny began to spend every summer, from May to October, at the castle. His return would signal the start of a social season in that corner of north-west Donegal and his presence acted as a catalyst, encouraging others, including the artist Derek Hill, to settle in the area. In 1984 McIlhenny donated Glenveagh to the nation, having already sold the lands to the State, and returned to Philadelphia, where he died unexpectedly in 1986.

Today Glenveagh remains as though awaiting his return and the arrival of the guests - including celebrities like Greta Garbo - he loved to entertain. The tradition of filling the rooms with flowers - McIlhenny would arrange no fewer than 74 vasefuls each week - is still kept up, and some of his staff are still cooking for appreciative visitors.

The house is furnished with the mainly Georgian and Victorian Irish pieces he loved to collect, and his collection of Landseer copies and engravings hang in the dining-room.

McIlhenny's reign re-created all the luxury of an Edwardian house party. There were picnics in the glens, complete with silver service, ladies breakfasted in bed and guests gathered in the drawing-room for drinks.

The castle's main features are a square battlemented keep, based on an Irish strong house, and a round tower and battlemented wings added later by Mrs Adair. The two principal reception rooms are the drawing-room, overlooking the lake, and the dining-room. The most original rooms are the tower rooms.

However, Glenveagh now seems a particularly blessed spot. The surrounding National Park ensures that the landscape is completely unspoiled. Visitors leave their vehicles in a screened car park and are shuttled to the castle by minibus, where the combination of house and gardens make for a thoroughly satisfying visit.

OPEN Easter to first weekend in Nov., 10am-6.30pm, tel. 074-37088.

ADMISSION £2, OAPs £1.50, family £5. Restaurant, visitor centre, castle, tea room, guided tours, walks, toilets.

DIRECTIONS Glenveagh is about 13 km from Churchill on the R251.

MOUNT STEWART

County Down

Mount Stewart is Ireland's answer to Vita Sackville-West's Sissinghurst Castle. Its situation - where the narrow arm of the Ards peninsula reaches around the coast of County Down to enclose Strangford Lough - is unique. The warm breath of the Gulf Stream gives the area a sub-tropical climate to bless the magnificent gardens which Edith, Lady Londonderry, created as a foil to the Londonderrys' Irish seat.

The interior of the house is very much as Lady Londonderry arranged it. The rooms, with the strong colours and informal style of the 1920s, still breathe the perfume of flowers from the pot-pourri she made from roses and carnations, and the scent of lilies and perfumed

rhododendrons in the garden drifts through the windows in spring and summer.

Lady Londonderry, known as Circe the Sorceress to her circle of powerful friends, was a remarkable woman. A brilliant society hostess, she was particularly known for her eve of parliament receptions at Londonderry House, glittering affairs for up to 2,000 guests, where the hostess, dripping with family jewels, shone most brilliantly of all. Warm and attractive, she was something of a *femme fatale*, and Ramsay MacDonald and Michael Collins were among the men who fell under her spell. A feminist and formidable organiser, she was the founder of the Women's League and instigator of the inner circle of politicians and socialites known as the Ark. Their animal alter egos (Winston Churchill was Winston the Warlock, Harold Macmillan was Harold the Hummingbird) are celebrated in the stone figures Edith had created for her whimsical Dodo Terrace.

Mount Stewart was Edith's happiest home, and one into which she poured her heart and creative energies, fuelled by the family coal fortune, and in celebration of the rekindling of her marriage.

While Edith's friendships were platonic flirtations, her dashing husband, the 7th Marquess Londonderry, known as Charlie the Cheetah (or more accurately the Cheater), had become involved in a serious long-term liaison. The child of the Londonderrys' rapprochement, Lady Mairi, had a special white-and-silver garden created in her honour as a baby and the house was eventually left to her.

On first seeing the house, however, Edith described it as 'the dampest, darkest, saddest place'. Without the softening effect of the garden, the iron-grey Scrabo stone mansion with its cavernous *porte-cochère,* under a leaden Ulster sky, must have seemed forbidding.

Linen merchant Alexander Stewart, founder of the Londonderry dynasty, purchased estates at Comber and Newtownards, funded by marriage to an heiress cousin, and built the first house on the site, known as Mount Pleasant, in 1744. His son Robert married twice into politically powerful families, continuing what was to become a family tradition of advantageous marriages. He rose through the peerage to become Earl of Londonderry and commissioned leading London architect George Dance to add an elegant wing to the north-west of his father's house, overlooking what is now the sunken garden. His son, another Robert Viscount Castlereagh, became the great politician and statesman who steered Britain through the Napoleonic Wars to victory. Charles, his half-brother, who became the 3rd Marquess Londonderry, married Frances Anne Vane-Tempest, the beautiful heiress to a Durham coal fortune - with the aid of which the pair had grandfather Robert's section of the house replaced by a very much grander version, designed by William Vitruvius Morrison and executed after Morrison's death in 1838 by Charles Campbell.

Morrison echoed Dance's external theme for the house, uniting the long two-storey classical house with a heavy balustrade on the parapet, and adding a giant Ionic portico to replace the original entrance and a pedimented loggia to the centre of the garden front. Inside the house, the difference in architectural styles is more in evidence.

Beyond the entrance lies a dramatic octagonal hall, flagged in black and white, with a gallery supported by pairs of dark-green scagliola columns, designed to display statuary; the room makes an unexpectedly grand statement, in contrast to the more intimate scale of the rest of the house. Against its rather chilly grandeur, Charles Dance's imperial staircase and delicate cast-iron balustrade seem all the more light and graceful. One of the most arresting equine portraits, of the Hambletonian - still raring to go after his 1799 Newmarket victory and baring his teeth at a nervous groom - hangs on the half landing. Equally enchanting is Dance's music-room, in the centre of the west front, with the spiderweb motif of the ceiling repeated in John Ferguson's marquetry floor. The room which most clearly reflects Lady Londonderry's personality is her sitting-room (originally a library by Dance), with a delicate plaster-work ceiling and a bow window overlooking the garden, where Edith would sit, sorting through plant catalogues and seeds and keeping up her flow of correspondence with the key figures of the day and her beloved husband. Of their new daughter Mairi she wrote to him: 'She is a gift of God to us, surely, yours and mine. It is such joy we both have in her, now don't we. The truth is, we should not be separated.'

The drawing-room, divided by two screens of monumental Ionic columns, is in Morrison's more austere style. From 1920, when Charley became a member of the new Ulster government, Mount Stewart became the Londonderrys'

main home. Edith set about renovating and redecorating, making the house a warm and welcoming place for house parties of guests and a place of rest and relaxation for exhausted politicians. Bright colours were introduced, and the clutter was replaced by fine continental pieces. Typical of Edith's attention to detail, the twenty-two chairs from the Congress of Vienna in the Castlereagh room were re-covered with specially commissioned embroidery, with the coats of arms of the participants.

Charley, a keen aviator and Under-Secretary for Air, had an aerodrome built at Newtownards. VIPs were frequently flown in from London and regular guests at Mount Stewart included Ramsay MacDonald, W. B. Yeats, Sean O'Casey, Ribbentrop (during an attempt to promote Anglo-German understanding) and many leading political and artistic figures of the day. They were accommodated in bedrooms named for the principal European cities, from 'Madrid' to 'Moscow'. 'Rome' is a typical example of Edith's taste in décor, with wine-coloured velvet curtains, a baroque bed and blue-and-gilt cupboards.

In the grounds of Mount Stewart is the exquisite Temple of the Winds, an exact copy of the original Tower of the Winds in Athens, built as a banqueting house for the 1st Marquess to the design of James 'Athenian' Stewart (so-called because of his book, *Antiquities of Athens*). The inlaid floor by carpenter John Ferguson and the plasterwork by William Fitzgerald in the upper room repeat an exquisitely delicate cobweb design, and there is a marvellous, swirling spiral staircase.

Edith and Charles Londonderry lie together in Tír na nÓg ('land of the ever young'), the garden created by Edith overlooking the house and grounds. Their daughter, Lady Mairi, donated the house and its contents to the National Trust in 1977.

OPEN Easter & weekends in April & Oct., 1-6pm; May-Sept., daily except Tues. 1-6pm. Garden open March, Sun. only 2-5pm; Oct., weekends 11am-6pm; April-Sept., daily 11am-6pm, tel. 0044-12477-88387.

ADMISSION £3.50, children £1.75, family £8.75. Group rates available. Guided tours, teas, wheelchair access, toilets, parking, shop.

DIRECTIONS On the shore of Strangford Lough, 8 km from Newtownards on the Belfast-Portaferry road.

FLORENCE COURT

County Fermanagh

You have to hand it to eighteenth-century grandees for their unerring instinct in picking the most glorious sites for their increasingly imposing homes. John Cole, grandson of Elizabethan adventurer William Cole, must have become familiar with the beautiful sweep of countryside rising to the dramatic outline of Benaughlin mountain through his involvement in building the new road from Enniskillen to Sligo.

He chose the location some time before 1718 as a fitting setting for a grand house, named for his wife, Florence Bouchier Wrey. He showed all the bravura of his planter class, turning his back on the castles and tower houses of his forebears and laying down walks and opening up vistas around his undefended house.

It took three generations of Coles to complete the present Palladian building. John Cole mark two rebuilt on the foundations of his father's house in the 1750s, aided no doubt by an inheritance of an additional 2,000 guineas a year and spurred by his status as MP for Enniskillen. The Grand Tour undertaken by his son, William Willoughby Cole, provided the classical inspiration for the wings and pavilions. While his father and grandfather probably used architectural design books and collaborated with local builders, Davis Ducart - who was working nearby at the time - is thought to have been the architect for the final phase of the building. Similarly, the interior plasterwork dates from two different periods. The entrance hall, library and breakfast-room are in the earlier baroque style, while the magnificent rococo concoctions of birds, foliage, fruit, waves and shells which were the track-stopping decorative features of the staircase, the upstairs salon and dining-room are in the style of Robert West.

The Cole family fortunes followed a typical rise and decline. The second John Cole became the 1st Earl of Enniskillen. The 2nd Earl also served as MP for Enniskillen and received a baronetcy in 1815. Among the Coles who left their mark were his brother, Sir Galbraith Lowry Cole, whose monument to his generalship in the Peninsular War dominates the Enniskillen skyline.

The 3rd Earl, William Cole, did not follow the family tradition of soldiering, but became a passionate follower of the newly fashionable science of geology. He housed his magnificent collection of fish fossils (now in the British Natural Science Museum) in one of Florence Court's pavilions and - as a precautionary measure - caused the roof above the kitchen to be strengthened with a curious umbrella-like reinforcement. William Cole also carried out many of the improvements to the estate, and the water-powered sawmill, the icehouse, walled garden, thatched summer house and the tilery - all restored by the National Trust - provide a fascinating insight into the self-sufficiency and resourcefulness with which great estates were run.

The 4th Earl continued to represent Enniskillen, while the 5th Earl's son donated the house - by now shorn of its supporting estate - to the National Trust in 1954.

In 1955 disaster struck when the house caught fire, destroying almost two-thirds of the building. The National Trust spent nearly six years restoring the house, and much of the plasterwork - bar the study,

library and dining-room ceilings - is therefore not original. Many of the original contents of the house were returned in 1997. The most interesting is the Irish furniture. Often elaborately carved in mahogany with characteristic shells and animal masks, these pieces illustrate the wonderful imagination and skill of Irish craftsmen.

The basement of the house is open to the public, revealing the subterranean hive where servants serviced the upper floors, scurrying between kitchens, sculleries, lamp room, maids' and china stores, coal cellars, butler's pantry, housekeeper's room, post room, silver room, beer cellar and servants' hall. In the early eighteenth century there were twelve female servants and sixteen male servants, their accommodation strictly segregated, with the men housed in the yard buildings and the women in the house.

OPEN May-Aug., daily except Tues. 1-6pm; April-Sept., weekends & bank holidays 1-6pm. Estate open from 10am daily, tel. 0044-1365-348249.

ADMISSION £2.80. Toilets, parking, tea room, shop.

DIRECTIONS Take the A32 for Swanlinbar off the A4 from Enniskillen to Sligo road.

CASTLE WARD

Strangford, County Down

There are a number of colourful stories about the Ward family of Castle Ward. One concerns a stuffed bear offered in exchange for the hand in marriage of one of the Ward daughters (the offer was accepted). There was also a duel between a Ward and a Hamilton, in which each protagonist mortally wounded the other, and sibling rivalry which resulted in the contents of the house being sold off. But the best known concerns the architectural difference of opinion between Bernard Ward (later Baron Bangor) and his wife, Lady Anne Bligh, daughter of the first Earl of Darnley, which resulted in one of Ulster's stateliest houses being built with a classical front and a Gothic back inspired by Horace Walpole's Strawberry Hill.

The division in styles continues inside the house, which was built between 1761 and 1767, at the then enormous cost of £400,000, to the design of an unknown English architect. The rooms at the front of the house - the entrance hall, library and dining-room - are classical and masculine in style, and the distaff side of the house is as 'whimsical' (as the ubiquitous Mrs Delany described Lady Anne) as the woman whose taste they reflect.

Castle Ward is sublimely situated, overlooking Strangford Lough, with views across the water to the wooded hills and the village of Portaferry on the far side. Bernard Ward laid out the park, its pleasing undulations planted with cloud-like clumps of trees. Bernard could have chosen to live at the Queen Anne house built by his father as a home for his beloved wife, heiress Ann Hamilton - all that is left as a reminder of this house is one of a pair of long ponds in the grounds - but Bernard Ward was socially ambitious, and he inherited at a time when taste in architecture and gardening had changed markedly.

If the Wards wanted to impress, they certainly succeeded. The house has three storeys over a basement, with a seven-bay front and a central pediment carried on two-storey high Ionic columns. In contrast, the back of the house is altogether more light-hearted, with pointed ogee Gothic windows, and pinnacles and battlements adorning the parapet.

The entrance hall is exceedingly grand. The walls and ceiling are ornamented with elaborate plasterwork featuring arms, trophies and farm implements - the plasterwork on the walls is different in quality and was probably the work of local stuccodores from nearby Dundrum. The imposing doorcase leading to the saloon is surmounted by the coat of arms of the 3rd Viscount Bangor and guarded by a screen of scagliola Doric columns. The panelled dining-room is relatively small and the panelling is grained to represent oak. The Gothic saloon has the most elaborate ceiling, with quatrefoils and a fretted cornice. The doorway, mirror and fireplace are in ogee form and even the overmantel has battlements. The most extraordinary room of all is the boudoir, which has Gothic plasterwork billowing down from the ceiling like so many pendulous bosoms, apparently inspired by the vaulting in Henry VII's chapel in Westminster Abbey.

The morning-room is in Lady Anne's Gothic taste, while the staircase hall, with its wrought-iron balusters, is classical in style.

The furniture is not original to the house, as most of the furniture dating from before the 1820s was removed by Robert, third son of Bernard Ward, in a sad episode of the family history. Bernard's heir Nicholas was insane, the second son, Edward, remained at Castle Ward as his guardian on an inadequate allowance, while the third son, Robert, inherited Bangor Castle and estates. Despite this, Robert refused to increase Edward's allowance. Castle Ward fell on hard times and, after Edward died, outlived by his mad brother, Robert took most of the furniture. When Edward's son eventually inherited the estate, it was in a bad way. The estate and title then passed through the male line until, following the death of the 6th Viscount Bangor, the estate was accepted by the Northern Ireland government as payment for death duties, and the house and demesne are now in the care of the National Trust.

OPEN April, Sept. & Oct., Sat.-Sun. 1-6pm; May-Aug., daily except Thurs. 1-6pm. Estate open all year round, tel. 0044-1396-881204.

ADMISSION Adults £2.60, children £1.30, family £6.50. Group rates available. Shop, tea room, parking, wheelchair access.

DIRECTIONS Castle Ward is 2.5 km west of Strangford village on the A24.

SPRINGHILL

Moneymore, County Derry

Springhill is a rare example of a plantation house predating the battle of the Boyne, and a survivor of a particularly turbulent chapter of Irish history. 'Good' Will Conyngham, Overseer of the Woods and Forests of Ulster, began building Springhill early in the 1680s to satisfy the marriage contract drawn up with Anne Upton, which required him to provide a 'convenient dwelling house of lime and stone two storeys high'.

The Conynghams settled in Ireland during James I's plantation of Ulster. Stout Scottish dissenters, they supported Cromwell and William of Orange in turn, and the family owned lands in counties Derry and Armagh. Good Will played a leading part in the defence of Derry during the siege of the city.

The whitewashed façade of the original house built by Good Will has the appealing simplicity of a child's drawing, with the front door in the centre, symmetrical windows and the chimney stacks at the gable ends of the steeply pitched roof. Originally the house was surrounded by a defensive bawn, but this was taken down in the eighteenth century and two barns with Dutch gables were built flanking the forecourt. Beyond them are ranged the herb garden, a walled flower garden, sties, barn, and a bleaching green. Whether it is the modest scale of the place, the scent of musk roses, or the cooing of doves in the dovecot tower, Springhill breathes an enchanting air of peace and tranquillity.

Good Will's house became the hub of self-sufficient industry. Forests were cleared and replaced with orchards and fields of grain, a sawmill was set up to process timber and new trees planted for future generations. Herbs were grown for medicinal purposes and the inhabitants of the dovecot augmented the fare for the table.

The contents are original to the house and tell the story of eight generations of Lenox-Conynghams. The flintlock pistols used by Good Will in the defence of Derry hang in the oak-panelled gun-room. The library - unusual in such an early house - is lined with early calf-bound volumes collected by book-loving Conynghams. And the house is filled with family portraits: Good Will, his nephew William Conyngham - who built the two pavilions flanking the oi house in 1765 - and 'Wims' and Charlotte Lenox-Conyngham, who the dining-room in the 1820.

Part of the charm of Springhill is that you have the feeling walking through the century pass through its rooms. The oak-panelled seventeenth-century rooms and the shallow oak staircase, with its barley-sugar banisters, contrast with the grander eighteenth- and nineteenth-century rooms.

The house is a wonderful tribute to the Conyngham family. William Lowry Lenox-Cunningham gave Springhill, together with its contents at a fraction of their cost, to the National Trust. The house is still peopled with all the characters who made its history and with their possessions. It has been kept up in a sympathetic way, retaining the magic of a well-used and much-loved family home.

The three daughters of William Lenox-Conyngham, Hazzie, Jane and Charlotte, ran a sewing class for the girls on the estate and kept the house supplied with jams and cordials. There are reputed to be two ghosts at Springhill. One is associated with the death of George Lenox-Conyngham, who shot himself in 1816 in one of the bedrooms; the other is thought to be an ancestress who nursed her children through smallpox.

OPEN April, May & Sept., Sat., Sun. & bank holidays & Easter 2-6pm; June-Aug., daily except Thurs. 2-6pm, tel. 0044-16487-48210.

ADMISSION £2.40, children £1.40, family £6. Parking, toilets, shop, tea room.

DIRECTIONS 1 km from Moneymore on the Moneymore-Coagh road.

DERRYMORE HOUSE

Bessbrook, County Armagh

Derrymore House is a delightful example of a *cottage orné*, one of the few, together with the Swiss Cottage in Cahir, to have survived. Intended as an idyllic rural retreat, in the fashion first embraced by Queen Marie-Antoinette at Versailles, it is ironic that the fantasy cottage should have become the scene for a political decision which has caused strife in Ireland ever since.

The house was built some time before 1787 for Sir Isaac Corry, MP for Newry and last Chancellor of the Irish Exchequer. It may well have started life as a thatched manor and have been given the ornamental treatment at a later stage. Marie-Antoinette's Hameau de Trianon at Versailles was built between 1783 and 1788 and the vogue for the picturesque style, with naturalistic

landscaping and rustic buildings featuring thatch and logs, came later to England and Ireland. The Swiss Cottage was built in the early 1800s, but the enthusiasm for idealised peasant architecture never really caught on here, the realities of life in cabins and cottages being only too wretchedly apparent.

The single-storey house is U-shaped, with a bow-fronted centre block, with trefoil windows on either side of the bay linked to two flanking wings, and a thatched roof billowing over the eaves and bays. The mullioned windows reach the ground in some cases, with hooded eyebrow-like moulding over them.

Isaac Corry was a controversial figure, who was born in Newry in 1755, the son of a Newry merchant who represented the town as MP. Like his father, Isaac in turn represented Newry for nearly thirty years, but his policies were not popular in the town. To this day there is a road known locally as the 'Chancellor's Road', which Corry used to bypass Newry on his way back to Derrymore from Dublin. His infamous tax on windows, introduced in 1799 after he succeeded Sir John Parnell as Chancellor, may have had something to do with this.

Corry fought a duel with Henry Grattan. He is most remembered for his involvement in the execution of the Act of Union which came into effect on 1 January 1801, ending Dublin's role as the seat of Irish parliament, removing Irish autonomy and binding Ireland closer to Britain. The Act is meant to have been drafted in the drawing-room and it is this connection which caused the destruction of Derrymore by an IRA bomb, which had more to do with misplaced symbolism than the subtleties of Irish history.

The exquisite drawing-room section of the house, with its coved ceiling, marble fireplace, built-in bookcases, niches for statues and painted chairs, is a reconstruction. The house has an unusual layout, with stone-flagged passageways running round the inside of the U and all the light-filled, gracefully proportioned principal rooms looking outwards.

Corry lost his seat in 1806 and sold Derrymore in 1810, retaining his Dublin property. It was subsequently owned by Sir William Young and then the Quaker Richardson family had the estate from 1859. John Grubb Richardson had taken over the Nicholson linen mills at Bessbrook and had the model village built there. In its heyday, the mills at Bessbrook gave employment to 3,000 and the school, town hall, teacher's house and Friends' meeting house were also built by the Richardsons, who lived in another, larger, house on the property, known as the Woodhouse. The village of Bessbrook, in another ironic twist of history, is now dominated by the presence of a large British army barracks.

The property was donated to the National Trust in 1952. It is also home to the Baillie family, the knowledgeable and courageous custodians of Derrymore, who survived several bomb attacks.

OPEN Easter, daily 2-5.30pm; May-Sept., Thurs.-Sat. 2-5.30pm, tel. 0044-1693-830353.

ADMISSION £1.60, children 80p.

DIRECTIONS 2 km outside Newry on the A25 Newry-Camlough road.

CASTLE COOLE

Enniskillen, County Fermanagh

Were the 1st and 2nd Earls of Belmore to return from the Heavenly House of Lords to visit Castle Coole today, their lordships would find that very little has changed.

Earl number one would discover the cool, classical perfection of the palace he had designed by James Wyatt intact down to the last detail. Even the colour schemes of the rooms remain the same and the fine detail of the Grecian plasterwork is as sharp as ever - for the interior of the house has only been painted three times in the 200 years since it was built, while the furniture specially designed to complement Wyatt's magnificent interiors is still in place.

Earl number two would find his extravagant Regency furniture - including the great scarlet-draped state bed created for an anticipated visit by George IV in 1821 - in situ. The gilt-and-crimson furnishings of the splendid saloon are undimmed and the curved sofas designed for the circular room remain where they were placed on delivery from the Dublin furniture suppliers, Preston's.

The house is a magnificent example of Hellenism, reflecting the late eighteenth-century love affair with classical ideals. The combined effect of the 1st Earl's mansion and the 2nd Earl's furniture is stunning: a perfect period setting for one of Jane Austen's haughtier heroes. 'It is a truth universally acknowledged that a gentleman in possession of a fortune must be in want of a wife', wrote Austen in *Pride and Prejudice*.

Armar Lowry-Corry was certainly in possession of a fortune: by the age of 40 he had inherited three large family estates, totalling 70,000 acres. The £12,000 income generated - approaching £1 million in today's terms - allowed Armar to pursue his political and social ambitions. He was less fortunate in love, however, and his first happy marriage, to Lady Margaret Butler, ended in tragedy, three children and five years later, when Margaret caught her death of cold out riding, having given her coat to a poor woman.

Four years later Armar was smitten by the beauty of young Lady Henrietta Hobart. 'Henrietta has made a conquest of Mr Corry, who is from every account the best match in this kingdom', wrote her father, the Earl of Buckingham. The match furthered Armar's upward mobility, and his father-in-law, the Lord Lieutenant of the day, recommended his elevation to the peerage.

But the marriage (à la Charles and Di) between the 40-year-old country gentleman and the 18-year-old society beauty failed after a year. They separated, and Henrietta began a fling - having fallen for the highland charms of Lord Strathaven. Later, Armar - now Baron Belmore - sensationally divorced Henrietta. He formed a liaison with a woman who lived on the demesne and bore him three children. Lady Louisa, Armar's daughter by Henrietta, continued to live at Castle Coole and her three illegitimate siblings shared the nursery, even after Armar's third marriage in 1794 to Mary Ann Caldwell.

Armar continued to engineer his social rise, extending his political influence by buying up boroughs, and was created Viscount in return for his support of the government.

His elevation to earldom was then certain in due course.

He also devoted a huge amount of energy to building a suitable seat for a peer, determined to outdo the magnificence of his sister's home at Florence Court. He chose a hilltop site, near his earlier house, overlooking a lake with views of the Belmore mountains. He sacked his first architect, Richard Johnston, in favour of James Wyatt. Wyatt's design for a Palladian house with a central block is dominated by a portico with four great Ionic pillars.

The house is of silvery Portland stone - specially shipped from England - and was built between 1788 and 1798 at an eventual cost of £70,000; staggering even in those days. The central block has two storeys and nine bays linked by Doric colonnades to two small pavilions. In 1795 the Belmore estates were settled on Armar's heir, Somerset, when he came of age.

Somerset, like his father before him, lived way beyond his means, spending as much on furniture for Castle Coole as his father had on building it. He maintained houses in London and Kilkenny and on the Isle of Wight. He was a passionate sailor and traveller, maintaining a 32-man brig on which the entire extended family voyaged around the Mediterranean and to Egypt and Syria. Somerset also became governor of Jamaica in 1828, sailing to take up the appointment in his own cutter.

The extravagance of the first two earls left family fortunes straitened and subsequent generations could not afford to put their stamp on Castle Coole, so its interiors remain frozen in time, perfectly reflecting the lifestyle of the Regency period. You can imagine visitors being dazzled by the austere splendour of the entrance hall, dominated by four great porphyry scagliola pillars, or marvelling at the massive elegance and drama of the galleried first-floor lobby, with its classical peat-burning stoves set in alcoves. It seems as though the separate spheres occupied by gentlemen and ladies during the day have only just been vacated. You can picture Lady Juliana, Somerset's wife, at work at her needlework with her companions in the first-floor bow room, and the gentlemen returning from the hunt to smoke and read in the library, where the chimney piece by Westmacott was carved to resemble the drapery of the scarlet-and-gilt pelmets.

It was, above all, a house designed for entertaining, with a sumptuous succession of rooms - drawing-room, saloon and dining-room - arranged enfilade. Most sumptuous of all is the oval saloon, lined with grey scagliola pilasters with Corinthian capitals and a frieze of swags, and its walls lined with mirrors, niches and gilt-and-scarlet dressed settees. The fabulous plasterwork was carried out by English plasterers, under the supervision of Joseph Rose. The walls of the drawing-room and Chinese breakfast-room are hung with portraits of all the family members, so that you can imagine Lady Juliana leading the musical entertainment at her Broadwood piano and Somerset enthralling guests with tales of the family's adventures on the Nile.

The succeeding earls inherited massive debts, exacerbated by the famine. Only astute management and a reduction of the estates by over two-thirds enabled the 4th Earl to rescue the family finances. In 1951 the 7th Earl of Belmore passed the house and part of the demesne to the National Trust.

OPEN Easter, daily 1-6pm; April & Sept., Sat. & Sun. 1-6pm; May-Aug., daily except Thurs. 1-6pm, tel. 0044-1365-322690.

ADMISSION £2.80, childen £1.40. Toilets, parking, guided tours, tea room.

DIRECTIONS On the outskirts of Enniskillen on the A4 Belfast-Enniskillen road.

INDEX